THE GOSPEL SOLUTION
Was Jesus looking for "a few good men" ?

The
Gospel Solution

Was Jesus looking for "a few good men"?

Tom Weaver
with John Souter

TRUE
LIGHT
PRESS
JOHN 1:9

Bremerton, Washington

Library of Congress Catalog Card Number: 99-93713
ISBN 0-9670611-0-5

Unless otherwise noted, Scripture quotations are from the
New American Standard Bible®, ©copyright The Lockman
Foundation 1960, 1962, 1963, 1968, 1971, 1972, 1973,
1975, 1977. Used by permission.

Printed in the United States of America

True Light Press
3912 Steelhead Dr. NW
Bremerton, WA 98312-9671
(360) 830-2734
(800) 479-3208
FAX (360) 830-2436

Tom Weaver is very interested in your feedback. He can be e-mailed at tweaver@tscnet.com.

What Others Are Saying

"Have you ever been perplexed by what Jesus says in the Gospels? Get ready for an intriguing exploration of His life-changing message in the highly thought-provoking book by Pastor Tom Weaver."
Dr. David L. Jones, Vice President of Administration, CFO, Luis Palau Evangelistic Association, Portland OR

"Author Tom Weaver raises some penetrating questions about the Gospel message in his book, *The Gospel Solution.* He helps us wrestle with the aspects of grace and law that are so foundational to our understanding of the New Testament."
Dr. Daniel Mitchell, Assistant Dean, Liberty Baptist Theological Seminary, Lynchburg, VA

"Tom Weaver has looked hard into God's Word and he has unveiled some startling truths about the words of Jesus Christ in the synoptic Gospels of Matthew, Mark, and Luke. Truths that will bless your life immensely and also answer hard questions that may have troubled you. Lights will go on inside your soul bringing freedom and peace. Chapter 6 and Chapter 10 alone are worth the price of the whole book. But then again I loved every chapter. I taught this book to a class of thirty adults and the comments were always the same, 'This book is terrific!' Buy it and get blessed."
Wilma Stanchfield, author of *Struck By Lightning Then By Love*. She is also an internationally known speaker and seminar leader and lives with her husband in Winter Haven, FL.

Dedicated
to the memory of
two men who impacted my life for Christ

Harvey A. Simmons
and
Dr. Donald B. Fullerton

Table of Contents

WARNING!
Read at Your Own Risk

As the ghostwriter who helped Pastor Tom Weaver put *The Gospel Solution* together, I can confidently predict that reading this book will challenge some of your beliefs. I must admit that as I first began assisting Tom in organizing his ideas, I wasn't sure this book would ever find a publisher.

In the beginning I just didn't "buy" all that Tom had to say because of my twenty-five-year history as a Christian writer and pastor; I felt pretty well versed in the New Testament. On several occasions as I started to rewrite one of Tom's chapters, I remember thinking, *He's not going to convince me on this subject.* But halfway through this project, a flash of insight finally zapped me, and I began to comprehend what Tom was saying.

After reading one of our early drafts of the manuscript, an editor made a statement which sums up my feelings: "This is indeed startlingly simple, yet fundamentally profound material. It is an exciting set of thoughts to ponder and let sink into the fabric of my life, and it takes time for all the potential ramifications to be felt." The material in this book has had a dramatic impact upon my own life and ministry, and it has changed my outlook like few other books.

This manuscript presents a whole new perspective on the Christian life by reexamining the teachings of Jesus. There are millions of wounded Christians who don't know how to reconcile what they believe with what they feel Jesus demands of them. I believe this book will dramatically alter that conflict for many believers.

I've written almost fifty books, and I can confidently say that no other project has impacted my life more than this volume. Because this book presents a radical challenge to many of our cherished "private interpretations," I expect that some will ignore it, others will dismiss it as lacking substance, and some will even reject it as a harmful new wind of doctrine. But I believe the message of this book, and the potential it has for good within the church, is greater than anything with which I have ever been involved. For that reason, I fully expect its message to consume most of my remaining years of ministry.

You'll see as we examine different passages from the Gospels that our task has been to get to the bottom of what the Lord was really teaching. We have asked the hard questions so we could make sense of all those difficult passages.

For best results, I encourage you to turn the pages with an open mind. But if you can't do that, by all means, read anyway. Even if you disagree with the views expressed here, I think you'll still find much in this book that will encourage your walk with the Lord. At the very least, this book should help you better understand the ministry of Jesus and the New Testament doctrine of grace.

As we worked on the manuscript for *The Gospel Solution*, we labored to make its message easily grasped by people who are untrained in theology. At the same time, we knew that many of the answers we provide here would create their own set of questions in the minds of our readers. Therefore we have provided footnotes and chapter summaries in an attempt to give a little more help in answering the many questions that will inevitably arise from this significantly different approach to understanding the Gospels.

You can be sure that this will not be the last book written on this subject. We are already laying plans to produce several more volumes in the light of this new approach.

May God stimulate and challenge you as you read.

—John C. Souter

Chapter 1

The Gospel Dilemma
My Faith Challenged

In a climactic, bittersweet scene from the Hollywood movie *Shadowlands,* C. S. Lewis, the Oxford professor and noted author (played by Anthony Hopkins) faces the impending death of his wife and discovers anew that experience is a brutal teacher.

"I don't want you to go," he says to his attractive younger wife (played by Debra Winger). Lewis had been hesitant about allowing himself to fall in love with the woman, and now she was dying.

"Too much pain," she replies softly. The ravages of cancer have taken their toll.

"I don't know what to do, Joy. You have to tell me what to do." Now the professor was the student. He had questions rather than answers.

"You have to let me go," she answers simply.

"I'm not sure that I can," he replies.

Over the course of the film, William Nicholson's masterful script reveals that Lewis had suffered the tragedy of his own mother's death at age nine. That event was a turning point for him, and as an adult he chooses the single life and the isolation of academia over the pain of close relationships.

As a noted skeptic who experiences an awakening to Christ, Lewis became a popular lecturer. His treatise on faith, *Mere Christianity,* the popular *Chronicles of Narnia,* and his other writings made him renown. One of his readers, American divorcee Joy Gresham, comes to Oxford to meet the world-famous author and upsets his cloistered existence. Despite his best intentions as a confirmed bachelor, the film chronicles how the outspoken woman challenges his thinking and reawakens the feelings which have been dormant since his mother's untimely death.

When Joy's son Douglas arrived, the boy explored the house, including the attic where he found an old wardrobe closet like the one in *Chronicles of Narnia*. Douglas tries to push through the coats stored in the wardrobe to see if it just might lead to Narnia. Later, shortly after Joy's death, the filmmaker places Douglas back in the attic in front of that same wardrobe. If he could, the boy would surely crawl through that closet and off to Narnia to reach his mother.

"Douglas," Lewis begins, speaking more to himself in a feeble attempt to salve the boy's grief, "when my mother died I was your age. I thought that if I prayed for her to get better, and if I really believed she'd get better, then she wouldn't die. But she did."

"It doesn't work," says Douglas, agonizing over his own unanswered prayer.

"No, it doesn't work," Lewis agrees. The scene ends as they shed bitter tears of grief over their mutual loss.[1]

The reality of Joy's death overwhelmed C. S. Lewis, and in the process challenged his theology. Experience was a brutal teacher for the wise old professor as he struggled over unanswered prayer. Lewis made a telling observation when he said: "Every war, every famine or plague, almost every deathbed, is the monument to a petition that was not granted."[2]

Unfortunately this is the experience of many, both inside and out of the church. The problem stems from the promises Jesus made—such incredibly limitless promises—

---

[1] A Richard Attenborough film, *Shadowlands*, Spelling Films International, A Savoy Pictures Release, 1993

[2] C. S. Lewis, *Letters to Malcolm: Chiefly on Prayer*, A Harvest/HBJ Book, 1963, 1964, p. 58.

that he would give us what we prayed for. Lewis admitted to struggling with these biblical promises; he searched to find someone who might be able to explain this apparent contradiction between the Lord's statements in the Gospels, the events in Gethsemane, and the reality of unanswered prayer. But no one was able to offer an acceptable answer to satisfy his keen mind.

Sometimes this problem is compounded by well-meaning Christians who encourage others to embrace the Lord's promises. I'm acquainted with a woman who was told in her youth that she should pray for her terminally ill mother; if she prayed and believed, they claimed, her mother would get well. So the girl prayed for her mother to be healed—but then her mother died. While Lewis continued in his faith after his wife's death, for this woman, the experience became the defining moment in her unbelief. For many, the Lord's promises turn out to be both hollow and frustrating.

When prayer doesn't work, we wonder if something is wrong in our lives, or if the Lord doesn't care about us. Worse, we may begin to doubt our faith. Anger and despair often envelop Christians who are confronted by God's silence to their desperate prayers.

A Sense of Loneliness

In my own spiritual journey, unanswered prayer was only one of many issues with which I struggled. At first I assumed I was alone in my struggle; I never realized how many other Christians despaired over their own experience that seemed so contrary to the words of the Lord Jesus. Slowly I comprehended that many, like Lewis, suffer under their inability to make sense of Christ's words. Many Christians feel a disturbing powerlessness brought on by the teachings of the Lord.

A friend of mine, who had grown up as a member of an evangelical church, admitted to me that he used to hate church. Communion Sundays were always the worst for him because he felt unworthy to participate. He had such an awful sense of guilt; he would look at the people around him and wonder, *How can all these people be so good, when I'm so bad?*

His experience is far from unique. Many have a strong desire to be in church, but they fear God can't accept them with their futile attempts at being good. It seems the harder they try, the more unrighteousness they uncover in themselves. When they think about their moral failure they conclude that they're too corrupt for the church. Because of this, many have tremendous struggles with guilt. A woman in my congregation recently sent me a letter detailing a similar past:

"Years ago in other churches," she wrote, "Sunday morning service and Wednesday Bible study felt like atonement days—'face your failure' days. We would get all pumped up with enthusiasm by listening to other Christians tell how long they had gone without committing this or that sin. We'd write down their methods, then the next day was the start of a new program of being good. My attempts to change were always like going on a diet. How long can I keep this appearance of always being loving (let alone actually be loving)? How many hours in the day can I go without a bad thought? Forgive totally, work diligently, be a perfect wife and mother? It was impossible—so defeating. I was inch-by-inch extricating myself from involvement in church. I could not believe I was a Christian when faced with such monumental failure on a daily basis."

This is the norm for many Christians. They often end up doubting their salvation. After all, they reason: *I haven't obeyed what Jesus demands of me, so why should he let me into heaven?* These confused Christians are often uncertain about what constitutes salvation. They're confused because what they find in the Gospels seems so different from what they read in the rest of the Bible, or even what they hear from the pulpit.

Philip Yancey, an editor with *Christianity Today,* shares his own experience of the difficulty of living up to the words of the Lord in his book *The Jesus I Never Knew*:

> The Sermon on the Mount haunted my adolescence. I would read a book like Charles Sheldon's *In His Steps,* solemnly vow to act "as Jesus would act," and turn to Matthew 5–7 for guidance. What to make of such advice! Should I mutilate myself after a wet dream? Offer my body to be pummeled by the motorcycle-riding "hoods" in school? Tear out my tongue after speaking a harsh word to my brother?
>
> Once, I became so convicted about my addiction to material things that I gave away to a friend my prized collection of 1,100 baseball cards, including an original 1947 Jackie Robinson and a Mickey Mantle rookie card. Anticipating a divine reward for this renunciation, instead I had to endure the monumental injustice of watching my friend auction off the entire collection at a huge profit. "Blessed are those who are persecuted because of righteousness," I consoled myself.
>
> Now that I am an adult, the crisis of the Sermon on the Mount still has not gone away. Though I have tried at times to dismiss it as rhetorical excess, the more I study Jesus, the more I realize that the statements contained here lie at the heart of his message. If I fail to understand this teaching, I fail to understand him.[3]

My own experience was so similar to Yancey's. Jesus required so much more than I could do; his demands left me feeling hopeless. I don't know anyone who measures up to the Lord's standards. Just the other day I came across a book

[3] Philip Yancey, *The Jesus I Never Knew,* Harper Collins, Zondervan, 1995, p. 105.

put out by a respected evangelical publisher that stated that the Sermon on the Mount is "the righteous lifestyle of those who belong to the kingdom of heaven." On the back cover the author promised: "You can be godly all the way to the core. You can become the person you long to be and live a life that pleases God." And the author claimed that this would all take place in only nine weeks! Forgive my impiety—*but I don't think so.*

Why Can't I Do This?

I remember a woman who came for counseling who had begun to question her salvation. When I asked the reason for her doubts, she replied:

"I was reading in Matthew and became convicted. The Lord says if I don't forgive others, he won't forgive me." An expression of guilt flooded the woman's face. "You see, I want to forgive. I've prayed the Lord would help me forgive. Sometimes I even think that I have forgiven, but then something happens that triggers the memories of what certain people did to me, and . . . when the pain and anger flow over me, I know that I still haven't forgiven."

This woman felt particularly burdened every time she recited or sang the Lord's Prayer. Whenever she prayed, those words cut like a knife into her soul: "Forgive us our trespasses as we have forgiven." She knew she just couldn't do it, no matter how hard she tried. The wounds were too painful and deep. What does a pastor say to a woman who feels unforgiven because she cannot forgive—especially when, if the truth is fully known, I still have similar bitterness lurking deep (maybe not so deep) within my own heart?

Over the years, I've run into so many Christians who feel haunted because they know that they simply have not measured up to something they feel that the Lord wants them to do. A man once related how he came upon his mother as she read her Bible. He overheard her anguished voice: "I just can't, Lord! I just can't be a missionary!"

You've probably read the words of the Lord when he calls people to follow him—and you've read their excuses. "I just bought a piece of property," or "I have to bury my father," or that wimpy excuse: "I have this wife." We read the Lord's words and we hear those sermons on discipleship, and we feel so guilty because there are just too many things in our lives that distract us from following him. We don't really have the resolve to follow the Lord to the extent he demands, and we know it. So we end up wallowing in guilt.

Are You Upset with God?

But there's another side to this coin. The chances are good that instead of just feeling inadequate, we may even be angry with the Lord. This is often one of the hardest things for Christians to admit—that we have a problem with God. How can we admit we're angry with him? (After all, it might make him mad at us.) Such feelings—whether we repress them or not—are very common among Christians.

I went to see a man who had visited our church. As we began to speak about the possibility of his attending Crosby Chapel, his story began to pour out. It seems that he had been in a particular church for many years—until he divorced his wife. As he explained what had happened in their relationship, I had sympathy for what he had experienced with her. Christians had told him that according to the Lord's teaching, he didn't have "scriptural grounds" for his divorce and then they sided with his ex-wife and eventually disciplined him in front of the whole church and ostracized him.

While I was in his house, the man kept shaking his head.

"I just can't understand it. Why did the Lord let this happen to me? I can't tell you how much pain I experienced at the hands of that church."

Here was a man who felt that he was the victim, yet both the Lord's statements on divorce and the church's discipline had been used against him—and he was deeply wounded. He told me that he wouldn't be able to start back to church yet because of all the anger and pain he still felt. He didn't know if he could handle it. I wish I could tell you this man's experience is unique. But I can't. There are many walking wounded like him.

Do the Gospels "Offend" You?

Perhaps I'm more sensitive to those who are struggling because I too labored under these same difficulties. These conflicts made me feel like a second-class Christian. I was taught to believe in salvation by grace through faith in the work of Jesus on the cross, but as I read the first three Gospels, I discovered they often did not say what I believed. The words of the Lord in Matthew, Mark, and Luke actually offended my theology. Now isn't that an awful thing to say, "the words of Jesus offend my theology"?

I picture you thinking: *Well then, you ought to change your theology.* But I was unable to do that and make it work. My problem was, if I changed my views based upon the words of the Lord in the first three Gospels, I would then be at odds with the teachings of the apostle Paul and the Gospel of John. I just couldn't get them all to agree. New Christians are often encouraged to read the Gospel of John because of his grace teachings; his book meshes with Paul's writings, while the first three Gospels seem at odds with the New Testament letters.

This conflict stems directly from the teaching of Jesus himself. For years I wondered if there could be an answer to this dilemma, but no one I talked to and none of the books I read offered anything approaching a satisfactory answer. I began to wonder if I could believe the Bible as a whole and maintain my intellectual integrity.

Even as a young Christian the words of the Lord confused me. But when I became a pastor and started to teach from the Bible, I found that the problem did not get any better; in fact, it seemed worse, because I felt a greater obligation to be honest. The more I read, the more problems I discovered, and the less hope I felt. None of the scholars I consulted suggested an adequate explanation of this New Testament difficulty. Many scarcely acknowledged there was a problem. Everyone seemed so conditioned to mixing grace with the Lord's teaching that few acknowledged the disparity between the two.

C. S. Lewis was one who grasped the nature of this problem. He wrote: "A most astonishing misconception has long dominated the modern mind on the subject of St. Paul. It is to this effect: that Jesus preached a kindly and simple religion (found in the Gospels) and that St. Paul afterwards corrupted it into a really cruel and complicated religion (found in the Epistles). This is really quite untenable. *All the most terrifying texts come from the mouth of Our Lord*: all the texts on which we can base such warrant as we have for hoping that all men will be saved come from St. Paul" (emphasis mine).[4]

Lewis saw what many scholars apparently are unwilling to admit: The words of Jesus are often terrifying in the light of their eternal implications. When it came to my assurance for obtaining eternal life, the Lord's words caused me to question my own final destiny; so I hung onto the hope that somehow grace would win the day.

How Does One Become a Christian?

The most basic problem troubling me was my concern over how someone becomes a Christian. I heard different

---

[4] Lewis originally wrote this as part of his introduction to J.B. Phillip's *Letters to Young Christians: A Translation of the New Testament Epistles,* (London, 1947). The quote appears in *God in The Dock* , Eerdmans, 1970, p. 232.

"answers" on salvation, depending on whom I listened to. For example, many teach that a Christian is someone who receives the Lord Jesus in faith, has his sins washed away in the blood of Christ, and then keeps the Ten Commandments as the principle of his Christian life. This can be summarized in the formula: Grace is God's response to us, and Law is our response to God.

That view sounds reasonable, but I was unable to keep the Ten Commandments before I knew the Lord, and I was still unable after becoming a believer. I wanted to obey, but I just couldn't do it. I might give lip-service to following those laws in order to convince myself that I was obeying, but whenever I became serious in my attempts, I would immediately become frustrated with how far I fell short.

When I was young, I had a strong hunger for God, but I remember reading the words of Jesus and thinking the Lord's teachings in the Gospels seemed so difficult. I felt awed by such high standards and his words greatly discouraged me. As a ten-year-old, I still vividly remember closing my Bible and saying to myself: "If this is what it takes to be a Christian, then I guess I can never be one." Those who struggle to be Christians by keeping God's standards only end up frustrated, seeing Christianity as an impossible dream.

Another approach to salvation that I encountered emphasized repentance and confession. Jesus said in Luke 13:3, "I tell you, no, but, unless you repent, you will all likewise perish." Now I believe that repentance has a part in salvation, but this view claims a true Christian turns away from his sin when he feels convicted and then he stops sinning. Unfortunately, experience quickly showed me that I couldn't achieve this goal of sinless living. This view calls for a "self-atonement," as we are forced to retreat to the Lord for regular confessions due to the sin in our lives.

I confessed and repented, and I believed God forgave each new sin, but then I would begin to wonder: *What if I die before I confess a sin? Will I enter eternity lost and condemned?* Either I was saved before confessing that specific sin, or I would always be in danger of falling into hell if I failed to confess even one offense. Try as I might to "turn over a new leaf," I always slipped back into that same swampland of sin. I was left frustrated, wondering if I had fully confessed all of my sins. Would God ever find me good enough?

The Problem

My frustrations came directly from the pages of the synoptic[5] Gospels: Matthew, Mark, and Luke. But whenever I turned to John's Gospel, everything seemed different. With John's slant on the life and teachings of Jesus, my theology was at rest. John 3:16 is a classic example: "For God so loved the world that He gave His only begotten Son, so that whosoever believes in Him shall not perish, but have everlasting life." That is what I was taught; that is what I believe. Yet that's not what I found in Matthew, Mark, and Luke.

I was taught in church that you are saved by faith in the work of the Lord Jesus Christ on the cross. This certainly fits well with John's Gospel and the letters written by the apostle Paul. But whenever I read the words of the Lord in the other three Gospels, I wondered if that were really enough. Jesus seemed to contradict Paul and even his own words as they are recorded in the Gospel of John.

The Lord told one man if he wanted to inherit eternal life that he must keep the commandments.[6] John doesn't teach that. The apostle Paul doesn't teach that. Whenever the Lord was asked about eternal life in the synoptic Gospels, I found myself troubled by his answers. Those three Gospels seemed to set up standards alien to salvation by grace.

---

[5] They are called the *Synoptics*, meaning "seen with the same eye," because they are so similar in content.
[6] As in the example of the rich young ruler (see Matthew 19:17).

Once I discussed this dilemma with another pastor who (by my standards) is fairly liberal in his theology. I discovered his problem was the opposite of mine. He had no particular struggle with the Synoptics, but he felt conflict with John's Gospel. It was his opinion that a person had to reach a certain level of goodness to demonstrate the reality of his Christian faith, and he thought the apostle John made Christianity too easy. The words he used were, "John is too Pauline." He and I really had the same problem, only from opposite sides.

The more I studied the Bible, the more striking this contrast became between Jesus' teachings in the Synoptics and the gospel of grace taught by the apostles John and Paul. Jesus placed such high demands on those who heard him, which is so different from the emphasis on grace taught in the rest of the New Testament. The contrast mystified me. I couldn't reconcile the Lord's teaching with the message of grace for the forgiveness of sins.

A particular area of struggle for me was Matthew 5:17-20, where the Lord said: "Don't think that I came to do away with the Law or the Prophets. I didn't come to abolish, but to fulfill. For truly I say to you, until heaven and earth pass away, not the smallest letter or stroke shall pass away from the Law until all is accomplished. Whoever then annuls the least of these commandments, and so teaches others, shall be called least in the kingdom of heaven."

Those verses were a problem for me, because as a pastor I teach we are not obligated to keep the Sabbath (based on the teachings of the apostle Paul). Keeping the Sabbath is one of the Big Ten. I don't keep it, and I don't encourage others to keep it, nor do I keep Sunday as the Sabbath.[7]

Now this might not seem like much of a problem until you read what happened when someone broke it back in the Old Testament. When the children of Israel were camped

[7] Sunday isn't the Sabbath; the Sabbath begins at sundown on Friday night and runs to sundown on Saturday.

in the wilderness, a man was caught picking up firewood on the Sabbath. They brought him to Moses and asked what should be done with him. Moses detained the man so he could ask for God's verdict. The Lord commanded Moses to have the man stoned to death for this crime.[8] Woe!

If you study God's law in an attempt to keep it, you quickly discover that there are no optional commandments; they aren't the "Ten Suggestions." And Jesus says, "Whoever annuls one of these commandments will be least in the kingdom of heaven." I've annulled the Sabbath and taught others to do the same. Is the Lord condemning me? When I read these verses in my earlier years of ministry, I had to pause and give this serious thought.

But when I leafed back to Paul's writings and read: "You are not under Law but under grace,"[9] I would be reassured. Paul definitely presents a different view of the law than what I read in the synoptic Gospels. The apostle said: "Before faith came, we were kept in custody under the law, being shut up to the faith which was later to be revealed. Therefore the Law has become our tutor to lead us to Christ, that we may be justified by faith. But now that faith has come, we are no longer under a tutor."[10] Paul says we are no longer under the law, but Jesus says we must not annul even the least of the commandments. So who's right? Do we just pick the teaching we like best and forget the other?

Other Difficult Teachings

Let me ask you, how does it make you feel when you read where the Lord instructed his hearers to give up all of their possessions to the poor in order to follow him? Do you feel that teaching applies to you? Was that message included when you first accepted the gospel? (I imagine if it was, there would be a lot fewer conversions.) Not only can I not find

[8] Numbers 15:32-36
[9] Romans 6:14
[10] Galatians 3:23-25

that teaching in the epistles, I find it personally frustrating. How am I supposed to live if I give all my possessions away? Or is the gospel so individualized that each person has different demands placed upon him? If so, how are you to know your own individual requirements? Some spiritualize away this demand to give up one's wealth, but if you do this, don't the words then essentially become meaningless?

On one occasion Jesus was asked about the greatest commandment. He said we should love the Lord with all our hearts and in a second summary commandment he said we must love our neighbor as much as we love ourselves. Now that sounds fine as long as you don't give it serious thought, but I find this to be impossible. How can I love everyone as much as I love myself? If my salvation is dependent on doing that, I'm lost. Only if I trivialize the Lord's teachings can I ever hope to make a semblance of obedience. I can give lip service to these commandments and express admiration for Jesus' high morality, but I don't dare look critically at myself, because there's no chance I'll ever obey it. Some attempt to resolve this conflict by taking a relativistic approach. They say: "God knows you can't do this, so just do the best you can." Unfortunately, my best isn't very good.

Jesus wanted the weak and heavy-laden to come to him, yet he also made the rather troubling statement that if a man divorces his wife and remarries another, he would be committing adultery. That certainly isn't a message that would be designed to bring weak and divorce-laden people to Christ. There are millions of Christians in the church who have been divorced. Was Jesus saying they are all living in adultery? If they are, can they even be Christians? This is certainly not the gospel to which I was originally introduced. It seemed the "interpretation" of these Gospels as I understood them just didn't fit the stated purpose for which Jesus had come: "to seek and save the lost." I knew there had to be an explanation or solution to this dilemma.

A New Operating System?

A friend of mine recently bought a computer on which the operating system was improperly installed. He found that although most of his programs worked, almost all of the software had subtle little "glitches" in performance. The programs just didn't run like they should, and he had to fight to make his software perform. If you have suffered under any of the spiritual struggles that I've mentioned in this chapter, it just might be that your interpretation of the Lord's ministry has been "improperly installed." You are a Christian, but the program doesn't seem to be working well for you. Perhaps this is why you've struggled to make your beliefs work as you know they should.

I have come to some conclusions that I believe can open up the Gospels for you in a fresh, new way. When you hear the solution, you may be tempted to say, "That's just too simple!" Yet I think you'll find once you've embraced this view of the Lord's ministry in the Gospels, his words will start to make sense like never before. For the first time, you'll see the incredible power behind what the Son of God was saying, and you'll develop a whole new appreciation for the gospel of grace.

Chapter 2

The Gospel Solution
My Problem Resolved

For a period of fourteen hundred years, most of the great minds in Western civilization believed the sun, the moon, and the planets all revolved around the earth. This teaching was formulated by Ptolemy.[11] Telling time and predicting seasonal events could easily be accomplished using his model of the universe, and although there were problems with his theory,[12] the teaching seemed so logical it was universally accepted and became the official position of science and the church.

It was not until the sixteenth century that a scientist named Copernicus first seriously questioned Ptolemy, but the theory was so entrenched that even seventy years later, when Galileo attempted to popularize the idea that the earth was not the center of the solar system, he found himself bitterly rebuffed. The more those astronomers studied the heavens, the more problems they had making their observations fit Ptolemy's theory; yet society had been convinced it was a fact.

I can identify with the plight of those astronomers as they struggled with the incongruity of that outdated theory and the data they observed. The more I read the Gospels, the

[11] Claudius Ptolemaeus (known as Ptolemy) was a Greek born in the second century A.D. He taught in Alexandria, Egypt, and developed trigonometry for use in navigation and astronomy.
[12] The retrograde motion of the planets, the variations in the brightness and size of planets (like Venus), and the variations between total and annular eclipses of the sun could only be explained with great difficulty using Ptolemy's theory.

more I saw that they just didn't fit what I had been taught. I was taught Jesus was the world's greatest teacher—and I believe that to be true—yet he often tried to confuse people. In Mark, the Lord candidly admits he used parables "in order that while seeing, they may see and not perceive; and while hearing, they may hear and not understand lest they return and be forgiven."[13] This certainly was not what I expected from the world's greatest teacher. *Why*, I wondered, *would the Lord camouflage his message so people wouldn't be forgiven?* Sometimes, and I would suggest often, the Lord did not even make sense to his own disciples, and his teaching certainly confused me.

Like Copernicus and Galileo, I discovered that the current popular interpretation of Jesus' teachings just didn't match what was said in the Gospels. But where should I turn for answers? I could not find any books or published articles offering any solution for this dilemma. In time I became convinced the answer must be found in the words of the Lord himself. I sensed if I probed deeply enough, I might discover why his teaching seemed so out of sync with the doctrine of grace in the rest of the New Testament.

Discovering the "Catalyst"

My personal awakening began while I was studying a story in the Synoptics that I found particularly troubling; the incident that I grappled with is when Jesus tells the rich young ruler he can obtain eternal life by keeping the Ten Commandments. As I probed the elements of this encounter, several insights jumped off the page at me. (I'll share these insights about this particular story in the next chapter.) I felt as if I had discovered the Lord's overriding purpose.

I can still vividly recall being struck by how the entire story became consistent with salvation by grace when I viewed it from this new vantage point—a position I think

---

[13] Mark 4:12

represents the Lord's overall purpose in his teaching. Suddenly, I felt like one of those two disciples who heard the risen Lord explain the Scriptures after his resurrection[14]—for me the Gospels opened, and for the first time, the light snapped on. The words of Jesus made sense like never before, but I wasn't absolutely certain that I could duplicate this success with other Gospel passages.

My experience reminds me of the discovery of Teflon, used on those no-stick pans. When I took chemistry in the sixties, I was told that Teflon had first been synthesized by accident. A chemist working with materials in a fire extinguisher noted the canister had gained weight after an experiment. The residue he had accidentally produced could withstand high temperatures, was relatively inert, and had a low coefficient of friction. DuPont patented that substance before they fully understood how it had been created. They had to perform what we now call "reverse engineering" to discover how it was made. Eventually, they determined that the presence of a silver washer in the fire extinguisher was a catalyst to allow the chemical reaction to take place so the material could be synthesized.

In the same way, I had discovered a "catalyst" that made sense of the incident of the rich young ruler—and I soon found it worked well with other Gospel portions. Over the next ten years I began to examine difficult synoptic passages from the same reference point and found this basic interpretive approach consistently made sense out of these troublesome texts. As I applied this framework, I felt freedom for the first time to preach through the Gospel of Luke and then through Mark a few years later. Everything made sense at last. This new solution led me out of my despair and brought me to a new level of joy and excitement in the Lord.

I've developed four principles for the interpretation of the Gospels which I believe make sense of Jesus' ministry.

---

[14] Luke 24:25-32

You'll find these principles will help you understand the Lord's teaching in a simple, meaningful, and consistent fashion. I call this approach *transitionalism* (or a transitional interpretation of the Gospels, if you prefer). The ministry of Christ is set in a transition period between the Old and the New Testaments. The key to understanding this approach—the catalyst, so to speak—is this transitional period into which the Lord's earthly ministry falls.

A Case of Covenants

Let's begin by asking a question: Where does the Old Testament begin? The typical answer I receive when I ask that question is: "Why, in Genesis Chapter 1, of course." But let me suggest another answer. We are used to thinking of the Old Testament as a book or a collection of books rather than a contract. In reality, that collection of books is named for and characterized by a covenant, testament, or contract which was made when the children of Israel camped at Mount Sinai. That's where the Old Testament historically begins, in Exodus 24.[15] In fact, all 39 books are properly called the Old Testament because they are dominated by this covenant made at Sinai.

Let me paraphrase what God said to the Israelites upon offering that covenant: "I would like to make an agreement with you, Israel. I want you to be my special people. This is my law. If you keep my law, I will bless you; but if you fail to keep it, I will curse you. Is that okay with you?" The Israelite nation agreed to accept this covenant, and it was sealed to them by the shedding of the blood of animals.[16] Genesis and the first half of Exodus belong in the Old Testament because they provide the historical setting for this cov-

---

[15] In the rest of this book, I will refer to the written documents as either the Old "Testament" or New "Testament." When referring to the way God deals with his people, I will use the term old "covenant" or new "covenant."

[16] Hebrews 9:11-22

enant. The rest of what we think of as the "Old Testament" are all the books that fall under the dominion of that agreement on Mount Sinai made between God and Israel. It is important to point out that the rest of the Old Testament is a study in failure and frustration. The people were never able to keep God's law.

When does this old covenant come to an end and the new covenant begin? *Why, at the birth of Jesus*, you might be thinking. That's what many Christians assume. But the New Testament book of Hebrews tells us that the Lord is the mediator of the new covenant, and that Christ had to die before it could come into effect. "For where a covenant is, there must of necessity be the death of the one who made it."[17] This is why on the night before his death, Jesus introduced the Lord's Supper to his disciples by announcing: "This cup is the new covenant in My blood."[18]

Now keep in mind that the first covenant stayed in force until it was replaced by the second covenant. That means that all of the material before the death of Jesus in the Gospels—from the birth of Jesus through his earthly life and teachings—*all belong to the old covenant period.*[19] This is very important, because this means that the earthly life and teachings of Jesus can only be correctly understood when they are seen as having taken place within the context of that first covenant between God and Israel. Only the last few chapters of each of the Gospels can properly be considered to have taken place under the new covenant from a chronological perspective. So the Lord's purpose was not to present the gospel of grace but to prepare his people for it. This is the starting point for the four principles of transitionalism.

---

[17] Hebrews 9:15-17
[18] 1 Corinthians 11:15. See also Matthew 26:28; Mark 14:24; and Luke 22:20.
[19] According to Galatians 4:4, Jesus was "born under the Law."

Principle #1: Transitional

The ministry of Jesus is lived under the old covenant. While it prepared people for the coming new covenant, it was primarily directed towards those still living under the law.

Now you might be wondering: *Didn't the Lord present the gospel[20] message?* Because most Christians have read the glad tidings given by the angels at Christ's birth and the heralding that declared the kingdom of God was at hand, they assume the Lord's birth introduces the gospel to the world. But although Matthew, Mark, and Luke are called "Gospels," much of what's in them is not what we would consider the new covenant gospel message. Paul defines the gospel in 1 Corinthians 15:1-4 as the "good news" of our salvation through the death, burial, and resurrection of the Lord Jesus Christ. So although the synoptic Gospels tell the story of the Lord's death, burial and resurrection, the explanation of the meaning of those events is left to the rest of the New Testament.

This has been somewhat modified in John's Gospel. Although his book covers the same time period as the Synoptics, John's stated purpose and style are different. History tells us that John was an old man at the time he composed his Gospel.[21] It was one of the last volumes of the New Testament to be written. Eusebius, a church historian in the fourth century, relates that when John wrote, he had the other three Gospels available to him. The apostle chose the events and messages from the Lord's ministry, editorially commenting upon them to teach that salvation was by grace through faith.

---

[20] To clarify my intention I am capitalizing the use of the word Gospel whenever it refers to one of the four books called Matthew, Mark, Luke and John. When I talk about the doctrine of the good news of our salvation, I will not capitalize the word gospel.

[21] It was about the year 90 A.D.

"The Law was given through Moses," John says, but "grace and truth were realized through Jesus Christ."[22] He even proclaimed his purpose in John 20:31, where he wrote so "that you may believe that Jesus is the Christ, the Son of God; and that believing you may have life in His name." His Gospel is a clear presentation in agreement with Paul's gospel in 1 Corinthians 15.

John's style is full of editorial comments that clarify the hidden purpose of the Lord's words. John seems to anticipate our questions. For example, in Chapter 2, Jesus is quoted as saying: "Destroy this temple, and in three days I will raise it up again." But John clarifies that the Lord was speaking of his body.[23] In Chapter 3, when the Lord makes the cryptic statement, "You must be born again," John goes on to explain those words editorially in John 3:16 and the verses that follow. John does this in his book because his purpose is to clarify the gospel of grace within the context of the Lord's life.

The balance of what we now call the New Testament clearly declares the gospel of grace through Christ's death on the cross. Paul and the other New Testament writers focus on the meaning of his death and resurrection because that is the heart of the new covenant message. *This* is the gospel of the New Testament as distinct from the gospel of the kingdom (found in Matthew, Mark, and Luke). Many of the Lord's words are simply *not* the Christian gospel, yet they prepare the way for it. So the first principle of *transitionalism* is that we must understand the transitional nature of the Lord's ministry if we are to understand what his teaching message was designed to accomplish.

The Need for Conviction

What then was Jesus trying to achieve in his teaching ministry through his parables and sermons? I believe that

---

[22] John 1:17
[23] John 2:21-22

Jesus' teaching ministry, especially as it is recorded in the Synoptics, has as its primary purpose the bringing of the covenant people to a realization of themselves as sinners. They were people who had broken the law and who were therefore in danger of being condemned. Because the Jews had learned to live with a cultural approach to the law, many convinced themselves that they were actually keeping it.

The Lord's purpose was to break down this belief. His goal was to undermine their self-confidence. They needed to be crushed under the full weight of the holiness of God's law. Therefore, the Lord used it as his "tutor" to prepare them for the coming message of the cross.

Principle #2: Conviction
The purpose in the Lord's teaching ministry was to bring his people, the Jews, to a conviction of sin so that they could grasp their need for a savior and be ready for grace.

To understand the Jewish mind-set of the time, it helps to realize that the rabbis had constructed an elaborate system of at least 613 commandments that interpreted the law. A religious Jew could know exactly what he was allowed to do in every situation. The Pharisees therefore believed that they were keeping the law. This explains why they found the Lord's accusations so offensive. Jesus attacked them at the place of their greatest pride.

The primary purpose of the Lord's teaching ministry, then, was an attempt to clarify for the Jews God's righteous demands through the old covenant law. He did this with only a veiled presentation of the coming hope that would be available after Calvary. His goal was to break down self-righteousness, not to present a salvation that wasn't yet available. This is consistent with Paul's statement of the law's purpose to 'shut up all men under sin.'[24]

[24] Galatians 3:15-22 and Romans 3:10-20

When you examine many of the Lord's parables and sermons from this old covenant perspective, you can clearly see his emphasis was upon conviction of sin. His purpose therefore *was not an attempt to offer the new covenant to the Jews.* They were simply not ready for that message. This is consistent with the parallel ministry of John the Baptist.[25] Jealousy developed among the disciples of John because the Lord's disciples were baptizing more people than John. This would indicate that Jesus and his disciples were carrying on a ministry that approximated that of John—the nature of their two water baptisms was the same. John's baptism was for repentance and I'm confident that the baptism that Jesus' disciples performed was also for repentance (because sorrow is a natural outgrowth of conviction).

The people who crowded around Jesus to hear his parables and marvel at his miracles heard messages which impacted each of them differently, depending upon their need and the degree of conviction under which they fell. Some felt little desire for salvation because they possessed so little consciousness of their own guilt—after all, they prided themselves on being keepers of God's law. Others, like the tax collectors and prostitutes, recognized their great need and felt drawn to the Lord like metal filings to a magnet. Although they still didn't know how Jesus would save them, at least now they had a renewed sense of hope.

Early in his ministry, during the Sermon on the Mount, Jesus stunned his audience by declaring "unless your righteousness surpasses that of the scribes and Pharisees, you shall not enter the kingdom of heaven."[26] That was an incredibly bold and incomprehensible statement, because the Pharisees had committed themselves to obeying every detail of the Mosaic law as well as all the traditions of the elders. If their righteousness wasn't sufficient to qualify them for heaven, who could make it?

[25] John 3:22-4:2
[26] Matthew 5:20

When Jesus arrived on earth and began to speak to his people, his main task was to reveal to his audience the foolishness of depending on self-righteous deeds. The gospel is unnecessary for anyone who can keep the law. The Lord wanted to bring his people into a right relationship with God, but before that could happen, they had to understand their failure to keep the law.

So the Lord's primary teaching mission during his earthly ministry was to crush his people under the full weight of God's law, driving them toward what we now know is the cross. When you examine the ministry of the Lord throughout the synoptic Gospels, you see that preaching for conviction under the law was his primary purpose; in fact, this message is so consistent and powerful, you'll find it steaming off virtually all of the pages of Matthew, Mark, and Luke. These three Gospels, in particular, record the Lord's blow-by-blow struggle to convict his religious audience of their sin.

Our Major Misunderstanding

Once you understand this, it is easier to see that the Lord was not aiming his teaching toward the church, nor did he ever intend that these public messages should become a rule for Christian living. This is the major misunderstanding of his purpose that confuses so many Christians today. We have come to assume that the Lord's teachings are for the church under the new covenant; but in truth, he was clarifying the old covenant and its implications in order to reveal the futility of trying to keep the law. The Lord simply was not teaching rules designed for new covenant living.

The first three Gospels are an honest history of the Lord's attempts to reveal man's inability to keep the law, but the Lord never meant his words to be interpreted as a new standard by which Christians were to live. But out of love and genuine faith in Jesus, many believers have accepted the

Lord's challenge to keep the law, not realizing that his message was meant to produce frustration and a sense of need. Jesus was clarifying the law by revealing the full ramifications of God's incredibly high standard. When Christians try to live by his teachings, they place themselves under bondage to a new form of Christian legalism that can only lead to frustration.

Now I know this might seem a little radical. So let me clarify that I am not saying the Lord's words are uninspired. Nor am I saying that they do not contain many things both pertinent and applicable for the church today. What I am proposing is that the Lord's *primary* intention was not to instruct the church; this conclusion is completely consistent with what we find in the epistles.

The apostle Paul wrote 13 books in our New Testament, and in all of his letters, there is only one place where he ever quotes Jesus. That's in 1 Corinthians 11, when he teaches about Communion, quoting the Lord on the night of his betrayal.[27] In the Book of Acts, Luke records that Paul quoted Jesus, saying it is "better to give than to receive,"[28] and there are two other places where Paul appeals to the teachings of Jesus but doesn't actually quote him;[29] but in all of his many letters, the apostle largely ignores the teachings of the Lord given before the night of his arrest.

Why does he have this seeming lack of interest in the teaching ministry of Jesus? If the words of the Lord were meant to be the new rule for the church, doesn't it seem strange that the apostle would make so little use or comment upon them? It is certainly true that these two teachers can easily take a believer in one of two radically different directions. The message of Jesus in the Gospels is so dramatically different from what Paul gives us that it appears like trying to

---

[27] 1 Corinthians 11:24-25
[28] Acts 20:35
[29] 1 Corinthians 7:10 and 1 Corinthians 9:14

mix water with oil. The obvious solution is that Jesus was simply not speaking to the church but convicting men of their need, and preparing them to repent and receive grace so they could later enter the church.

One of the rules of biblical interpretation is that a passage of Scripture may have many applications, but it has only one primary interpretation. This is why we do not interpret passages written in the Old Testament to the Jews (such as in the Book of Deuteronomy), as we do those written for the church. We can certainly draw applications from such books, but if we attempt to interpret those passages for the church when they were written for men who had no knowledge of the cross, we will only confuse and confound our understanding of God's intentions. In the same way, if we attempt to apply to the church the Lord's messages in the Gospels that were given to the Jews, we will seriously misunderstand what Jesus had in mind when he spoke.

Catch the Lord's "Flavor"

The third principle of transitionalism will give you a greater appreciation of the beauty and subtlety of the Lord's teaching style. I do not believe you will be able to fully understand what Jesus is saying in most cases unless you understand what was going on under the surface. Whenever the Lord teaches, he is attempting to evoke—even provoke—an unexpected response from his audience. We often assume that the Lord was trying to be clear, attempting to communicate in such a way that everyone would understand, yet this was precisely *not* what he was trying to do. The Lord's teaching ministry was meant to evoke responses rather than to clarify ideas.

Principle #3: Evocative

Jesus meant to evoke (or even provoke) a response from his audience rather than just to clarify his meaning. The significance of what he said was often meant to dawn on his hearers with unexpected and subtle power.

The Lord's method reminds me of statements made by Alan Greenspan, the head of the Federal Reserve Bank. In 1992, when some senators were trying to pin him down on the possibility of future cuts in interest rates, he responded: "I try to be as oblique as possible." On another occasion, he prefaced a speech by saying, "If anything I say tonight seems particularly clear to you, you have probably misunderstood me."

Jesus was often unclear, and I submit that it is because he *meant* to be obscure. In fact, he was almost *never* clear. Even when he was clear (from our vantage point), he still wasn't understood by his audience or the disciples. He uttered those baffling parables to hide some of his cryptic insights from his audience, knowing that they would later figure out the meaning of his words. He answered the fool according to his folly, and only later did the real meaning of his words become apparent. He preferred to be unclear, even confusing, because it served his purposes.

Unfortunately, the church has often misunderstood what the Lord was trying to say because we have not understood his style, nor have we grasped his purpose. His approach was meant to evoke a feeling in order to lead the hearer toward a desired attitude or response, not just to convey facts or ideas.

John Dewey, the "father of modern education," taught that it was best to communicate abstract truths by first pointing to concrete objects. For instance, a child is shown five balls, and then the teacher introduces the concept of the number five to the child. Bible teachers often suggest that Jesus used this principle when he used illustrations, mentioning tangible everyday objects because they believe it made his teaching clearer. But the reality is that the Lord never used John Dewey's principles. He was far more interested in arousing feelings than he was in helping people fully understand the content of his message. Jesus' approach seems more inclined to create an emotional feeling, just as music does, than in teaching specific information.

A High-Risk Offense

A high-risk approach to teaching can be especially powerful. In my son's fourth year of language study, his teacher took the class to hear a Spanish lecture. With 60 other students he listened to a guest professor discuss the economic class system in Latin America. Near the close of the session, a Domino's pizza man delivered four large pizzas to the platform. As it was close to lunch, my son's mouth instinctively began to water.

When the lecture ended, the speaker passed out slips with the letters A through E on them. He said that all of the students with the letter B could come up and each take three pieces of pizza. There were only two B's. He then invited the four students with the letter C to come up and select one piece each. Next he called those who had D's to come and receive a quarter of a piece each. Seven more came forward. The speaker announced that the rest of the pizza belonged to those who had the letter A, but when he looked down he noticed that he had the letter A. In fact, his was the only A in the hall. The speaker began to eat his pizza while my son and the other 47 students who had the letter E looked on with growling stomachs. Finally, the lecturer paused and glanced at the remaining pizza and then gazed up at the many hungry students in the hall, as if realizing for the first time that they didn't have any pizza.

"I have way too much pizza," he announced. "I can't eat all of this."

So the lecturer picked up the pizzas and slammed them into the trash can beside him, stomping on them for good measure. For the first time my son, and the rest of class, understood emotionally how the economic class system in Latin America impacts the disenfranchised. The teacher had provoked their emotions so that anger and despair rose to the surface. His goal had been to bring those students from the passive stance of saying "So?" to the dynamic place of saying "Oh!"

That's the type of response Jesus meant to achieve through his teaching as it is recorded in the synoptic Gospels. The Lord often gives what Henry James would call a "turn of the screw," a new twist that shocks his hearers and in some respect calls their behavior and world view into question. His speeches were not meant merely for mental instruction but for shocking these people into a new way of thinking and feeling. His primary goal was to impact them, first by gaining their attention, then by preparing their hearts to fathom their need for personal forgiveness. Jesus confronted their "so what?" attitude, so that after the cross, they would say: "O God! Now I see my need!"

You can often spot this methodology whenever someone asked the Lord a question. It seems as though he's responding to a different question than the one being asked. If you look at the answers the Lord gave, they so often reveal an underlying unasked question, motive, or need on the part of the questioner. Just as Sherlock Holmes solved his mysteries by being drawn to the element that is out of place in the story, so we understand Jesus best by examining the seemingly out of place elements in the gospel accounts.

Jesus understood that people are not converted by coming to a clear understanding of the gospel message; conversion comes only after someone is convicted of their desperate need. I once discussed sales techniques with a life insurance salesman who mentioned that he had been trained not to spend much time explaining the plan of insurance. He had been instructed to concentrate on the person's need and to help his clients picture the benefits being paid to his dependents. He would talk about what life would be like if the man's loved ones were bereaved and financially destitute because they didn't have insurance. In the same way, people don't buy insurance because it is such a great plan, neither do they become Christians because the plan of salvation is reasonable; they trust Christ when they discover how helpless and lost in sin they are without him.

The Lord used this high-risk offense to provoke his listeners with these quaint stories that had stingers attached at the end. His purpose was to arouse their attention. If his words didn't always seem to make sense, it was so his listeners would get curious, maybe even angry. He intended to polarize the crowd, causing some to seek the truth while others would seek his death.

You will not understand what the Lord is saying unless you understand what is going on under the surface; if you miss that he is trying to provoke an unexpected or delayed response, you'll miss what's happening. Jesus took a long-range view and he never intended to finish his lesson until after the cross.

Seeing the Bigger Picture

The fourth and final principle of transitionalism is that the ministry of Jesus is best understood by looking at the larger sections of Scripture that surround any particular incident or teaching event. I've discovered that whenever a passage in the Gospels seems to be particularly out of place, it isn't.

Principle #4: Interwoven Context

Any single passage within the synoptic Gospels should be viewed and understood in the light of the larger context of the Scripture surrounding it. Adjacent passages are often interwoven together to interpret one another.

This fourth principle is particularly fruitful in comprehending the Lord's intent in certain portions of the Gospels. You might be tempted to pass this up as being reserved for pastors and scholars, especially if your motivation is simply to alleviate any pain you might feel in your struggles with the words of Jesus. But let me explain its importance by comparing it with the need to lay the proper foundation.

A few years ago, when I built my home, I placed a beam under the house, which was set by stretching a string across the foundation's outside walls. Due to the natural sag in the string, the beam ended up being two inches low. That two inches proved a great difficulty for me for the rest of the project. From the framing of the walls to hanging of the wallpaper, I fought those two inches. Ignoring the context of the Gospel stories is a little like that sagging string; you can still achieve significant success in your understanding of what the Lord is saying, I have a really nice house, but you'll end up struggling with many of your final conclusions if you don't seriously examine the context.

Most preachers have a tendency to treat the "preaching sections" of the Gospels as if they were a collection of proverbs, each one standing alone. This becomes a problem when the passage was not meant to stand alone. Because preachers are trained theologically, they generally reach orthodox conclusions. Unfortunately, these theologically correct conclusions are often thrust upon a text where they aren't taught, rather than coming from the intent of the Gospel writer.

My son first brought to my attention the fact that I tended to combine significantly larger segments of the Gospels in order to allow them to interpret one another. Shortly after he made this observation, I was reading a commentary on Mark by James Brooks, in which he pointed out that the stories in the Gospels are interwoven together in groupings in all of the Gospels. Brooks defined this interweaving[30] as a bracketing or sandwiching of material; he sees it as a literary and theological device to indicate a lapse of time, to heighten tension, or draw the reader's attention to something. It can show a contrast, and even more importantly, it can be used to let two accounts interpret one another. This interweaving is exactly what the Gospel writers intended.

Many of the situation comedies on television use this interweaving development for their programs. There will be two or three plots running parallel during a half-hour show. Each of the plots is independent, but all are related to the central theme found in the moral (or "immoral") at the program's conclusion. The use of this interweaving approach is what the Gospel writers use to heighten tension and drama and to allow one event to interpret another. If you fail to see the way the Gospel writers handle the material, you will often miss much of the bigger picture they are trying to present. The grouping of the various events in the Lord's life were designed to produce unique consolidated messages in each of the Gospels.

Following this approach has taught me from experience that when I cannot grasp the intent of a Gospel passage, it is quite often because I am too close to the story. To get a clearer view, it is often necessary to take a step or two back so I can examine the context. By studying those seemingly unrelated passages that surround any particular event, it's often possible to see the bigger image God has painted on his

---

[30] James Brooks, *The New American Commentary, Mark*, Broadman, 1991, p. 73. The actual word Brooks uses is "intercalation," but for the sake of clarity I have chosen to use the term "interwoven."

inspired scriptural canvas. It seems that there is always more to glean than what you can find by harvesting only the information on the surface.

Learning how to view the context is a little like taking the time to practice touch typing. At first you can still type faster using the old hunt-and-peck method, but that may lead to a false economy if you abandon touch typing. In the end, a typist enhances his results greatly by sticking with it. In the same way, the words of Jesus are best understood in the light of the larger interwoven context in which they're found.

Some Final Thoughts

Before we apply these four principles to specific portions of the Gospels, let me offer two suggestions that should help you navigate successfully through this book.

First, it's important to note that a distinction should be made between the teaching ministry of Jesus and what he did through the cross. The Lord's arrest, trial, and crucifixion are so important that all four Gospel writers devote more than a third of their books just to cover these events.[31] The cross is the primary reason Jesus came; his entire earthly life focused upon his journey to Calvary because it was there that he would atone for the sins of the world.

But the primary purpose of the Lord's *teaching* ministry was to radically establish man's shortfall from God's holy standards. Remember, Jesus did this at a time when the cross and its purpose were veiled that not even the inner group of disciples had a clue about what he was doing. Therefore, whenever a modern-day believer struggles with the Lord's teaching ministry, it is often because he does not realize that the Lord was speaking in this transitional way to prepare the Jews for the future preaching of the cross. Jesus' goal

---

[31] John devotes seven full chapters to the twenty-four-hour period from the last supper to Christ's entombment.

in his teaching ministry was to convict men making them ready for the radical solution that the cross presented.

Second, keep in mind that *The Gospel Solution* is not meant to be a comprehensive study on any of the subjects introduced in the various chapters. For example, when I conclude in Chapter 4 that our salvation is not dependent upon our forgiving others, I do not mean to discount the importance of forgiveness. As believers, we should use the teaching of Jesus as a model to understand how God views forgiveness and we should certainly nurture it in our own lives. But to demand that believers must forgive as a condition for salvation is a *tragic misunderstanding* of what the Lord was saying. Perhaps I may have gone to an extreme in maintaining a sharp distinction between the interpretation and application of a passage of Scripture, but the failure to make that distinction has precipitated many difficult problems for hurting believers.

As you read on, you will see how easy it is to miss the intent in many of the Gospel passages. Transparency was not Jesus' goal. The Lord doesn't overtly reveal what he is trying to accomplish, so we must carefully examine his audience, the flavor of his words and the larger context within which they are spoken in order to understand what is being said. Perhaps this is why Jesus declared, "If you have ears—use them."

As we apply the four principles of transitionalism, I believe you will be able to understand the Lord's purpose in his teaching ministry as never before. Like Galileo, you'll be looking at the Gospel events through a new lens, and I think you'll be amazed how this approach will make sense of the Lord's words in a way you've never understood before. This book comes out of my own struggles, I hope it will answer many of your questions. May God bless you as we study the teachings of the Lord together.

Chapter 3

Is Jesus Looking for a Few Good Men?

The Rich Young Ruler

A few weeks ago, one of our Sunday school teachers rushed up to me between the early and late worship services.

"Pastor," she said, "I don't know what to do. I'm teaching on the life of Jesus, and the story I'm supposed to present is where Jesus tells this young man how to get to heaven." Her brow furled as she shook her head. "Pastor, this isn't what I believe. How can I teach this?"

That look of frustration on her face brought back my own experience when I first encountered that same Bible story. The question this Bible character uttered is the one I would have asked had I lived in the first century: "What must I do to inherit eternal life?" When I read that, I thought: *Great question! What will the answer be?* But then when I read the Lord's discussion with the man, I ended up like my Sunday school teacher—completely confused.

The Lord's encounter with this fellow is recorded in all of the synoptic Gospels.[32] All three writers reveal that he was rich; Matthew informs us he was young; Luke adds that he was a ruler of the Jews—so throughout history he's been known as the rich young ruler. When I first read it, I tried to understand it as best I could, but my conclusions seemed unacceptable.

Jesus informed us through his dialogue with this man that there are three things one must do to get into heaven:

[32] Matthew 19:16-29; Mark 10:17-30; and Luke 18:18-30

Keep the Ten Commandments, give everything to the poor, then follow Jesus. The obvious implication I saw was that if I couldn't do those three things, then I would be lost.

It particularly bothered me that Jesus asked the man to give everything he owned to the poor. *Is this really what the Lord requires of me?* I wondered. It seemed so unreasonable to try to live in this world without owning anything. Besides, many believers in the New Testament had wealth. *Why is the Lord asking this?* The truth was that I couldn't keep the Ten Commandments, and I wouldn't give all my money to the poor, so I probably wasn't following Jesus either. I figured God must certainly be unhappy with me.

As I studied this story in Luke's Gospel in an attempt to determine what the Lord was saying, four questions formed in my mind: (1) Why did Jesus question the man's reference to his being good? (2) Why did the Lord suggest that keeping the commandments was the way to inherit eternal life? (3) Did Jesus really expect his followers to give everything away to the poor? (4) What was the Lord saying by using this camel and needle illustration?

How Good Is Good?

The man addressed the Lord as "good teacher," but Jesus quickly challenged his use of the term "good" by saying that only God is truly good. Now some have suggested that here Jesus was actually denying that he is God. I can't accept this because the Gospel accounts, and the rest of the New Testament make it obvious that Jesus was God in human flesh. If the Lord was denying his deity, the rest of the New Testament doesn't make sense.

A second suggestion is that Jesus was telling us never to call anyone "good." But later in the book of Luke, we read about another rich fellow, "a man named Joseph, who was a member of the Council, a *good and righteous* man"[33] (emphasis mine). Luke uses the same Greek word to call Jo-

---
[33] Luke 23:50

seph "good," even throwing in that he was "righteous," so if the Lord's purpose was to stop us from calling people "good," even Luke missed the point.

I believe Jesus' statement about goodness is meant for clarification. In all languages, words derive their meaning, from the context in which they are spoken. Hot weather, hot food, and a hot fire indicate a wide spread of temperatures, even though all use the same adjective. Because of this, when we enter a serious discussion, we sometimes define what we mean by a particular term to avoid confusion. I believe the Lord's declaration that "no one is good except God" is meant to clarify his intention in this particular discussion; he intends to talk about morality specifically from the standpoint of God's absolute standard.

A few years ago, Sears used to sell three qualities of merchandise in their catalog. Faucets, for example, would be labeled: *Good, better,* and *best.* Now what did *good* mean in one of those catalogs? It actually labeled the worst quality the store was willing to sell.

Suppose I were to ask you, if you consider your spouse to be a good person. You would probably answer *Yes.* In a relative sense, compared to other people you know, your spouse is probably a good person—but not compared to the absolute standard by which God is measured. So let me paraphrase what I believe Jesus is saying: "Young man, don't misunderstand what I'm about to tell you by inflicting your relative standard of goodness upon it. Get that out of your mind. I'm going to talk to you about good and bad and right and wrong from God's point of view."

Keeping the Commandments?

The Lord tells this man to keep the commandments in order to inherit eternal life. For me, this statement is the most troubling part of the whole encounter. I've been in church all my life, and I have never heard a preacher say, "Do you want to go to heaven? Well then, keep the Ten Commandments!" I've heard many preachers say, "Do you want to go to heaven? Then place your faith in the Lord Jesus and his work on the cross." But I've never heard a single preacher quote the Lord's words here as the way to obtain eternal life.

This is contradictory to Paul's teaching that the law *isn't* the way to get to heaven. In Romans the apostle says, "by the works of the law no flesh will be justified in His sight."[34] In Galatians he adds, "a man is not justified by the works of the law but through faith in Christ Jesus."[35] Paul even goes so far as to call the Ten Commandments a "ministry of death engraved on stones."[36] Why then does Jesus instruct this man to keep the commandments in order to obtain eternal life?

Let me make a suggestion. This may sound radical to you at first, but I believe there are *two ways* to heaven. One is by keeping the commandments—the other is by placing your faith and trust in the work of Jesus Christ on the cross. Now before you reject this premise, remember that when the Lord says, "keep the commandments," he does not mean keeping them in a *relative* sense—as in being better than your neighbor—he means keeping them in the *absolute* sense of being perfect, just as when he says "no one is good but God."

This is why Jesus says in the Sermon on the Mount, "Therefore you are to be perfect, as your heavenly Father is perfect."[37] The first way to get to heaven is the method of the old covenant, the second way is the method of the new covenant. Because Jesus preached at the close of the old covenant period, he talked to the Jews living under the law only in terms that applied to them at the time. His goal here is to startle this man so that he will recognize his failure to keep the old covenant.

---

[34] Romans 3:20
[35] Galatians 2:16
[36] 2 Corinthians 3:7
[37] Matthew 5:48

Remember at the time Jesus made this suggestion to keep the commandments, that's what every God-fearing Jew was already attempting to do. Because the Lord had not yet gone to the cross, the Jews saw no other way to reach God except through keeping the law. So there are two ways to heaven: (1) by keeping the commandments in their absolute and complete sense (which can never really be achieved), and (2) through faith in the finished work of Christ on the cross.

If our attempts to keep the law are futile, why did the Lord suggest it to this young man? Because no one is ready to receive the Lord in faith as his Savior until he has first been broken under God's standards. The recognition of your sin and guilt becomes the passageway through which you must travel to obtain salvation. This is why Paul says, "through the law comes the knowledge of sin."[38] When we have failed to qualify for heaven by the first method, we are left only with the second. Let me make it clear that no one has ever made it by the first method. Although there are two ways, only the second succeeds in getting people into heaven.

How Were Old Testament Saints Saved?

Sometimes Christians think of the old covenant and the law as God's first attempt to find a solution to the sin problem. Perhaps they picture God thinking: *I'll try a little law and see if that works. Hmm. No luck with that. Well, maybe let's try grace and see if that's any better.* Nothing could be further from the truth. God never intended that the law would save man. He knew from the beginning it would not improve man's character. It was designed to bring men to their knees so they would acknowledge their need for a savior.

The old covenant was always meant to be a temporary thing. Even in the middle of the old covenant period, God

---

[38] Romans 3:20

declared through Jeremiah that a new covenant was coming.[39] The New Testament tells us that "the just shall live by faith." Although this statement is found in three New Testament letters, you'll find that it is actually a quote from the Old Testament book of Habakkuk.[40] Salvation has always been by faith.

That means people in the Old Testament were not saved by works, by offering sacrifices, or by keeping the law. They were all saved by faith. In fact, the book of Hebrews confirms this. Abraham, Moses, and David, along with all of the other Old Testament saints listed in Hebrews 11, were all made righteous by their faith in God, just as we are today. In their case they looked *forward* to the veiled remedy for sin that God was going to send—the Messiah's death on the cross. In our case, we look *back* to the unveiled remedy that God has already provided through Christ. So, no one in the Old Testament was ever saved or made righteous enough to enter heaven by any other means than by faith in God's ability to wash away his sins.

How Much Does Salvation Cost?

Does Jesus expect all who come to him to give away everything they own to the poor? It certainly seems that is what the Lord said to this rich young man. In the very next chapter, in Luke 19, we discover a second encounter that Jesus had with another rich man who desired eternal life. Zaccheus was a wealthy tax collector in Jericho. As the Lord traveled through the narrow streets of Jericho, a large crowd thronged about him, so short Zaccheus ran ahead and climbed up into a sycamore tree to get a view of Jesus. But the Lord stopped under the tree and gazed up. "Zaccheus," he said, "climb down. Today I'm coming to your house for lunch." When the crowd saw why Jesus stopped, many must have grumbled, wondering how Jesus could go into the house

[39] Jeremiah 31:31-34
[40] Habakkuk 2:4

of this "known sinner."

Tax collectors were hated more in the Lord's time than they are today because they worked directly for the Romans, who held Israel under the oppressive grip of military force. Rome contracted with these Jews to raise a set tax quota; anything beyond this amount could be pocketed by the collectors. The Jews hated these men who became rich at their people's expense, but especially because they worked for the Romans.

Zaccheus' encounter with the Lord impacted his heart. He seems to have spontaneously announced: "Lord, half of my possessions I will give to the poor, and if I have defrauded anyone of anything, I will give them back four times as much." Notice how Jesus responds to the man. He says: "Today salvation has come to this house."

Now here's a rich fellow who actually gets salvation and for only *half* his possessions. Because this takes place just a chapter away from the deal offered to the first man, you might be tempted to think this is the "drop down close." You know: "Would you like salvation at the cost of all your possessions? No takers? Okay, let's try a new deal. How about salvation for just half your possessions?" No, I don't think so. The answer to why Jesus treated these two men differently is found in what the Lord *didn't* say about the Ten Commandments.

The rich young man in Luke 18 was a ruler of the people. Whenever we speak of a New Testament Jew who holds a government position, it almost always implies someone who was quite religious. [41] The man confirms this when he claims to have kept the commandments from his youth.

When Moses received the Ten Commandments on Mount Sinai, God inscribed them on two tablets, or tables. The message of the first table clarified the Jew's duty toward

---

[41] The top governmental leader in the nation was the high priest.

God, while the second summarized his duty toward other men. Here's how the commandments lined up on the two tablets:

FIRST TABLE	SECOND TABLE
Toward God	*Toward Man*
1. No other gods	5. Honor parents
2. No idols	6. Do not murder
3. Do not take the Lord's name in vain	7. Do not commit adultery
4. Remember the Sabbath	8. Do not steal
	9. Do not bear false witness
	10. Do not covet

In the three versions of the rich young ruler's story, the Gospel writers all list the same commandments. Although the order is slightly different, you can see that Jesus says the same thing in each account:

MATTHEW	MARK	LUKE
19:18-19	*10:19*	*18:20*
6. Murder	6. Murder	7. Adultery
7. Adultery	7. Adultery	6. Murder
8. Steal	8. Steal	8. Steal
9. False witness	9. False witness	9. False witness
	Do not defraud	
5. Honor parents	5. Honor parents	5. Honor parents
Love your neighbor		

Now look carefully. When you compare these lists of commandments with the second table of the law, can you see which commandment is missing? The young ruler failed to notice the absence of one commandment—the tenth, banning covetousness. He simply did not hear what Jesus was implying by leaving out the commandment with which he struggled the most. Often what a person doesn't say is as important to the conversation as what he does say, and it's easy to misunderstand someone's intent if their message is subtle. In 1995, when I was in Egypt, my wife and I arrived at the airport in preparation to fly out of the country. People are stationed within the rest rooms in Egypt to hand out paper towels when you come out of the stalls. You're supposed to tip these people, but because I was about to leave the country I had already used up all my Egyptian pounds and had nothing to give the man. In response, he offered me some of his lunch and I thought to myself: *What a generous man.* Hours later on the flight to Greece, it dawned on me what he had really been saying. While he appeared to be offering me some of his lunch, he was upset because I had not paid him. He had meant to insult me as a cheapskate, but because of his subtlety, it had sailed over my head.

The Lord's omission of the tenth commandment is a similar subtle indication of the condition of the man's heart. But even after the young man apparently misses the implication and utters his claim of obedience to the law, Jesus still does not challenge him directly by quoting the missing law. Instead, the Lord says, "One thing you still lack; sell all that you possess, and distribute it to the poor, and you shall have treasure in heaven; and come, follow Me."

It wasn't because this young man owned great possessions that he reacted with such despair to the Lord's words; it was because his possessions had such a firm grip of ownership on his heart. Having the distinct advantage of being God, Jesus knew what held the man's affections. The Lord's request that he sell all was designed as a test to *show him* just how much he coveted, and by extension, how he had not kept the commandments.

My guess is that what Jesus said to the man that day was not at all obvious to him. Maybe as he walked home it dawned on him, but I doubt it. It probably took days, weeks, or even months before he realized what Jesus had been saying to his dull ears.

Unfortunately, many faulty sermons are preached on this Scripture. They'll say something like: "This man was asked to give up everything—what have you given up for Jesus?" Or, "The Lord's request here shows the high price of discipleship." Teaching such messages is to misunderstand the encounter. This story is not about giving, or discipleship, or sacrifice; it's about obtaining eternal life. Jesus' purpose was to bring conviction of sin on the part of this young ruler. Rich or poor is not the real question he's dealing with, but rather: "Do you see that you have not kept the commandments and that you need a Savior?" Faulty sermons based on this passage only cause believers to struggle, making them feel they are disappointing God by their failure to give all. The reality is that Jesus is not making that demand in this passage.

The correct response would have been for this man to acknowledge that God's standards are absolute. Once he admitted that he had only been superficially keeping the law, he would have been ready to plead for mercy. In contrast, Zaccheus revealed his desire to turn away from his self-serving lifestyle and repent of his covetousness. The Lord rewarded his faith accordingly. Zaccheus was not given salvation because he gave up some of his money. The act of giving only showed the joy that he had, having understood his need and then embracing Christ and the still veiled salvation.

Threading the Camel through the Needle

Why does the Lord say it is easier for a camel to go through the eye of a needle than for a rich man to get into heaven? Most churches today have their share of rich Christians, so preachers have felt compelled somehow to get that camel through the hole in that needle.

One popular suggestion has been that perhaps Jesus wasn't talking about a real needle. In the ancient world, walled cities had main gates that they kept open in the daytime for commerce but which would be closed at night to prevent bandits from sneaking into the city, robbing, and then rushing outside with their loot. It has been reported that there was a small gate in some cities that men could walk through single file; that little gate was called the "eye of the needle." The earliest existing recorded mention of this gate is in the ninth century (many years after the time of Christ). Supposedly, if a merchant's camel came to the city at night, he could bring his load into the city by first unloading the camel and then forcing the beast to kneel down to go through the smaller gate. The kneeling camel could be seen as a demonstration of humility and the unloading of the cargo would represent a willingness to free ourselves of the burden of possessions. Although I believe this is somewhat far-fetched, it is certainly more possible than threading a camel through a real needle.

Another suggestion has been made that camel hair thread, being coarse, can only be threaded through a needle with great difficulty, implying that Jesus meant only the hair would have to go through the needle. A third suggestion says that the expression is a play on the words in the original Greek, and that the Lord was actually referring to an anchor and cable; an anchor cable can be spliced, but only with difficulty. All three of these explanations present the same concept: It is difficult, but it can be done. I believe all three of these "solutions" are wrong.

Jesus is talking about a real camel—one hump or two (take your pick)—and he's talking about a regular needle. By making this comparison about how it would be easier to put a camel through the eye of a small needle than for a rich man to enter the kingdom of heaven, he's showing its utter impossibility. The disciples didn't miss this; they were flabbergasted by this statement, because Jesus *meant* to communicate it was impossible for rich men to enter heaven.

"How can this be?" said the disciples. "Who then can be saved?" They drew the logical conclusion that if what the Lord said was true, no one could get into heaven—not just the rich—because greed is an all-too-common sin, that knows no economic class barriers.

Based upon the Lord's words to the rich young man, the disciples could no longer see how anyone could be saved and enter the kingdom of God. Yet the original question asked by the ruler was, "How do I inherit eternal life?" The man made no reference to salvation, because he never saw himself as being lost. He felt he kept God's law and now desired to perform some great deed to seal his place in eternal life. But the disciple's question is different: "Who then can be saved?" They shift away from *inheritance* to that of being *saved*, which implies the condition of being lost. The Lord replies that with men this is impossible, but with God everything is possible.

We often equate having eternal life with salvation. This is natural, because salvation is the way we receive eternal life. But these two concepts are not equivalent. The interrelationship of the two is much more complicated than first meets the eye. God and his angels have eternal life, but they are not saved. Salvation is what removes the penalty and judgment of sin, and God and his angels have never sinned. For human beings, eternal life is the natural result of being in right relationship with God through salvation from our sin.

To understand what Jesus is saying, you must understand that the focus of the Lord's message here is salvation—not a man's net worth. He could just as easily have said: "It is easier for a camel to go through the eye of a needle than it is for a *poor* man to get into heaven." It isn't a man's money that keeps him out of heaven—it's his sin. Perhaps a case can be made that rich men are more consumed by greed than poor men (although I would seriously doubt that), but the amount of money one possesses is ultimately unrelated to the question of salvation because the Bible and heaven are filled with rich believers.

Abraham, Job, and David in the Old Testament; Joseph of Arimathea, Philemon, Lazarus, and Zaccheus in the New Testament, are all believing rich men. Being rich did not keep these men out of heaven. The issue was, did they trust in God's ability to save them? The camel (the big one), and the needle (the little one), demonstrate our potential of getting into heaven based upon our own merit. Jesus is ultimately saying: "Your hope of entering heaven based upon how you keep the commandments is the same as that of a camel getting through the eye of a needle." The chances are not slim—they're none. Even Houdini couldn't pull it off. Someone has suggested it can be done, but is awfully hard on the camel.

Jesus rejected the man's classification of goodness to force him to face God's standard of perfection. The Lord then suggested he keep the commandments in order to confront him with how far short he fell from that perfection. Believers do not need to give away all their possessions. The issue is not being rich or poor, but do you see your need? The camel and the needle graphically demonstrate our potential of getting into heaven without dealing with our moral failure. The cost of salvation was paid by Jesus on the cross. We can never earn it with an act of self-atonement like giving away all of our possessions.

A Few Good Men?

If this young ruler showed up in many of our modern churches, most preachers would make certain he ended up at the altar. Whether or not he was willing to give up his possessions, my guess is that he would certainly be encouraged to fill out a decision card. Today we wonder why Jesus made it so difficult on this young man. After all, he was asking the right question. But the truth is that most of the Lord's ministry produced this same meager number of decisions. Jesus preached to vast crowds numbering in the thousands, yet at the end, only a few hundred still remained with him. From our viewpoint, the Lord should have been in a hurry, worrying about all those "fish" slipping through the net.

There are many good non-Christians in this world. You might even think: *They're so good, I'm sure God will let them into heaven.* By our standards, some are quite good, better than many believers, but if they attempt to enter heaven based upon their own righteousness, they will have a rude awakening. Their very goodness may ultimately send them to hell. By being good, in a relative sense, they may fail to see their desperate need. If they don't allow Jesus to break through their defenses, they're doomed. They'll never respond to the Lord's offer of salvation because they'll never feel they need it.

In his encounter with the rich young ruler, the Lord was not in the business of enlisting "a few good men" to keep the law, give away their possessions, and follow him. What Jesus told this man should certainly never be put in a tract and given out as a way to heaven (or, for that matter, as a way to discipleship). The Lord customized his message for this man, turning his biggest weakness back upon his head in order to break down his self-confidence. The Lord's purpose was to provoke his need.

When the curious thousands thronged Jesus to glimpse a miracle or participate in one of his "free lunch" programs, they heard similar troubling messages that cut their hearts like a knife so sharp one doesn't realize he's even been cut. His quaint stories slowly awakened a painful throb of guilt. And as they walked back to their homes, it's not difficult to picture them struggling with a new awareness of their own sinfulness. John the Baptist had first kindled the fire, challenging men to change. Jesus poured fuel upon those flames and increased the heat. I can imagine the rich young ruler's thoughts that day: *Lord, I can't. There's no way. What you're asking is just too hard!* But that is precisely the reaction Jesus sought.

For when the day of Pentecost arrived, the crowds heard a significantly different message: "This Jesus God raised up . . . whom *you* crucified!" Suddenly the purpose of Jesus' teaching started to make sense to those thousands who had heard his troubling messages. The church burst into life as the seeds that the Lord had sown sprouted in those hungry, hurting hearts. I am virtually certain the rich young ruler stepped out of the crowd, perhaps even on the day of Pentecost, and received eternal life. His respect for Jesus, and the Lord's love for him, give me confidence that once he encountered the power of the cross, he would have fallen to his knees and repented.

Understanding this story is so important, because when we comprehend why Jesus taught the way he did, those troubling passages in the first three Gospels start to make sense. For the first time, the New Testament begins to meld and mesh as we know it must.

Do I keep the commandments? No. I'm unable to. But it's those very commandments that convicted me of my need to respond to Christ as my Savior. I used to think I was pretty good, now I know that I am awful. I'm depending completely on Christ's ability to wash away my sins—not on my own goodness.

If you stood before Jesus and asked, "Lord, is there anything I need to do to inherit eternal life?" What do you think the Lord would say to you? Would he mention (or even skip) one of the commandments that sums up your greatest point of rebellion? Do you think he would subtly turn your attention to some personal sin that's eating you up inside? The Lord knows that the camel will get through the eye of the needle easier than you'll get into heaven if you don't look deeply into your own heart to see the evil that lurks there.

Don't come to the Lord, accepting his grace, without first seeing your need for mercy. If we sign up to get the love, the joy, and the peace before we experience conviction about our sin, we come backwards. And we'll doom ourselves to a life of never being able to measure up. That's why the Lord did not bring this rich young ruler to a quick decision. He knew that a decision not based upon brokenness would never stand.

Why am I going to heaven? Not because I'm good. Not because I keep the commandments. And certainly not because of all the money I give to the poor. I still fall far short of God's standard of perfection. I'm going to heaven because I am depending upon what the Lord did on Calvary's cross. Jesus accepts losers like me. Me and Zaccheus. He's short and I'm tall, but we're going through the same pearly gates. Salvation has come to my house too, because I've turned, in faith, from the old life to trust in the Lord's power to save me.

A Recap of Transitionalism

Note: At the end of the chapters I have included a "recap," a brief summary supporting the four principles of transitionalism as applied in that chapter. This may seem redundant, but it has been of help to some who questioned the wide application of these principles. Feel free to skip them if you like. Why make life harder than it needs to be?

As you read this chapter, the first three elements of transitionalism are fairly clear to follow.

1) Old Covenant. The Lord's encouragement to keep the Ten Commandments couldn't be more old covenant in nature. Jesus addressed how well the rich young ruler kept the law.

2) Conviction. That the Lord's purpose was to arouse conviction in this man is easily seen by the way he turned the ruler back to the law and challenged him to forsake all. This created a depression in the man's materialistic heart, just as it was meant to.

3) Evocative. The evocative nature of the Lord's ministry is particularly subtle, but it can still be grasped by his question over the meaning of "goodness." Here he helps the man understand that for God, goodness means perfection. Also, the subtle absence of the tenth commandment in the Lord's list, and the more direct test to sell all, reveal this rich young man's affections and bring his covetous self-centered nature to the surface (thus establishing his need for a Savior).

The Lord's message in this passage is like the submerged iceberg—almost all hidden underneath a veil of subtle but meaningful statements. While enticing the rich young ruler towards conviction, he weaves a tapestry for the disciples and the rest of us that we can fully view only when we take a few steps backward and allow ourselves to be struck by the wonder of the Lord's incredibly subtle presentation.

4) Interwoven context. This principle is important because isolated interpretations have caused so much grief among believers. The story of the rich young ruler is found in all three of the synoptic Gospels, but in each case the context is slightly different. I find Luke's use of it the most interesting. I believe the starting point of the context that impacts this incident should be the parable of the Pharisee and the Publican, and its conclusion is the story of Zaccheus.[42] I would label this section "Humility and the Individual."

Luke begins the section with the parable of the self-righteous Pharisee, which is unique to his Gospel. Both the self-righteous Pharisee and the penitent tax collector go up to the temple to pray. The Pharisee thanks God for his own goodness and announces he is not like the sinful tax collector. In contrast, the publican will not even raise his eyes to heaven but cries out, "Lord, be merciful to me, a sinner." Jesus concludes that only the tax collector leaves the temple justified before God.

I believe Luke then proceeds to develop this parable by giving us a series of events that create a living parallel. First, he depicts the disciples as viewing those babies brought to Jesus for his blessing with the same contempt the Pharisee showed in the parable. The rich young ruler also becomes an example of the self-righteous Pharisee when he makes the statement that "All these (commandments) I have kept from my youth."

Jesus then stuns the disciples with his statement about the camel and the needle, which they interpret to mean that rich people will not be able to get into heaven; they further draw the logical implication that *no one* will be able to gain entrance into heaven. Jesus replies with his vague and incomprehensible answer that with man it is impossible, but that with God all things are possible.

---

[42] Luke 18:9—19:10. This is a portion of the larger context from Luke 9:51—19:21, as the Lord is on his long journey towards Jerusalem and the cross after Luke 9.

In the next portion of Luke's Gospel, Jesus makes one of his three announcements about his impending death on the cross, but the disciples do not comprehend what he is saying. This clear presentation is to fill in the vague hint given earlier, that "with God all things are possible" (which is a faint prediction of the coming new covenant).

After this, Jesus arrives in Jericho, where he is met by a blind man. The blind man is representative of lost mankind, living in the kingdom of darkness. He is excluded from the temple of God by his physical defect, and lives as a beggar. When he approaches Jesus as his Messiah, those around him try to shut him up—but he forcefully gains the Lord's attention. Jesus gives the man sight, which I believe is symbolic of eternal life.

The final event in the context is the story of Zaccheus, which parallels the tax collector in the Lord's earlier parable. The tax collector felt unworthy to approach God directly in the same way Zaccheus feels unworthy to come to Jesus. Just as the imaginary man in the parable went down to his house justified, so salvation is brought to the house of Zaccheus.

The larger interwoven context of all these stories illustrates the great gospel truth, that by the works of the law no flesh will be justified. While the disciples see themselves as superior to others, and the Jewish nobles picture themselves as keeping the law, both are rebuked by the Son of God. The ultimate purpose of Jesus in coming as the Messiah, the Son of David, is to go to the cross and bring salvation to those who are willing to humble themselves before an almighty God. The key verse in the Gospel of Luke is 19:10, which says, "For the Son of Man came to seek and to save what was lost." This key verse aptly summarizes this smaller portion of Luke.

In the other two synoptic Gospels, the sections surrounding the story of the rich young ruler are slightly different. Matthew develops the idea of "humility and the kingdom of God," while Mark develops the story in a section that deals with "humility and the servant."[43] Where Luke contrasts the rich young ruler and Zaccheus, Matthew and Mark present both the ruler and the disciples as carnal and proud. I mention these other two Gospel passages, because it is important to learn that within the Gospels these larger interwoven contexts always help by interpreting individual passages. Even though you are dealing with the same story, it has a different impact within another context.

---

[43] Matthew 19–20 and Mark 10

Chapter 4

What if I Just Can't Forgive?
Forgive Us Our Trespasses

One afternoon I tuned in the story of American missionary Diana Ortiz on my car radio. She had served in a remote Indian village in Guatemala, where she greatly enjoyed teaching the Mayan children. The military government had razed over 440 Indian villages, and she received threatening letters warning her to flee the country, but a strong sense of calling caused her to remain.

In 1989, two armed men kidnapped her, incarcerating her in a secret prison inside Guatemala City. Interrogators tried to force her to divulge names of people working against the government, but when she failed to provide any names, they tortured her. They inflicted over a hundred cigarette burns on her back, raped her repeatedly, and then lowered her into a pit of human bodies and infested with live rats.

While being held, Ortiz overheard a man who spoke Spanish with a North American accent angrily tell her captors that she was an American whose disappearance had become public. When he took her out of the prison, she asked if he was an American, but he wouldn't answer, so at a stoplight she bolted from his car and escaped. Arriving in the U.S. a week later, she had been so thoroughly traumatized she had difficulty recognizing her own family.[44]

Almost in tears during the radio interview, I heard Ms. Ortiz cry, "What bothers me most is that here I am, a missionary, and I can't forgive these people!" I felt a great

[44] See *Christian Century*, April 28, 1995, pp. 449-450.

deal of compassion for her, doubting that any Christian would be able to handle such experiences and forgive. I realized it was the words of Jesus himself that were causing her pain. How could she expect to be forgiven if she could not forgive?

Over the years I have met many who struggle to forgive. One woman told me of the abuse she had received at the hands of her stepfather. She is still experiencing deep pain because of her inability to forgive him for the wrongs he had committed against her while she was growing up. In an act of self-preservation, her mother refused even to listen to her grievances, and that made her embittered towards her mother as well. Because of her inability to forgive, the woman has questioned whether or not she could even be a Christian. The evil done to her is now compounded by her self-doubts surrounding her inability to forgive her family.

These stories express a reality for countless individuals, people who want to forgive offenses done in the past but who have recurring bouts with hot waves of overwhelming anger. If this lack of forgiveness is not your difficulty, I'm sure you know someone who is tormented by past problems. What would Jesus say to these people?

How Must We Forgive?

In the synoptic Gospels Jesus made some startling statements about the need to forgive. In Matthew 18 it is recorded that Peter asked: "Lord, how often shall my brother sin against me and I forgive him? Up to seven times?"[45]

In the Lord's day, the Jews argued over just how many times a person must forgive someone who had offended them. Rabbi ben Haina stated: "He who begs forgiveness from his neighbors must not do so more than three times." And Ben Jehuda stated that "the fourth offense they do not forgive." So when Peter suggests the answer to his own question, I suspect he was pretty proud of himself. He was prob-

45 Matthew 18:21-22

ably trying to portray himself as being a gracious individual, and no doubt he expected the Lord to say: "Pete, you're sure a forgiving sort of a guy. You know, you're my favorite disciple."

The Lord's answer to Peter's question is unimaginable. "I do not say to you, up to seven times, but up to seventy times seven." I can imagine the disciples trying to run the numbers over in their heads, trying to get a total. Not three, not seven—*but 490 times!* On another occasion Jesus tells his disciples they are to forgive offenders up to *seven times a day.*[46] That's a lot of offenses in one short day. If someone were to injure you to that extent, you might easily be pushed beyond the breaking point.

But the Lord then adds to the impact of what he's just announced by crafting for Peter and the other disciples a disturbing parable. He says a certain king wanted to settle his financial accounts and in the process discovered that one of his slaves owed him ten thousand talents. Since the man had no way of repaying, the king sentenced him and his family to be sold so some compensation could be paid. But the slave fell down and begged for patience, saying he would repay everything. The king felt compassion and decided to release the slave from his debt.

But that slave went out and found someone who owed him a hundred denarii. He seized the man and began choking him, demanding that he pay back what was owed. This second slave also fell down and begged for patience so he could make repayment. But the first slave was unwilling, and threw him into prison.

When the king heard of it, he called the first slave in. He told him he was wicked because while his large debt had been forgiven, he was still unwilling to offer mercy to his fellow slave. So the king had the man handed over to the torturers until he should repay everything.[47]

[46] Luke 17:4
[47] Matthew 18:23-34

When the disciples listened to that story, I imagine they must have shuddered, hearing the terrible price that was required of the slave because of his unforgiving act. His pardon was revoked and he ended up in the hands of the torturers. But what must have struck the disciples even harder was the moral Jesus used to close the story: "So shall my heavenly Father also do to you if each of you does not forgive his brother from the heart."[48]

Is the Lord saying that if we don't forgive, we'll face eternal judgment? His words, "from the heart," add to the haunting nature of his story. Jesus gets pretty personal here, condemning mere lip service. The implications are powerful and have wide ramifications. He is saying that you can't just go through the motions, or you're going to end up on the rack.

Besides this passage in Matthew 18, there are several sections in the synoptic Gospels where the Lord presents some pretty terrifying statements on forgiveness. In Mark, he says, "And whenever you stand praying, forgive, if you have anything against anyone; so that your Father also who is in heaven may forgive you your transgressions."[49] Jesus ties in the condition of receiving God's forgiveness with our willingness to forgive others.

But probably the best known statement in the Gospels is found in the Lord's Prayer.[50] Jesus teaches us to ask the Father's forgiveness for our trespasses *just as we forgive* those who trespass against us. Again, the implications are powerful and have wide ramifications. Most of us have glibly prayed that prayer, in effect asking the Lord to not forgive us because we do not forgive others!

I must admit that when I have repeated the Lord's Prayer in public church services, I have often prayed mentally: "Oh Lord—not that! Don't forgive me as I forgive

---

[48] Matthew 18:35
[49] Mark 11:25
[50] Matthew 6:12; Luke 11:4

others." While I was mechanically repeating the proper words, my heart was admitting that I could not forgive like the prayer seems to demand. My spoken prayer, although part of the liturgy of many churches, is not my real prayer. If you really think about what the Lord's Prayer says, you'll see it is a true condemnation of our lives—because we simply don't forgive all that well. No one in their right mind would really want God to forgive him in the way he forgives others.

To make it even worse, Jesus goes on to explain this phrase of his prayer in Matthew by saying: "For if you forgive men for their transgressions, your Heavenly Father will also forgive you. But if you do not forgive men, your Father will not forgive your transgressions."[51] How can this be? If this is really true, what hope do I have? If this is what it takes to get into heaven, I'm afraid I'll be lost.

Is There Any Hope for Us?

In the past, when I read the words of the Lord on this subject, I would often say to myself: *I can't measure up to this.* I try to forgive. I want to forgive. I teach others to forgive. But when it comes right down to reality, I know that I only forgive shallowly at best. I'm afraid to admit that I find it difficult to forgive offenses committed against me.

Resentments by their very nature are often replayed in my head, and angry feelings often well up over past offenses. I've found that the years often don't soften the pain at all, but increase it so that it can overwhelm me, even if I've attempted to forgive the offender. The other day I was taking a shower, and I began to think of a man who had once publicly embarrassed me. Even though the offense took place eighteen years ago, I suddenly felt waves of anger flowing over me. The man who offended me, if he's still alive, is probably now in his eighties. He probably doesn't even remember me. What

---

[51] Matthew 6:14-15

am I to do? I want to forgive him, but I find it so difficult to forget the pain he caused me, even after all these years.

Before my wife and I celebrated our twenty-fifth anniversary, I suggested we purchase new wedding rings. The stone in my wife's engagement ring had fallen out and disappeared, and my wedding band was almost worn through. Originally, all three rings had cost me less than a hundred and fifty dollars, but now I wanted to spend about five hundred to purchase matching bands so we could exchange them at our twenty-fifth anniversary celebration. It wasn't a lot of money, but my wife saw it differently because of the bill we were running up for the celebration, the reception, and the cost of a second honeymoon. So we didn't purchase the rings.

This is the kind of emotionally charged encounter that is so common in most homes occupied by sinners, whether they are Christians or not. It became a source of conflict between my wife and I for the next two years. Several times after the ceremony, my wife told me she was sorry and suggested that we buy the rings. (She probably wasn't really sorry; I just wore her down by my incessant complaining.) I pointed out my vision had been to exchange the rings at the time of the renewal of our vows. I no longer wanted the rings; in my opinion, she had miserably failed me.

I share this illustration, because it reveals just how poorly I forgive. I fear that I may not fully have forgiven my wife to this day, even though we did purchase the rings. I don't want to have lingering bitterness, but it's still there. I'm not so sure that my forgiveness really came from the heart, but rather to eliminate my guilt and the tension in our relationship. If I can't fully forgive over a wedding band, what hope would there be for someone with experiences like Diana Ortiz?

Many Christian teachers have picked up the Lord's words and used them to encourage Christians to forgive. C. S. Lewis, for one, claimed that the only requirement the

Bible makes for forgiveness is that we forgive others.[52]   I wonder what Lewis would have said to Diana Ortiz. It's one thing to encourage Christians to forgive—we all want to do this—but the reality of our inability to perform is so daunting in the face of the Lord's stern warning. Perhaps you're like me. As much as you want to forgive those who have offended you, you find that you're not always able to do so. If forgiving others of their trespasses is a requirement for your salvation, then you and I are in danger of not making it into heaven. If we take an honest look at the reality of our situation, we will confess that we simply can't live up to this standard. While we must take the words of Christ seriously, for many Christians it seems impossible to reconcile them with the New Testament teaching on grace.

Forgiveness in the Rest of the New Testament

The apostle Paul makes it clear that we're saved by grace, not as a results of our works, which would surely include the work of earning our salvation by our attempts to forgive others. His view of forgiveness is quite different than Jesus' view. In 2 Corinthians 2:7, he refers to a Christian brother who wronged the church at Corinth but who had since repented. Paul says, "On the contrary you should rather forgive and comfort him, lest somehow such a one be overwhelmed by excessive sorrow." (Note the subjunctive use of the word *should* expressing a hypothetical doubtfulness.)

Three verses later he says, "But whom you forgive anything, I forgive also; for indeed what I have forgiven, if I have forgiven anything, I did it for your sakes in the presence of Christ in order that no advantage be taken of us by Satan; for we are not ignorant of his schemes."[53] The apostle claims that our forgiveness is not the basis of receiving forgiveness

---

[52] C. S. Lewis, *Mere Christianity*, Barbour and Co., 1943, 1945, 1952, pp. 97-98.
[53] 2 Corinthians 2:10-11

from the Lord. Instead, he introduces it as a basic motivation of the Christian life. He gives two reasons to forgive: (1) because it benefits one another, and (2) by doing it we keep Satan from gaining an advantage over us.

Even more explicit is Ephesians 4:32, which says: "And be kind to one another, tender-hearted, forgiving each other, just as God in Christ also has forgiven you." In Colossians we read similar words: "Bearing with one another, and forgiving each other, whoever has a complaint against anyone; just as the Lord forgave you, so also should you."[54]

How dramatically different is this teaching! Paul does not say we are to expect forgiveness because we have forgiven others. Instead, he reverses the order: We are to forgive *because we have already been forgiven by God*. And he makes no mention whatever of the Lord's teaching found in Matthew, Mark, and Luke, leaving us to wonder how these two messages are to be reconciled.

In his parable, Jesus indicates we are in danger of being handed over to the torturers if we don't forgive from the heart—the clear motive is the fear of punishment. But Paul encourages us to gratefully forgive because God has so graciously forgiven us when we didn't do anything to deserve it. Even the words they both use are different. While the Lord uses such phrases as "you shall," indicative of a command, Paul uses passive phrases like "you should do this." Christ makes our forgiveness *conditional*, while Paul makes our forgiveness *motivational*. Although the subject is the same, Jesus and Paul come to two radically different conclusions. Finding the true answer to this dilemma is so very important, especially because the Lord ties our eternal destiny to the deed. These teachings simply must be reconciled.

---

[54] Colossians 3:13

What Was the Lord Saying?

The answer to understanding the Lord's teaching on forgiveness lies in how well we comprehend what Jesus was trying to accomplish. Christ was speaking to Jews who were still under the law. By nature, religion often creates intolerance. Certainly the Jews during the time of Christ tended towards self-righteousness and found forgiveness a difficult quality to maintain. The Lord's primary purpose in uttering these statements was to challenge these people, including the disciples, to reach a place of being uncomfortable. He was trying to make these people anxious about their eternal destiny.

The Lord's use of numbers is an obvious exaggeration; 490 is meant to represent an unlimited number, because if someone actually kept a running score, a good case could be made that he wasn't really forgiving. This is an exaggeration meant for effect. Although the deed is possible, it is not likely. This statement is somewhat similar to threading a camel through the eye of a needle. It is meant to represent an impossible feat. From God's perspective, there can be no limit on forgiveness.

To understand the impact of this story we must realize why the Lord uses these amounts of money. It is hard to translate Bible money into modern equivalents because our economies are so different. Israel's society at this time was composed mainly of subsistence farmers, and therefore what little money they actually saw consisted of only a small portion of their total income. (American farmers around the turn of the century had a similar situation, their total annual cash income might have been only fifty dollars.)

The first slave owed 10,000 talents of gold. To give you an idea of the worth of these talents, I have heard that the combined revenue of Judea and Samaria was *only 600 talents per year*! Jesus has made an obvious exaggeration by using such an incredibly high figure. For the sake of understanding, I suggest a meaningful comparison might be that the slave's debt to the king was something like 6 trillion dollars. The second slave owed the first slave one hundred denarii. One denarii was generally considered to be a day's wage. So again, using our income for comparison, we might translate that to be about 10,000 dollars. The exact exchange rate is not as important as the comparative values.

It's important to grasp that the second slave's debt was a healthy amount of money. We're not talking about five, or even fifty dollars. Ten thousand dollars would be a significant debt to most of us. But in comparison to 6 trillion dollars, it almost becomes meaningless. I don't believe that Jesus is discounting the reality or significance of those who have sinned against us; such sins are real and painful. But the Lord is demonstrating their comparative magnitude with our sin against God. While 10,000 dollars is a significant amount, 6 trillion dollars is overwhelming.

Whenever we sin, it is really an affront to our Creator, a slap in his face, because everything we own ultimately comes from him. It is clear that the king in this story represents God, while the first slave represents the one who is listening to Jesus. The Lord uses this parable to contrast the wrongs that the Jews had committed against God with the relative insignificance of the wrongs others commit against them. That's why the amounts of money are so dramatically different. Jesus was demonstrating the magnitude of a man's sin against God when compared with the sins that men have commit against that man.

When you read this story, don't you feel that the first slave gets what he deserves? The story probably reveals a certain amount of intolerance in our hearts toward that man who had no forgiveness in his heart. We all hate hypocrisy (*in others*). After all, how could he choke his friend and throw him into prison after he himself has received such incredible mercy?

The Lord uses this illustration to touch the emotions of the audience and put them "in the picture." Yet, at precisely the moment the listener is feeling superior to that wicked slave, the Lord utters the statement that unless we forgive others from the heart, we'll also be in danger of being tortured. It's as if, at that moment, the slave turns toward the audience and as you look at his face you see yourself.

This unnerving story throbs with conviction. The reality of the image it presents of our sin leaves us with a sense of being undone. Until a man sees how much he's like the slave in this parable, he will never be ready to hear the good news of salvation. He will still be feeling smug and comfortable—like Peter—in his meager lip service in the name of forgiving others.

I was sharing the gospel with a young woman who had a difficult time understanding her need for the Savior. When I asked her if she ever struggled with anger and bitterness towards others, she insisted she had no problem in that area. But earlier in our conversation she shared how she had once been violently assaulted by two men. Remembering that incident, I asked if she had been able to forgive the ones who assaulted her. Immediately she became silent, because she realized that she had not been able to forgive those men. We may think we have forgiven everyone, but chances are good we just haven't looked deeply enough into our own hearts.

Are Unforgiving Christians Bound for Hell?

Why did Jesus condition our forgiveness on our forgiving others? Why did he lay this condition upon us? The more one reads the words of Jesus, the more clearly they see that Jesus is constantly challenging his audience to impossible feats, precisely so they will recognize that those tasks are impossible.

Go ahead, just try to forgive everyone. Try to always be loving to those unlovable people who inflict pain upon you. (I have found that those little slights, whether real or imagined, are often the hardest to overcome.) Try as hard as you can, and you'll see the frustration that comes with the task. Unless you are a master at self-deception (which many of us are), you will see that you fall far short in this impossible dream of forgiving all of the things others have done to you. Again, this is as difficult as trying to cram that camel through the tiny eye of a needle. Once you realize the nature of the challenge, you will have learned the lesson Jesus was trying to teach.

If you could actually forgive everyone (from the day you were born), you would be perfect and God would *owe* you eternal life. You wouldn't need grace, because you would have earned heaven. Because Jesus is asking the impossible, his goal is to drive us to the cross. It is certainly not to drive us towards a hypothetical quest of Christian perfectionism. Self-centered, proud people will not come to the cross, because they feel no sense of need.

When a lifeguard sits beside a pool, he watches over the swimmers, promotes safety by keeping the kids from diving into the shallow end, enforces the ban on running, and ensures that only qualified swimmers are allowed in the deep end. While he does his job by enforcing those safety rules, he really couldn't say that he saved anyone's life until someone comes in danger of drowning.

If there is no imminent danger, no saving is possible. The same thing is true with the kingdom of God. Until a person recognizes that he is lost, he cannot be saved. Until he sees himself as a sinner, he is not "suitable" for forgiveness. Only the lost are candidates for salvation, and that is exactly the message Jesus is trying to communicate with his teaching on forgiveness. He's taking those happy little masks off of our faces so we can see how truly self-serving and unforgiving we really are.

I'm sure it can be shown that all Christians have some areas in their lives in which they have been unable to forgive. If unforgiving Christians are bound for hell, there will be no one to populate heaven. The very fact that we even care about this problem is a sure sign that God has performed a work of grace in our hearts. Imperfect as we are, we now want to forgive because we have been forgiven.

But what about a Christian who knows that they are wrong and still finds that they cannot forgive? Will this failure short-circuit their Christianity and bring about spiritual death? I don't think so. When you consider the fact that almost all Christians have moments when they willfully sin, it becomes easier to understand that God is patient toward us, and certainly does not give us what we deserve. Even after you become a believer, you still wouldn't want what you truly deserve, because Christians are *always* less than perfect. These areas of personal failure continually drive us back to the cross. The feeling that we have "arrived" is contrary to the gospel or grace. We did nothing to become believers and we can do nothing to stay believers—but believe. Our fellowship will be impacted by any lack of forgiveness, but not our salvation.

What Color Is Your Parachute?

Let's imagine that the next time you take your seat in an airplane, the flight attendant approaches you with magazines, pillows, and something a little different.[55]

"Would you like a parachute?" she asks. "These chutes are wonderful. They come in designer colors, and we probably have one that will match what you're wearing. They'll make you look like a flyer, and you'll find they improve your flight."

---

[55] I am indebted to Ray Comfort for this striking illustration. He is an evangelist from New Zealand, currently living in California and ministering through Living Waters Ministry, located in Bellflower, CA. www.raycomfort.com   1 (800) 437-1893

You're interested in anything that will improve your flight.

"You've talked me into it, Miss," you say, pointing. "I'd like one of those tan-colored chutes."

You put on the parachute, but soon you discover that it's rather bulky. In fact, you find that you can no longer lean back comfortably in your chair. When you go to the rest room, the chute makes it much more difficult to get down the narrow aisle, and you find it extremely tough to use the small lavatory. On your way back to your seat, you notice most of the other passengers have not accepted parachutes. You even see several snickering at you. So you take it off and throw it into the aisle, feeling that its value has been misrepresented to you. After all, it really has not made your flight better—it has made it worse.

But then the pilot's voice sounds over the intercom.

"Ladies and gentlemen, this is your captain speaking. I have good news and bad news. The bad news is that our airplane is having engine troubles and we've used so much fuel that we will not be able to reach our final destination. The good news is that there are some parachutes available for you to use."

At that moment, you would quickly pick up that parachute from the floor and immediately strap it on your back. It would no longer matter to you what color it was or how uncomfortable it made you feel. Nor would it bother you that other passengers refused to wear them. And if someone walked down the aisle and asked if they could take your chute so that you would be more comfortable, you'd reply: "No way!" You would refuse to be separated from that parachute. The thing which had seemed so uncomfortable and inconvenient now becomes an absolute necessity.

The same result happens in our understanding of the teachings of Christ. When someone comes to the Lord and makes a decision for Christ because they think that the Lord will make their life more comfortable, they often end up feeling that Christianity just does not deliver as they envisioned it would. Keep in mind that there are many things about being a Christian which make our lives less comfortable and less convenient.

But when we see ourselves as sinners in danger of the judgment of God, as brands for the burning, suddenly the good news of the gospel becomes an overwhelming relief. For the first time, we see how marvelous and powerful and life-changing this message is, and as we wouldn't be talked out of the parachute, so we won't let anyone talk us out of being a Christian. We hold onto our faith with a tenaciousness that is born of a sense of desperate need.

I have noticed in my years of ministry that those people who come to Christ with a great sense of their own sinfulness are inevitably those who have the most significant conversion experiences. They often end up having radically altered lives. Because they know that there is going to be a jump at the end of this flight called *life*, they make certain their parachute is ready (and encourage their friends to get their chutes on as well).

Much of Jesus' teaching in the three synoptic Gospels was designed for the conviction of our sins so that we might see our need and come to the cross. Because we will *never* be able to forgive as we should, we are broken under the burden of our need. Paul's teaching in his New Testament letters is for our instruction after we have come to the cross. He encourages us to forgive because we have received so much grace from our Father. These two messages are really not in conflict, they are in succession. The message of our need comes first from the Lord. When it has brought us to conviction, we are then ready to receive God's grace.

Our continued brokenness and desire to forgive the grievous wrongs of the past are signs of the work of the Holy Spirit in our life. Our inability to fully accomplish this stands as a memorial to what we were saved from. We may never be able to forgive some grievous wrongs, but as we dwell on the gracious forgiveness we have received, our lives express more and more the joy of receiving full forgiveness. And our lives grow to more closely follow the teaching and life of our Savior.

A Recap of Transitionalism

1) Old Covenant. In Matthew 18 Jesus once again speaks to people who are living under the old covenant. They are therefore trapped in the legal mind-set that assumes the only way one can please God is through a relationship of works. Jesus says to them, in essence, "If you want to work your way to heaven, you should understand how the Father sees each of your good deeds. Unless you can forgive your brother from your heart, the Father won't forgive you."

2) Conviction. The Lord's message is clear; he meant to convict the disciples (and others who read this encounter) so they would be driven to their knees. Jesus asks the impossible of these people to bring them up short. An honest attempt to fulfill the Lord's words can only result in hopeless failure, and failure is a perfect stepping stone to reach the message of the cross.[56]

3) Evocative. The evocative nature of the Lord's approach here is revealed by Christ's use of numbers, both in the degree of a man's forgiveness,[57] as well as in the contrasting amounts of debt given in his story.[58] The message is not in the literal use of these numerical symbols but in their implied significance. The parable the Lord gives is a subtle but dark story designed to trouble and provoke a greater sense of urgency to get right with God.

---

[56] It is important to point out that even in the Lord's Prayer, Jesus is attempting to show the futility of working our way to heaven by forgiving others. It cannot be done. While the Lord's Prayer certainly contains many things that we can use and apply in our churches, we must remember that it was not spoken to the church, but to the disciples, who were at the time still under the old covenant. We can apply much of this prayer to our lives, but it was not meant directly for us.

[57] The number 490 was designed to represent unlimited forgiveness.

[58] The large debt and the small debt illustrate how far short our forgiveness falls when compared with God's forgiveness toward us.

4) Interwoven Context. The dialogue between Peter and the Lord on forgiveness is woven into the larger context of a major section that begins in Matthew 16:13 and continues on through the preparation for Palm Sunday. To fully understand the larger scope of this section, it is necessary to take a few steps backward. During these chapters of Matthew, the Lord attempts to reveal more about his true identity to prepare the disciples for what is coming. We find, however, that they fail to grasp the significance of this new information.

At this point the disciples view the Lord as a prophet like John (at least four of the Lord's disciples had been followers of the Baptist). John declared to them that Jesus was superior to him, but they still do not comprehend just how superior he is. Although Peter makes progress when he calls Jesus "the Christ, the Son of the living God,"[59] he obviously fails to grasp the truth of his own statement when we find him rebuking the Lord in his next breath.

On three occasions during this section, Jesus declares that he must go to the cross, die, and be raised from the dead. However, the disciples are unable to accept these predictions. At his transfiguration, the Lord reveals his glory, but Peter again shows his limited comprehension by offering the Lord advice in the midst of the phenomenon. Upon coming down from the Mount, Jesus discovers that the other disciples have been unable to cast out a demon, and he points out their lack of faith.

After Peter attempts to answer for the Lord about his willingness to pay taxes, Jesus sends him off on an outlandish mission to catch a fish that will contain a valuable coin inside its mouth. This incident is not about God's miraculous provision; rather, it is another strand in the tapestry the Lord is weaving that answers the bewildering question: "Who is this man Jesus?" Despite all of this revelation, the disciples re-

---

[59] Matthew 16:16 ff.

main essentially clueless as to the Lord's true identity.

Matthew 18 continues in the same pattern, showing how out of touch the disciples are with the Lord's origin and his message. The event with the young children shows that the disciples are focused on themselves rather than in truly hearing him. Jesus emphasizes to them the importance of humility to enter the kingdom of heaven. He also stresses the value of the individual through the parable of the lost sheep.

When Simon offers to forgive his brother seven times, he is caught in another attempt to second-guess the Lord. But his solution is only to "upgrade" his forgiveness level from three to seven times. This is similar to the view the disciples have of Jesus when compared to John the Baptist; he is "better," but only by degree. They do not really understand that the Lord is wholly different because he is holy God.

Peter's question and the Lord's answering parable were never meant to show him (or us) how we must forgive in order to get into God's kingdom. Upgrading our forgiveness level (as Peter has suggested) is only another form of "Phariseeism". The parable of the unmerciful servant demonstrates that we cannot please God by being a little better. Neither can we measure up to the Lord's summary at the end of the parable; when it comes to forgiveness, God demands perfection. This teaching reveals that Peter saw no need for something greater than the law. He will not fully comprehend how God can wash away our sin, as an act of grace without any merit upon our part, until the cross and the coming of the Holy Spirit.

Chapter 5

How Can Anyone Be This Good?
The Good Samaritan

Gordon MacDonald spotted a skunk one Sunday morning on his way to church. In the small town of Lexington, Massachusetts, where he pastored, skunks are a common sight in the early morning hours, but this one seemed greatly agitated. He careened violently back and forth, from curb to curb, and MacDonald realized the animal had a box over his head.

He slowed his car to watch the unusual sight. He guessed that the skunk had raided someone's garbage during the night and, in his efforts to reach a few grains of chocolate, had lodged his head in a cocoa box. For a few moments as he watched, MacDonald even considered getting out of his car to assist the critter.

As he drove away on the other side of the road, he felt a distinct twinge of guilt and was reminded of the Levite in the biblical story who, traveling down the road to Jericho, chose to pass by the mugged man lying beside the road. Like the Levite, MacDonald had religious duties to attend to that morning, and besides (he told himself), he couldn't have helped the skunk anyway.

As he began his sermon that morning, MacDonald shared the incident with his congregation. "I was faced with a momentous moral dilemma," he replied, deadpan. The people exploded in laughter because of the obvious nature of the "moral challenge;" they could *smell* a no-win situation without further explanation. He had prepared his message that morning to challenge his congregation to understand that caring for one another and for the oppressed would inevitably mean conflict and personal sacrifice.

"These were the sort of things that had been going in my mind when I asked myself if I shouldn't do something for that skunk on Grant Street," he said. But he added, "Now some of you are probably wondering what happened to the skunk." MacDonald could tell that his congregation had now become sympathetic to the plight of the animal, so he questioned why they found it so easy to sympathize with a poor, defenseless skunk, when they could so easily ignore human beings in similar tough predicaments.[60]

Today we only have to turn on the evening news to be assaulted with the desperate images of people facing great tragedies throughout the world. International catastrophes come to us in living color from faraway places like Bosnia, Cambodia, and Rwanda via satellite, so that their plight can easily become our entertainment. If we are moved at all, it is often only to change the channel rather than to risk getting involved. Over the years, the actions of missionaries like Mother Teresa condemned us all as they sought out poor, suffering souls in places like Calcutta while we sit comfortably in our stuffed chairs. Maybe sending off ten dollars will make us feel better and less like the Levite on the road to Jericho.

No other story in the Bible creates more of this type of guilt for me than the parable of the Good Samaritan. Now you might question my conclusion, because, after all, the story seems so "beautiful." But for those sensitive souls who carefully examine it, the parable can arouse tremendous guilt.

The story is found only in Luke 10:25-37. You might read it again to refresh your memory. The incident that led the Lord to utter this parable has many similarities to the encounter Jesus had with the rich young ruler. In both cases the men asked Jesus: "How do I inherit eternal life?" The rich

[60] *Leadership*, a journal for Christian Clergy, Spring 1983, Vol. 4 No. 2, pp. 28, 29.

young ruler came because he honestly wanted to know the answer, while we are told that the lawyer's purpose was to put Jesus to the test. Not all questions are equal, even if they use the same words. Whenever we say "lawyer," we immediately think of the lawyer's mind-set. In the Lord's day, a lawyer was a scholar who dedicated himself to the study of the law of Moses. Israel was different from most countries today in that its religious rules were mixed together with its civil law. This lawyer seemed to have a mind-set quick to question and find a loophole; lawyers are usually detail oriented, and they can often interpret the facts to suit their purposes.

So Tell Me *Your* Answer

It's important to note that when this lawyer comes to Jesus, he does not ask to be saved. The reason for this is that he doesn't feel lost. He certainly felt he was "okay" with God. It is also highly likely that he didn't feel he really needed the Lord's answer to this question. As an expert on the law, he no doubt felt that he already knew the correct answer. He was merely testing this itinerant teacher who had risen out of the Galilean backwater.

Notice that the Lord takes a significantly different approach to the lawyer than he used with the rich young ruler. Jesus responds with a question: "What is written in the Law? How does it read to you?" Now, those seem like fair questions to a man who studies the law every day.

But have you ever wondered why the Lord doesn't talk about the gospel? Certainly it would seem that Jesus should have informed this lawyer that the law would soon be replaced by grace. Yet he makes no reference to his coming crucifixion, nor does he allude to the new covenant or salvation by grace. Instead, he directs the focus of the discussion back to the law of Moses as the place where eternal life is found. This is so out of sync with the message of the apostle Paul.

Lawyers, like preachers, often have large egos, and I'll guess that this man probably loved the sound of his own voice (as many of us do). When Jesus asked for his opinion, I can picture him clearing his throat before speaking aloud with a projected voice, so everyone in the crowd could hear his wisdom and be amazed by his brilliance.

"You shall love the Lord your God with all your heart, and with all your soul, and with all your strength, and with all your mind;" he said, "and your neighbor as yourself."

Such a great answer! It's an orthodox, wonderful answer. The crowd probably murmured its approval. The phrase "love the Lord your God" comes right out of Deuteronomy 6; and "love your neighbor as yourself" comes from Leviticus 19:18. This answer is actually the same one Jesus will give later in Matthew 22, when he's asked which commandment is the greatest. You can't fault the lawyer's answer. Jesus commends him.

"You have answered correctly," replied the Lord. But then he adds six terrifying words: "Do this, and you will live."

Now that's a problem, isn't it? Even though the man's answer is correct, how can he follow his own advice? The lawyer finds himself in the midst of a real dilemma. He's spoken out an orthodoxy which he firmly believes, and which the Lord even seconds, yet if he really faces it, he knows that he cannot follow his own advice.

Whenever Jesus talks to people who need a clearer picture of themselves, he almost always deals with the second table of the Ten Commandments. While the first table presents man's duties toward God, the second deals with his duties toward his fellow men. The Jewish people were so convinced that they had a great love for God, that it was difficult to reach them on that level. A person can convince himself that he greatly loves God, especially because God is not bodily present to protest the man's shortcomings, but he finds it much more difficult to face his neighbors. Their glaring presence easily substantiates his failures.

Who Is My Neighbor?

When Jesus turned the man's answer back on him, the lawyer apparently felt the need to cover himself, or, as the passage says, to justify himself. So he immediately looks for a loophole through which he might crawl.

He responds with another question: "Well, then, who is my neighbor?"

I believe he asks this question for a very simple reason. He knows that if he can narrow the definition of who his neighbor is, then the chances become much better that he can avoid failure. Historically, the Jewish religious leaders had done impressive work in creating exact definitions about every part of the law so they could convince themselves that they were obeying it to the letter. If the lawyer defines his neighbors properly, he can beat this law.

I live in a rural area in the State of Washington. Next door to me is a vacant lot. I can honestly say that I love that neighbor. He and I have *a lot* in common—he doesn't bother me, and I don't bother him. On the other side of me there's another vacant lot owned by the man who lives on the property on the far side of it. They go to another church, but I guess I can love him too, from a distance. The only other neighbor I have lives up the hill, across the stream, a great distance away. Now this man is extremely easy for me to love. Whenever I see him, which isn't often, I just wave. You know, like the lawyer, I think I can do this! I can love my neighbors—*because I don't really have any!*

Jesus knew that the man was trying to justify himself, and that it was foolish to argue with him. (No matter what answer you give to a lawyer, if he's any good, he can turn it around. Isn't that what lawyers are trained for?) So the Lord answers the man's question with what we now call the parable of the Good Samaritan.

How Can Anyone Be This Good?

Jesus tells a story about a man who goes down the road from Jerusalem to Jericho and is attacked by robbers, who strip and beat him, leaving him half dead. Later, a priest travels down the same road, and when he sees the man lying there, he crosses over to the other side, ignoring him as he walks away. After him, a Levite passes by and he, too, crosses over to the other side of the highway and hurries off.

Finally, a Samaritan comes along and spots the wounded man, only he feels compassion for him. He bandages up the man, puts him on his donkey, and takes him to an inn. He pays for the man's stay and tells the innkeeper: "Take care of him; and if you have to spend any more, when I return, I will repay you."

Today we would think of the priest as someone who is like a pastor (or someone who might wear a turned-back collar). By his status in life, we would consider him a righteous person with a prestigious position. The same would be true of the Levite. All the members of the tribe of Levi had been set apart to serve God in the temple. In a Protestant church, we might think of this man as being a deacon—only as a full-time employee. Both of these men would have been highly esteemed because of their place and position in the community and religion of Israel.

But the third man was a Samaritan. He was half Jewish/half Gentile, and in the Jewish culture, these half breeds were outcasts. It was bad enough that the ancestors of the Samaritans had intermarried with heathen peoples, but the Jews loathed the Samaritans because they still considered themselves to be Jews. When the Samaritans built their own temple, the irate Jews tore it down. Whenever a Hebrew man came into any physical contact with a Samaritan, he became spiritually defiled. John 4:9 tells us that "the Jews had no dealings with the Samaritans."

Through this parable, Jesus widens the definition of a neighbor. He lets us know that a neighbor is not just someone living next door—someone just like us—a neighbor is anyone who crosses our path, even if he is a member of another racial or religious group.

The Samaritan felt compassion for the wounded man, and compassion is a powerful thing. In this case, it caused him to meet the man's need. He doesn't even know the wounded man, and more pointedly, he realizes the man is a Jew—his social enemy. Yet he still rushes to the man's aid.

First he bandages him. My guess is that he wouldn't have carried bandages with him. Most people in this era had only one or two sets of clothing, let alone extra cloth for bandages. That meant he probably would have needed to rip up something he owned to make bandages to wrap the man's wounds. Then he takes wine and oil and washes out the man's wounds. Again, this was a real expense, because wine and oil would not have been cheap for him.

The Samaritan places the wounded man on his own beast, which is probably a donkey; which means that *he* has to walk. If you ever go to Israel, you'll appreciate just how hot it can be there, and this Samaritan walks in the heat for the sake of a wounded Jew. He brings the man to an inn, and Jesus tells us that "he took care of him." Now most men struggle with getting too close to other men. I once read that churches would probably never be more than 70 percent full, because people don't like to touch one another. But the Samaritan took care of this Jew.

He even pays his motel bill. One denarius was worth about a day's wages. To figure out how much this cost him (by today's standards), compute what you earn in one day and multiply by two. He paid out the equivalent of a couple of hundred dollars so his enemy could stay at the inn, but when he leaves, he does something even harder to comprehend. In essence, *he runs his Visa card through the machine!*

He says to the innkeeper, "Whatever his bill is, I'll pay it when I come back." And he does this for someone who would have spit on him under normal circumstances!

(I was once admitted to a Good Samaritan Hospital. The first thing the personnel asked for at the front desk was the name of my insurance company. If I hadn't had insurance, I might not have been admitted. The receptionist stressed to me what my financial responsibility would be if the insurance company didn't pay up. I certainly didn't find the Good Samaritan's attitude in this place that had borrowed his name.)

Most of us would be glad to call 911 to deal with a situation like the wounded man in the Lord's parable. We reason, after all, that those paramedics are trained to help people who have needs like this. We have our excuses for avoiding contact with such problems. This makes the actions of the Samaritan all the more impressive. His is an open-ended commitment to this man he doesn't even know.

The "Boomerang" Question

When the Lord was done telling the story, he asked the lawyer a "boomerang question." By *boomerang*, I mean a question that, if answered, will come back to hurt the one who answers it. He says to the lawyer: "Which of these three do you think proved to be a neighbor to the man who fell into the robbers' hands?"

In this case, the so-called "good guys" didn't act neighborly at all. The Samaritan, who all good Jews would have spurned just because of his race, turns out to be the hero of the story. The Lord's question forces the lawyer to point out the good deeds of a man who he was prejudiced against. The lawyer couldn't bring himself to say "Samaritan," but he did respond honestly.

"The one who showed mercy toward him," he said.

Jesus answers with five terrifying words: "Go and do

the same." The lawyer's answer comes back to hit him in the head.

Jesus turns the man's self-justification back upon him. Once the lawyer admits the truth, he is told to emulate that behavior. The Lord condemns this man to a purgatory of his own making, because he can never really treat his neighbor like he treats himself.

This parable is so much more troubling when we realize that it is absolutely impossible to measure up to its teaching. If this is the ultimate requirement that each of us must perform to attain eternal life, I'm afraid that we will all end up damned for eternity.

Such a Nice Story?

Many people find a way around the parable of the Good Samaritan by seeing it as a pattern for Christian living. That approach reminds me of a friend's father, who lived in Idaho during the Depression. The man could fix anything mechanical, and one day a farmer asked if he would come out and repair his tractor. In the summer, the farmer could ford the river near his property, but during the winter, the only way to travel across the river involved traversing two cables that had been stretched out for that purpose. The mechanic walked on one cable, carrying his toolbox, while holding the other cable stretched out at head height. He went back and forth several times, carrying tools and parts until he finally fixed the tractor.

"What you need is a bridge," he suggested to the farmer when the tractor job had been completed.

"I know," he replied, "but it's just too expensive. We can't afford one."

The fix-it man studied the span and said: "You know, I think I could build you a bridge for about two thousand dollars."

"Really?" answered the farmer. "I think we might be able to scrape that up." Several families who lived on that side of the river all chipped in the money.

My friend's father was great with metal, so he began to fabricate a couple of towers, which he built on both banks of the river. He journeyed down to Oklahoma, where he purchased some used oil-drilling cable, and just as the project was beginning to take shape, a county man came along.

"What you doing?" he asked.

"I'm building a bridge," replied the fix-it man.

The inspector scratched his head. It didn't look like any bridge he'd ever seen.

"Well, where are your plans?" he asked.

The builder pulled out an old post card and handed it to him.

"I'm building it just like this—only smaller."

On the postcard was the image of the Golden Gate Bridge. The county man was duly impressed and ended up providing planking for the floor of the bridge. The bridge was actually written up in *Reader's Digest*. The Golden Gate is one of the greatest bridges ever built, and it became a standard. And this country fix-it man patterned his bridge on its architectural greatness, just from the image printed on a postcard!

If you're going to look at the story of the Good Samaritan and see it as a pattern for Christian living, about the best you can do is to say, "Well, I'm going to live like this—only smaller." You might tell yourself: *I know I can't love my neighbor as myself, but maybe I can love him with half of the love I have for myself. No, that's too much. How about ten percent of the love I have for myself?*

Do you believe Jesus was trying to give this parable as a lovely example? If you believe that, you'll end up a hypocrite, only paying lip service to it. Now don't get me wrong. I do believe that we ought to love our neighbors, and I would encourage you to love your neighbors. (Please start with me, because I am clearly in need of help!) But I don't find this to be a satisfactory explanation of what Jesus is saying here. There simply has to be more to this story than just the presentation of a good example.

What Was the Lord's Purpose?

If we're going to understand what Jesus is actually saying, we must discern his evocative goals when he spoke this parable. I do not believe that it was the Lord's purpose to give this lawyer (or us) simply a good example to follow. In fact, I believe that he was attempting to give an example that was too good to follow. The Lord's purpose was to arouse some very real emotions on the part of that lawyer—and, ultimately, with us as well.

Years ago, I watched an episode of the *Twilight Zone*, where a spaceship visited earth from some other star system. The aliens who landed had come from a great distance, and because of their friendliness, their leader was allowed to address the United Nations.

"We've come to bring peace to your earth," he said. "We've been watching your planet for some time now, and it's obvious that you're not doing very well. We believe that your world can become like ours—full of peace. And we would like to show you how."

The alien accidentally left a book at the U.N. written in his language. He then proceeded to give the world great new scientific ideas that were beyond anything that had been discovered. Diseases were conquered. Huge increases in crop yields were achieved. Warfare was ended. But some of the people expressed skepticism about the extraterrestrial's motives and began to work on translating the book that the alien had left behind. They hoped it might provide some key to the visitor's motives. One skeptic finally accepted their good intentions when the title was deciphered to read: "To Serve Mankind."

The aliens were offering free immigration to their planet, and many began clamoring to be taken on the long journey to their world because all of their advice had proven so helpful. The skeptic who had been won over expressed a desire to travel to the alien's home planet, but a translator cautioned patience, feeling he was on the verge of cracking the entire language in which the text of the extraterrestrial's book had been written. Against his advice, the man signed up to travel to the alien planet. On the day he boarded the spacecraft, the translator came running into the airport.

"Don't go!" he shouted. But everyone was so caught up in the clamor to get on board the alien's spaceship that he was shoved aside. "Don't go! I've translated the book!" he yelled, catching his friend's attention just as they ushered him through the spacecraft door. "It's a *cookbook!*"

It is wise to understand what we're really reading, especially because words can have so many different meanings. As in the case of the alien who left his cookbook at the U.N., the Lord's parable has a different purpose than what we might assume. The story was never meant to be an example to follow. Whenever someone calls this parable a beautiful story, they've completely missed the Lord's point!

That lawyer was living under the old covenant, and he believed he was keeping the law. After he asked the man to express his beliefs, Jesus uttered the parable designed to show him where his beliefs ultimately would take him. The only honest conclusion that lawyer could have reached was that his religious life was a sham. He failed to live up even to his own beliefs. For him, the parable of the Good Samaritan was meant to be an *awful story*. If he really grasped what he needed to accomplish to inherit eternal life by keeping the law, he could only have walked away under a crushing weight of personal guilt and despair.

This was the Lord's purpose. He needed to puncture this self-righteous lawyer by turning the man's beliefs against him. Like most Pharisees, he was so locked into self-righteousness that he simply wasn't ready for the message of grace (had the Lord been ready to give it). A man must feel lost before he will allow himself to be found. The Lord's purpose was to provoke this man, because his self-justification would never produce eternal life.

The apostle Paul indicates the purpose of the law was "that every mouth may be closed, and all the world may become accountable to God; because by the works of the Law no flesh will be justified in His sight; for through the Law comes the knowledge of sin." Did you catch that? The law will shut our mouth before God, causing us to admit our guilt because we fall so far short. In fact, Paul goes on to say, "For all have sinned and fall short of the glory of God."[61]

I'm reminded of the man in a small town who appeared in court before his friend, the judge. He was sworn in by promising to "tell the truth, the whole truth, and nothing but the truth." The judge then addressed him:

"Jake, what do you have to say for yourself?"

"Well, Judge, with all those restrictions—not much."

The Lord's purpose with this lawyer was the exact opposite of what it appears to be on the surface. He is not telling this man to emulate the Good Samaritan so that he can earn eternal life. He is showing the man that it is impossible to love his neighbor as much as he loves himself. That's like trying to forgive all those who have offended you. It is clearly meant to be impossible, in order to expose your inability to measure up to God's standards. In short, Jesus is trying to close this man's mouth, to shut him up by knocking his spiritual legs out from under him so that he'll come to repentance.

---

[61] Romans 3:19; 3:23

How Does This Apply?

Perhaps you're not convinced that you cannot follow the Good Samaritan's example. Are you prepared to do all that he did? Would you walk to work so that your neighbor could use your car? Would you be willing to pay another's doctor bills, even if you didn't know the person? Would you spend your resources to help someone who had fallen on hard times? And would you be prepared to come to the aid of those who hate you?

We all have moments of magnanimous living, but such behavior is more often the exception than the rule. Unfortunately, for most of us, the honest answer is a loud "No!" I'm sorry to confess that I don't like what this story reveals about my own heart.

One day I drove past my daughter's car, parked beside the road. She was obviously having car problems, so I turned around to help her. When I reached the automobile, it became clear that it was not my daughter's car at all; it just looked like her vehicle.

"It's okay," said the owner as I pulled up. "We've already called for help."

"Yes, fine," I said. "I . . . ah. . . I just wanted to see if you needed any help."

Whew! I thought as I pulled away. *I got out of that one!* Some people are the type to stop and help people whenever they can. I'm sorry, but unless I know the person, I just don't stop. It's not that I'm afraid. If I'm honest, I just don't care enough. I'm sorry, but I don't make a very good Samaritan.

A few years ago my wife and I saw our son off at the bus depot on his way to enter the Army Reserves. After basic training, he went right to New York City to start his freshman year of college. Not long after, I talked to him on the telephone, and he seemed so discouraged and homesick. So Jean and I decided we would bring him home for a long weekend. New York is a long way from the State of Washington, and being a country preacher, I had absolutely no money in my budget for this expense. So I put the entire cost of the trip on my Visa card, because I love my son very much.

I want you to know that if your son is ever homesick because he's away at college, and you don't have any money to bring him home, come talk to me and *I'll pray for him!* Now what's my problem? It's simple. I don't love your son as much as I love my son. I'm sure he is a fine man, and I hope he grows up to make you proud, but he's not my son. I love my son very much. I love my wife very much. But I love my neighbor very little.

Jesus is asking me through this parable: "Tom, how much do you love your neighbor?" The Lord is indicating to me that I should love everyone I see who is in need. But even more, he's telling me that I should love my neighbor as much as I love myself. *Now that's a lot!* I love myself even more than I love my son. So this parable really scares me, because it shows me just how far short I fall from this ideal.

For me, this is not a wonderful story because it reveals exactly how corrupt I am. No wonder this parable causes so many people to sense that God is disappointed with them. The truth is that you'll never squeak into heaven by trying to be like the Good Samaritan; you'll only end up feeling completely inadequate.

This is true because the parable of the Good Samaritan was never meant to lead directly to heaven. When you examine what the Lord is saying more closely, you realize that you cannot inherit eternal life according to the two commandments that the lawyer lists out for Jesus. You cannot consistently love your neighbor in the same way the Samaritan did. Go ahead and try, but the moment you think you have arrived, you'll find that there is another neighbor somewhere whom you've ignored or shunned.

I want to live like the Good Samaritan, but I'm afraid I can't imagine it really happening in my life. Are you that much different from me? Do you really think that you could ever measure up to this standard? My guess is that you probably struggle, just as I do. You probably fight many of the same battles.

If this parable is our way into heaven, my only hope is to come through the back door. I can't go through the front door. I can't love the Lord with all my heart and love my neighbor as much as I love myself. No matter how I might try, I am realistic enough to know that it is impossible. I don't love many of my neighbors, and those that I do love, I don't love very much. I will never be able to measure up against this standard.

I don't believe there ever was a real "Good Samaritan" who did the things that Jesus outlines in this story. Samaritans are just like Jews, who are just like us. We're all sinners, and we put ourselves first. Now this isn't to say that there aren't people in this world who enjoy helping others, but no one really fits this standard as it is given by the Lord. The only man in all of human history who ever really measured up to this was the Lord Jesus Christ himself. He's the only one who could consistently do this, and that's only because he's God.

So the Lord's evocative purpose in this story was to bring the lawyer to a sense of sorrow over his sin. And his primary purpose was to convict him (and us) so that we would see our need. We must understand that we do not measure up to God's standard—and that we will never be able to measure up, no matter how hard we try. The Lord wanted to bring us to the place where we would see our need and fall to our knees, pleading for mercy.

What about the Church?

If you are not a believer, this parable should bring you to the conclusion that the only hope you have of inheriting eternal life is by accepting what Jesus did on the cross. In other words, you have to accept the holiness of Jesus as a gift, in place of anything good that you could possibly do to earn eternal life.

Because we cannot measure up to God's holy standard in order to get into heaven, there is only one way left to enter. Think about that for a moment. Jesus does not lower the standard by putting us on probation until we measure up. He does not say: "Okay, guys, since you blew the law, I'll give you one more chance by letting you accept the cross. But when you become a Christian, I expect you to be perfect, like that Samaritan." No way. We're either saved, or we're lost; we're never placed on probation.

So which is it? Are you going to hold on to the ridiculous notion, like that lawyer did, that you can save yourself by being good enough? Are you going to hope that God will let you into heaven because you've tried so hard? The only way you can get into heaven is to accept the fact that Jesus has already paid the penalty for your sin.

Fortunately, being a Christian can be joyful because we no longer have to strive to live up to God's high standard (which was impossible right from the start). Once we accept the Lord into our life, our love for our neighbors will be enhanced. But wonderfully, our eternal destiny is no longer connected to our obedience. As with forgiveness, we ought to love others because the Lord has loved us. His love becomes motivational. We don't need to love our neighbor so that we can win God's favor. We have God's favor.

Jesus did it all for us on that cross; he was the only real Good Samaritan. He set the perfect standard, both in his life and in his death, so that we might have salvation *and* eternal life. This is one of the most life-changing concepts in all of Christianity. Don't ever try to be good enough for God, because you'll never make it. Accept his remedy for sin, which is the finished work of Christ on the cross. Then live your life out of a sense of the joy and fulfillment that comes because God has already accomplished your salvation for you. The Christian life is not a life of works, but a life of faith. The apostle Paul said in Romans 4:5, "But to the one who does not work, but believes in him, who justifies the ungodly, his faith is counted as righteousness."

When he walked away that day, the lawyer certainly didn't know the rest of the story. The Son of God had come to live among men and personally purchase a brand-new way of salvation. He would allow himself to be spit on, mocked, and nailed to a cross. He would hang there so all of the *lawyers* of the world—people like me and you—could have our sins washed away. Jesus let himself be crucified for me! Because of that, I'm now free of the guilt of my own sin. I have received the holiness of the God of the universe, and now it's mine.

Hey, God sees me as being righteous! How incredible! You, too, are free of guilt if you have accepted what Jesus did for you on that cross. It is a marvelous thing to be a Christian! If you haven't already come to the cross—do it now!

A Recap of Transitionalism

1) Old Covenant. When Jesus communicates with this lawyer in Luke 10, he is definitely speaking to a man living under the old covenant, because this lawyer's whole life is centered around studying and interpreting the law. The man is trapped by the concept of earning God's favor by keeping the commandments found in the Old Testament. This whole discussion hinges on the two great commandments of the old covenant.

2) Conviction. When the lawyer comes to Jesus, his question is not inherently off base, but I picture him expecting the Lord to respond: "You're on a good course. You certainly don't need much improvement. In fact, God is lucky to have someone like you."

But the Lord's approach brilliantly destroys the lawyer's self-righteousness, using his own words against him. Jesus says, in essence, "If you want to love your neighbor as much as you love yourself, live like the Good Samaritan. But unless you can live like that, you won't inherit eternal life." The result of the Lord's challenge is clearly meant to bring this man to conviction, by showing him how far short he falls. An honest attempt to fulfill the Lord's words can only result in a sense of hopelessness.

3) Evocative. The evocative nature of the Lord's approach is again in evidence by the skillful way he uses questions to force the lawyer to face his own spiritual inadequacy. Again, the Lord uses a parable as a subtle tool to provoke the man's sense of need, asking him to do the impossible, because only that will truly break him.

4) Interwoven Context. The parable of the Good Samaritan is found in a major section of Luke, which begins with Peter's confession[62] and ends with Palm Sunday.[63] As we mentioned in the notes at the end of the last chapter, this is a period of increased revelation, with an accompanying failure on the part of the disciples to comprehend who Jesus is. Luke also shows that this period is one of increasing opposition to the Lord on the part of the Jewish religious leaders, and that the disciples have only the vaguest idea of what is happening or what Jesus is facing.

They fail to comprehend his predictions about the coming cross, and he settles their dispute about which is the greatest disciple by using a child to illustrate that the one who is least will end up as the greatest. When John boasts about protecting the Lord's "franchise" by forbidding outsiders from using Jesus' name to cast out demons, the Lord responds by saying: "He who is not against us is for us." This is followed by the rejection of the Lord by the Samaritans because he is headed toward Jerusalem. Disregarding Jesus' admonition, James and John offer to call down fire from heaven upon the Samaritans, prompting the Lord to declare that they don't know what spirit they're of.[64]

The disciples are completely oblivious to the significance of what is happening on their pilgrimage to Jerusalem.[65] Some have personal matters they feel should take precedence over the journey; others are sent out by Jesus to the cities, and they rejoice at the tremendous powers they have over the demons, without understanding that this is a sign of the coming grace. Jesus tells them that they should rejoice instead, that their names are written in heaven. He utters a final "impact statement," pointing out that many in the past have wanted to see and hear the things they are witnessing. In oth-

---

[62] Luke 9:18-22
[63] Luke 19:28 ff.
[64] Luke 9:43-56
[65] Luke 9:57—10:24

er words, "Guys, you are seeing some momentous events."
Right after he gives the parable of the Good Samaritan, Luke follows with the story of two sisters. Martha has decided to prepare a thanksgiving feast to honor Jesus. Much preparation is involved, and when her sister, Mary, does not fulfill all of the duties that encompass Martha's plan, she complains to the Lord, asking for his intercession to prod Mary back to work. Jesus gently rebukes Martha, indicating that a simple meal is enough, implying she should reconsider her priorities.

Now we know that Jesus is on his way to Jerusalem, and that he does not reach his destination until Chapter 19, but Mary and Martha lived in Bethany, a suburb of Jerusalem; it is therefore highly unlikely that these events follow chronologically. Let me suggest that the reason Luke placed this incident at this point in the narrative is because it ties in with the teaching given in the parable of the Good Samaritan. Martha is unhappy with her sister. If sisters cannot love each other as much as they love themselves, how can they ever hope to love their neighbors (or their enemies) at the same level? Luke weaves this story into the narrative to further illustrate the Lord's basic premise that we do not (and cannot) really love our neighbors as much as we love ourselves.

In the next chapter of Luke, Jesus offends the Pharisees, and one of the lawyers replies, "Teacher, when You say this, You insult us too." Jesus then levels his accusations directly at the lawyers, saying, "You weigh men down with burdens hard to bear, while you yourselves will not even touch the burdens with one of your fingers." After he declares that these lawyers have the same spirit as their fathers who killed the prophets, he finishes with, "Woe to you lawyers! For you have taken away the key of knowledge; you did not enter in yourselves, and those who were entering in you hindered."[66]

---

[66] See Luke 11:45-53

On the surface, it appears that Jesus deals differently with these lawyers than the one who heard the Good Samaritan parable. In reality, the message is the same, only the Lord's method is different. The parable is to help the first lawyer see how far short he falls from God's standard of keeping the commandments. In the second encounter, Jesus states the obvious: These lawyers are hypocrites, who say one thing and do another. Their behavior is despicable, because their hypocrisy keeps others from entering the kingdom of heaven. If they don't come to recognize their lost condition, they'll never enter the kingdom of heaven.

In the end, Jesus is remarkably consistent with his message throughout the Gospels. Over and over, with a variety of different methods and approaches, he states his one recurring theme: No one can keep the commandments; everyone is lost apart from the goodness of God.

Chapter 6

Do I Really Love God Enough?
The Great Commandments

I'm acquainted with a faithful Christian woman who teaches Sunday school, is quick to help people in need, and is always in attendance at her church. If you knew her, I'm sure you would consider her to be a model Christian. Yet, she confided in me that she doubts that her love for God is good enough.

"I hear other Christians talk about how much they love God and how he's their best friend and that makes me feel so inadequate," she said. "Sometimes I hear these believers share how they have such deep prayer lives that are so much better than their relationships with their spouses, and some even say they can't wait to go home to be with the Lord. I'm worried because I don't feel that way at all! Testimonies like that make me fear that maybe I don't love God enough. I never have those deep emotional feelings. Am I the black sheep of God's kingdom?"

What does it mean to love God with all your heart? Seminary student Marshall Shelley took several Hebrew courses from Rabbi Stanley Wagner. One night, after the professor had taught his class on the 613 laws contained in the Torah, he challenged the Baptist seminary students in his class. Gazing through his thick glasses, the rabbi asked: "You Christians claim to obey God. I've just described the laws of God that I live by. Tell me, you Christians, what laws of God do you obey?" Put on the spot, no one dared answer. After a prolonged silence, Shelley finally lifted his hand:

"Well, I guess I'd answer the way Jesus did when he was asked to summarize the law. He said to love the Lord *your* God with all your heart, soul, mind, and strength. And to love your neighbor as yourself."

Rabbi Wagner smiled, stroked his beard, and said, "That reminds me of a story." (Whenever a rabbi says that, I'd learned, you're in trouble.)

"Have you ever heard the story of the centipede with sore feet?" he asked. None of us had.

"He had 100 feet, and they all were sore. He couldn't walk, so he went to the wisest creature he knew, the owl, to ask what he should do. The owl heard his plight and then intoned his solution: 'Learn to fly, give your feet a rest, and you'll be fine.'"

"Oh, that's a wonderful idea," replied the centipede. "How do I begin?"

"The owl retorted, 'I gave you the principle. The specifics you'll have to work out for yourself.'"

We all chuckled.

"That's what you Christians do," said Rabbi Wagner. "You talk about loving God, but how? That's a nice principle, but it's not very practical. It lacks specifics. We Jews like things a little more well-defined."[67]

Recently, I had a conversation with a man who doesn't go to church at all. By evangelical standards, his commitment to God would seem low. Although he had attended church in his formative years, he's probably missed a couple hundred Sundays in a row since then.

"Do you love God with all your heart?" I asked, anticipating that his answer would open the conversation up so that I could present the gospel to him. I thought he'd say

---

[67] Marshall Shelley is editor of *Leadership*, a journal for Christian clergy. The quotation is taken from the Fall 1992, Vol. 13, No. 4, p. 3.

something like: "I'm afraid I haven't loved God like I should." So you can imagine my surprise when he answered: "I do love God with all my heart. Now, just because I don't go to church doesn't mean I don't love him. I love God very much."

Over the years, I have found that most people feel that they do love God. They may even have strong emotional feelings whenever they think about him. Let me ask you, how can we know if we love God enough?

The Great Commandments

There are many different opinions about what Jesus was trying to say when he quoted the two great commandments. In this chapter I will focus on Mark's version, which you may want to read in 12:28-34. This event took place on Tuesday of the last week of his earthly life. That day he was bombarded with questions by his enemies. You can picture the setting: He's in Jerusalem in the temple area. The crowd throngs into the courtyard because of the Passover Feast, and they gather around Jesus with rapt attention. But the Jewish religious leaders, jealous by what they see and fearful that he will arouse the people to revolt, desperately want to discredit him. Behind the scenes, they are already in the midst of hatching a conspiracy that will deliver him to the Romans for execution; but in the meantime, they send several clever fellows into the crowd in an effort to trip him up.

First, they challenge his authority; then they ask him if it is acceptable to pay taxes to Caesar. Each time the Lord sees through their intent and deflects their query in a way that confounds their deception. The Sadducees concoct a story to demonstrate that there can be no resurrection; his answer leaves them looking foolish. Then a scribe asks what appears on the surface to be an honest question, yet Matthew indicates that this man, who was also a lawyer, is trying to tempt Jesus.[68]

[68] Matthew 22:34-40

Mark records the question, "What commandment is the foremost of all?" Amazingly, the Lord does not treat this inquiry as a trick question, for he gives the man a straight answer. Jesus' reply is almost identical to what the other lawyer said to him, which resulted in Jesus telling the parable of the Good Samaritan.

"The foremost is, 'Hear, O Israel! The Lord our God is one Lord; and you shall love the Lord your God with all your heart, and with all your soul, and with all your mind, and with all your strength.' The second is this, 'You shall love your neighbor as yourself.' There is no other commandment greater than these."

When the scribe heard the Lord's answer, he expressed his approval. Jesus seems to applaud the man. One wonders why the Lord treats this scribe differently than he did the lawyer who had uttered almost the exact same commands earlier.[69] The scribe didn't have a clue about what salvation through grace was all about, nor was he able to keep the law any better than the other lawyer. So why didn't the Lord just say, "You know all about the law; what you need is to believe on me so that you can obtain eternal life"? Here is another passage that doesn't align with the teaching of salvation by grace found in the rest of the New Testament. There must be something hidden under the surface. What was the Lord saying?

The Purpose of the Great Commandments

How can someone measure his love for God? I believe that the Lord offered the first great commandment to help us do just that—to measure the depth of our love for God. Jesus does this by the use of four "all"s. We are to love God with *all* our heart, with *all* our soul, with *all* our mind, and with *all* our strength. Now ask yourself, if a man's affection for God included his whole heart and emotions, how

---

[69] See Chapter 5 of this book and Luke 10:25-37.

would he behave? How would his life change? If he were to love God with his entire soul, how would that affect him? If he offered to love God with his entire mental ability, in what ways would his thinking patterns be altered? And if he were to truly love God with all of his strength (and health), what intensity of life could we expect to see?

Christians are often moved emotionally toward God by beautiful worship music or compelling sermons, yet our love for him is really fickle, compared to this. When we contrast our affection for God with the depth of love Jesus requires in this great commandment, we quickly realize it will be impossible to measure up to this. I imagine that just to love God with ten percent of your heart, mind, soul, and strength would put one way ahead of the pack.

I know of a man who woke up one Sunday morning with no desire to attend his church. Emotionally, he just didn't have the energy to get out of bed. Like so many of us who experience the "spiritual blahs," he wanted to sleep in. The man's wife was up, already busy helping the couple's young children into their Sunday clothes. She stuck her head back into the master bedroom and called to her sleeping husband:

"Honey, do you realize what time it is?"

"I'm not going this morning," he replied. "You and the kids go without me."

Quietly, the woman entered the room and sat on the bed. She didn't want to upset her husband, but she was anxious that he should reconsider.

"Sweetheart, is something wrong?"

"Nothing's wrong," he replied in a matter-of-fact tone. "I just don't want to go today. Besides, I don't imagine that anyone will even miss me."

At that moment, his wife could picture arriving at church without her husband. She shuddered at the thought of having to answer all those well-meaning friends who would surely ask where he was. She could never tell them the truth—*he just wanted to sleep in this morning.* For a moment, her mind began to conjure up excuses she might offer to "cover" for her husband.

"Sweetheart, you have to go."

"Why? Why do I always have to go? Give me three good reasons why I should bother."

The woman scratched her head.

"Well, the kids and I want you to go with us."

He seemed unmoved by her feelings.

"Well, don't you love God and want to serve him?"

He smirked.

"God knows that I love him. Besides, missing one Sunday won't change how I feel about him."

With a flash of insight, the woman realized what would move her husband.

"Everyone in the church loves you and wants to see you there. After all, Sweetheart, remember—you are the pastor!"

If the truth were known, even we pastors would have to admit that we don't love God as much as we should. If we are all fully honest with ourselves, we will be forced to admit that our love for God pales in comparison with the love we have for ourselves. So when the Lord tells this scribe (and us) that we must love God with all of our heart, soul, mind, and strength, we are overwhelmed by the magnitude of the command. Of all the scriptural requirements found in the Bible, this is surely Mount Everest. Any rational person must conclude that it is flat impossible. We're not even close to obeying this command. No one has ever been able to love God this much. This being true, it becomes obvious that Jesus cannot be expecting us to actually live up to this law. There must be another purpose here.

Now it would have saved us all a lot of confusion if Jesus had answered this man with a message about grace, but as we pointed out in Chapter 2, he would not do this, because he had not yet made atonement for sin. Because the new covenant was not in force, it would have been premature for the Lord to present it before he had finished his work on the cross. But why did the Lord treat this man differently than the other lawyer?

Let's take a moment to examine the scribe's response to the great commandments. "Right, Teacher, You have truly stated that He is One; and there is no one else besides Him; and to love Him with all the heart and with all the understanding and with all the strength, and to love one's neighbor as himself, is much more than all burnt offerings and sacrifices."

Jesus responded to him by saying: "You are not far from the kingdom of God."

The scribe's answer indicates that he was grappling with the reality of God's standards. Unlike the earlier lawyer, he does not attempt to justify himself; nor does he pretend lifelong obedience as did the rich young ruler. Instead, he makes an insightful comparison; he states that to love God totally and love one's neighbor as you love yourself *is much more* than all the burnt offerings and sacrifices. In other words, the man realized that these two great commandments cut to the heart of what the law teaches.

But notice that Jesus does not tell the scribe that he has obtained salvation, like he did with Zaccheus. Actually, the full implication of "not being far from the kingdom of God" is that the man is still outside the kingdom, and he is still lost. Although Christ puts a positive spin on the man's condition, the result is still the same: If the scribe does not fulfill these commands, he will be lost. The Lord is encouraging him to continue in his pursuit of the truth, but Jesus does not let him off the hook.

We don't know what happened to this Jewish scribe, but by the Lord's evaluation of his spiritual condition, my guess is that this encounter was the beginning of the man's conversion. Over the next two days, this man would watch as the religious leadership conspired against Jesus, causing him to be nailed to a cross. Witnessing that treachery must have had an impact upon him. Then fifty days after the first rumors of the Lord's resurrection reached his ears, I picture the man following the curious crowd on the Day of Pentecost to hear one of the Lord's disciples. When Peter declared that the Messiah had come, only to be crucified by the citizens of Jerusalem, I can imagine this scribe's heart being torn with conviction. Was he one of those three thousand who stepped out of the crowd in repentance? I think it highly probable that he would have responded to the apostle's bold plea to be saved from that perverse generation either at Pentecost, or shortly thereafter.

The Two Covenants

Take a moment to reflect again upon the two major Bible covenants. Remember that the Old Testament is more than just a book or even a collection of books, it's a contract—a binding legal agreement that God entered into with the nation of Israel at Mount Sinai. After Moses read the Book of the Covenant to his people, they replied, "All that the Lord has spoken we will do, and we will be obedient!"[70] So he took the blood of an animal sacrifice, mixed it with water, then sprinkled it with a hyssop branch on both the people and the book of the covenant. This sealed the agreement, and Moses declared, "Behold the blood of the covenant, which the Lord has made with you in accordance with all these words."[71]

This covenant of law between God and Israel involved works. "If you do these things," God said, "I will bless

---

[70] Exodus 24:7
[71] Hebrews 9:19-22 and Exodus 24:8

you. If you fail to keep the contract, I will curse you."[72] So this agreement was conditional and depended upon Israel's performance. But after its ratification and all the way through the rest of the Old Testament right up to the Book of Malachi, we see repeated failure on Israel's part. The entire Old Testament is a study in failure for the Jews, who were never able to keep their end of the agreement. Theoretically, obedience was possible, but realistically, with their fallen sin nature, it was an impossible dream. The apostle Paul declares that no one could ever earn salvation by keeping the law.

Now, the new covenant was initiated at Mount Calvary when Jesus offered the sacrifice of himself upon a cross, which was to save us from our sin. Just as the old covenant was initiated through the blood of animals, so the new covenant is accomplished through the blood of Jesus. On the cross, Christ's blood flowed down and was sprinkled, in effect, upon the entire world.

Because he was the Son of God, his death on that cross was sufficient to take away our sin and guilt. The Bible tells us that when we accept his sacrifice, the penalty we deserve for our sin is removed. God gives us this salvation under the new covenant, based upon our trust in his finished work on the cross. We are not saved by a futile attempt to keep any laws or perform any works. It is by grace that he freely gives salvation to us.

How Should We Love God?

I believe that these two summary commandments that the Lord gives *are not part of the gospel of Christ.* That's right. When Jesus sums up the law by saying that we are to love God with such an all-inclusive love, I do not believe that he could possibly have been setting up a standard for the church.

---

[72] This is a paraphrase from Deuteronomy 28.

When Jesus was asked what the greatest commandments were, he summarized the essence of the Ten Commandments and the entire law with these two. Therefore, these commandments were meant to boil down the old covenant message into two easy-to-grasp, bite-sized statements that would declare what the law demands. These two great commandments were designed to get sinners down on their knees and convicted of their sin. In offering these commandments, Jesus gave the Jews two laws that could only result in frustration. This was exactly the Lord's intent. Jesus never meant these commandments as a way to get to heaven. They were to show the futility of depending upon works to reach God. Now if this was the Lord's purpose, what makes Christians think that we will be any more successful then the Jews were at obeying them?

I find it is interesting that this first great commandment of the old covenant is found only in Matthew, Mark, and Luke. In all of the rest of the New Testament, we are never again told to love God in this way. But you might be thinking: *So what? How many times does God have to tell me something for it to be true?* That logic certainly has some strength, but I believe the reason this commandment is never mentioned in the rest of the New Testament is because it is not part of the good news of our salvation.

It's important to remember that when the New Testament was written, the various books were penned separately. Each book stood alone, and a first-century believer might only have had access to a couple of these New Testament letters. It was therefore imperative that the most important parts of the salvation message should be clearly taught again and again. This is why subjects like "faith" are repeated over and over, so that all believers would be exposed to this essential doctrine during the early days of the church; we are told 150 times that we are saved by "faith."

It stands to reason that if the first great commandment was meant for the church, and necessary for salvation, that we could expect to find it repeated many times through the different New Testament letters. But it's simply not there—not even once. This is because it was never designed by the Lord to be a commandment for the church; it was given to the Jews who were under the old covenant. (For a discussion about the references to the second great commandment in the epistles, please see the Appendix.)

In the New Testament, from John's Gospel on, we are never given this command. Does that surprise you? It surprised me when I first discovered it. There are many passages that assume that we love God (for example, Romans 8:28), and believers are described as a people who do love him, but *we are never commanded to love God.*

If loving God is required for salvation, why doesn't the rest of the New Testament give instruction on the subject? You might expect one of the apostles to provide "five keys to loving God" or something similar. Yet John, the man who has been dubbed as the "apostle of love," says simply: "In this is love, *not that we loved* God, but that He loved us and sent His Son to be the propitiation for our sins."[73]

I believe that we are not taught how to love God because that love to some degree is supernaturally imparted to us by the new birth. How can a believer keep from loving God once he knows what the Lord has done for him on the cross? Indeed, John says, "We love him because he first loved us." Although you will never be able to love the Lord with the all-consuming dedication of the first great commandment, if you are a believer, you will love God simply because he first loved you. Fortunately, in his grace, the Lord does not lay upon us any quantitative level of expectations about how we must perform that love. If he did, probably none of us would be able to measure up.

---

[73] 1 John 4:10 (emphasis mine)

Now if you insist that these two great summary commandments of Jesus are part of the new covenant, I would suggest to you to do exactly what Jesus told the lawyer. Before giving him the parable of the Good Samaritan Jesus had said: "Go and do it!" But once you see the futility of this, come back and finish reading this chapter. I think you'll find grace is a better way.

New Commandments for the New Covenant

Just as there are two summary commandments for the old covenant, so there are two summary commandments for the new covenant. Probably the most concise presentation of these is given by the apostle John, who said, "And this is His commandment, that we believe in the name of His Son Jesus Christ, and love one another, just as He commanded us."[74] Again, one of these new commandments is directed towards God, while the second is aimed at our relationship with others. While they are similar to the great commandments, they are different in several significant ways.

The first of these new commandments tells us to believe on the Son. Notice that John does not give any measure or quantitative amount of this belief. If I would ask a church full of people, "Do you believe on the Lord Jesus Christ?" probably everyone would answer "Yes." But if we're honest with ourselves, most of us have mixed with our faith a certain amount of unbelief. Almost always there is some doubt in our minds. When we get in a tight situation, we often become worried or afraid. These are characteristics of unbelief. I'm reminded of the man who said to Jesus, "I believe, Lord, help my unbelief." This seems to be where most of us find ourselves.

But notice the apostle John's command to us is not to believe on the Son with unlimited measure, nor is it to have some incredible amount of faith—it is *just to believe*. Let me

---

[74] 1 John 3:23

suggest that the smallest amount of faith, even the size of a mustard seed, is adequate. I could never love God with *all* my heart, but I can believe in Jesus with mustard seed faith. I find that this is attainable.

The second command that John gives to us is to love one another. On first reading, that might seem to be the same as loving your neighbor like you love yourself. But it is distinctive. In fact, Jesus himself uttered this command in the upper room two days after he gave the great commandments to the scribe.

On the night before his crucifixion, Jesus gave a commandment to the disciples. He said, "A new commandment I give to you, that you love one another, even as I have loved you, that you also love one another. By this all men will know that you are My disciples, if you have love for one another."[75] Now the command to love your neighbor like you love yourself is an old commandment, given in the book of Leviticus at least 1400 years before the time of Christ. So what the Lord gave in the upper room had to be different for it to qualify as something new.

Note that there are two distinctive differences in this new commandment, compared to the second great commandment given to the scribe. The first is who we're to love. It's no longer our neighbor; now, it's our brother in Christ. And no longer are we told to love as we love ourselves. In fact, no measure of love is given.

Occasionally, someone will point out to me that Jesus said, "*As* I have loved you, that you also love one another." They will follow up with an observation like, "If we are to love our brother *as* Jesus loved the disciples, don't we have an even higher command?" Although this appears to be a strong position, it has several fatal flaws. The first shows up in a comparison of the places where the commands are repeated. The old covenant command always included the measure to

---

[75] John 13:34-35

love your neighbor as you love yourself. While Jesus does use the phrase, "As I have loved you," the Lord's meaning is clarified in 1 John 4:11: "Dear friends, *since* God so loved us, we also ought to love one another." The phrase "as you love yourself" always appears in the old covenant command and clearly means "as much," but the phrase "as I have loved you," which does not consistently appear in the new covenant command, means "since."

Another flaw with this argument is that if we are being told to love in the same way God does, we are being put under a law in the same way that the Jews were under the burden of keeping the law. In the Jerusalem Council (found in Acts 15), Peter asks the question: "Now then, why do you try to test God by putting on the necks of the disciples a yoke that neither we nor our fathers have been able to bear?" We couldn't begin to love our neighbor as ourselves, how can we ever hope to love our Christian brothers as much as Jesus did? If you want to love the brethren as much as Jesus did, I say: "Go for it." But you'll end up either as a dismal failure or a hypocrite. Love the size of a mustard seed is more my style. It may be small, but it is certainly real.

The Lord indicates that the world will be able to tell that we are his disciples because we have love for one another. Certainly our love for the brethren is a witness to the rest of the world. My wife and I have visited a lot of churches over the years and whenever we walk into another fellowship I just sense I'm "home." I may never have seen these people before in my life, but when I come among them, the witness of God's Holy Spirit within me proclaims: "Tom, these are your people. This is where you belong." Whenever we visit a church, and as they begin to sing it is as if the Holy Spirit leaps within my heart because I know that I am with "my troops." I can't love my neighbor as myself, but I do love the brethren. If some measure were given, I would probably fail. But I can fulfill this, because the smallest amount is enough.

Now if what I am saying is true, these two commands of the New Testament should be strongly supported in the letters written by the apostles, and they are. John's Gospel and every letter can be used to teach these two commands. Eight of the New Testament letters give these two commands in a sort of "formula pronouncement" (the best is in 1 John 3:23, quoted above.)[76] Six books of the Bible give clear parallel teaching on these two commands. I feel the best is in John 14:1 through 15:12. This is a lengthy and clear development of the concept that is paralleled in five other books.[77] There is supportive teaching in the remaining nine letters.[78] While the word *love* never appears in Acts, faith in Jesus is clearly taught, and the love of the believers is demonstrated.

The apostle John also tells us that our love for the brethren will indicate our love for God. He says, "If someone says, 'I love God,' and hates his brother, he is a liar; for the one who does not love his brother whom he has seen, cannot love God whom he has not seen."[79] This is an interesting piece of logic, and it is one of those indicators that the Lord gives to us to confirm that we really are children of God. If we have no love at all for other Christians, perhaps we haven't really trusted Christ.

Now a man's love for God is not created by his love for his brothers in Christ (or ultimately dependent upon it). But the apostle is pointing out that these two loves go hand-in-hand. If you have one of these loves, you'll have the other also; but if you don't have one of them, you will not have the other love either.

---

[76] Galatians 5:6, cf. 6:2; Ephesians 1:15; Colossians 1:4; 1 Thessalonians 3:6; 2 Thessalonians 1:3; 1 Timothy 1:14; and Philemon 5.
[77] Romans 5:1, 12:10, 14:15; 2 Corinthians 8:1-7, 24; (cf. John 13:34, 35), Hebrews 12:1-3, 13:1; 1 Peter 1:21-22 and 2 John 2-6.
[78] 1 Corinthians 15:1-11 and Chapter 16; Philippians 1:9-11; 2 Timothy 1:1-2, 5-7, 13, 2:22, 3:10; Titus 1:1, 2:2, 3:15; James 1:19, 2:1-5; 2 Peter 1:3-7 (cf. Chapter 3 for use of "beloved"), 3 John 4-7; Jude 4, 5 and 12.
[79] 1 John 4:20

The Power to Be Good

The primary characteristic of the Old Testament was law demonstrated with works, while the primary characteristic of the New Testament is grace revealed without works. Everything we have through the gospel is given to us on the basis of grace, and we earn nothing. "To the one who does not work, but believes in Him who justifies the ungodly, his faith is reckoned as righteousness."[80] Without works, when we believe on the Lord Jesus Christ, our faith is counted as righteousness. That's almost impossible for us to accept, isn't it? For some reason we feel we need to do something to deserve this salvation. But grace is grace precisely because God gives it to us without the necessity of our working for it.

The old covenant was conditional—if you performed, you would be rewarded; if you didn't perform, you would be judged. But the new covenant is unconditional. None of us could ever live up to the old covenant, but the new covenant involves being born into God's family. My daughter is always going to be my daughter—even if she disappoints me, she will still be my daughter; there is nothing she can ever do to not be my daughter. In the same way, our relationship with the Lord is unconditional, based upon our acceptance of what Christ did on the cross; it is not based upon our performance.

We can't keep the two great commandments that Jesus gave to summarize the law. Anyone who tries to live by them as a standard will fail to find the freedom that comes from a clear understanding of the gospel of grace. If you do not understand that these commandments no longer have jurisdiction over your life, you will live in defeat.

But, praise God, we can keep the two commands of the new covenant as they are found in 1 John 3:23. As believers in Christ and recipients of the new covenant, we discover an unusual thing. When we accept Jesus' death on the cross

---

[80] Romans 4:5

for our sins, God gives us the Holy Spirit; he enters our lives, and we find that he provides us with a supernatural love for other Christians.

Although I never *disliked* kids, when I was 19 or 20 years old, I remember thinking that children should be seen and not heard. You know, keep them in the back room. Then, wonder of wonders, my wife gave birth to a baby boy. The experience had an amazing impact upon me, because my son was so beautiful and marvelous; we even let him come into the living room. Being a parent changed my outlook towards kids. Still, I was never as bad as that goofy group known as grandparents; they seemed to get totally carried away. Yet after a few years, God did another work in my life: He made me a grandparent. Suddenly, I realized for the first time that grandparents are the only sane people in the world because only they know grandkids are what's important in life.

In the same way, when I received Jesus Christ, something changed inside of me. Suddenly, I had a whole new love for God's people that I had never experienced before. If I had tried to conjure up such feelings on my own, I'm certain that I would not have been successful. But when Jesus Christ invaded my life, God sent his Holy Spirit to live inside of me; and my heart changed, just as it had towards children.

When we face God at the judgment, we can know that we will be acceptable to him, because we have *his righteousness*, which has been given to us as a free gift from the Lord Jesus Christ himself. When I face God, I will not have to fear that I have not loved him enough, nor will I need to worry if I have done enough good deeds, because he will judge me on the basis of Christ's righteousness, not mine.

If you try to use the great commandments to earn God's love and forgiveness, you will find yourself beaten down. But if you believe on the Lord Jesus Christ in faith, God will give you a love for himself and his people. I've entered into the new covenant, and I've placed my faith (feeble and small as it is) in Jesus Christ. And Jesus never fails. He's worked a work within me, and that gives me a whole new love for the brethren and for my Lord. It is so good to be a Christian!

You're under the new commandments of the kingdom of God, which says you are to believe in the Son of God and love the brethren. God doesn't indicate the measure; he doesn't give you a scale against which you are to be compared. Any amount of faith is sufficient. Any amount of love is adequate. This message of Christ is designed to free you and to change your life. You no longer attempt to please God by being good enough; *you do please God simply by your faith in Jesus Christ.* So praise him!

A Recap of Transitionalism

Let's recap the four principles of transitionalism found in Mark 12:28-34.

1) Old Covenant. When Jesus answers this scribe, he is responding to a specific question about the old covenant. This time we find a man who seems to be questioning the concept of earning God's favor by offering sacrifices. Jesus' answer comes right from the Pentateuch.

2) Conviction. When this scribe comes to Jesus, his question is initially given as a test. By his response, he seems moved by the Lord's answer. Once again, it appears obvious that the Lord's purpose is to arouse conviction in this man (and in all who read about the great commandments), leading him to repentance.

3) Evocative. The great commandments are a hypothetical unreality from the perspective of fallen mankind designed to evoke in the scribe and later readers a sense of unworthiness. It seems likely that this man was probably selected by the religious leaders to question the Lord and discredit him before the crowd. For a man who is attempting to trick Jesus, he seems unusually touched by the Lord's answer. Could it be that this is the same lawyer who challenged the Lord in Luke 10? In that earlier passage (see Chapter 5), *he* is the one who utters these two great commandments. If this is the same man, how appropriate for the Lord Jesus to respond to his question by repeating back his own earlier answer! Often, when our words come back to us, we find new meaning in them. This could explain why he is so quickly touched and responds the way he does. This is certainly a realistic possibility, given the fact that the two encounters are so similar, while the differences in the two incidents reveal that they are two separate events.

4) Interwoven Context. This passage is part of the larger events that occur from Palm Sunday through the trial and crucifixion (Mark 11—15). But more narrowly, it would include the events of conflict that take place on Tuesday of Holy Week from Mark 11:27 through the end of Mark 12. The major theme of this section of Scripture is that those who are making a show of religion are really falling far short of giving God the glory that is his due. While these men are being religious, they are still violating the basic tenets of their own religion.

This section begins with the Jewish leadership questioning Jesus' authority, and the Lord responding with a challenge to their leadership. He asks what authority John the Baptist had; because they had not received John (but the common people had considered him to be a prophet), the leaders were unable to answer for fear of arousing the crowd against them. Jesus follows this with the parable of the wicked tenants, which is a blatant attack, causing the leaders to seek his arrest.

This section is filled with a series of questions by the Lord's enemies to discredit him, but he destroys each of their positions. The teacher of the law who asked the question that I have dealt with in this chapter seems to have had an attitude of genuine interest. To him Jesus presents the highest and clearest standard of how one must live to please God on their own merits. The purpose of the Lord's answer is to destroy any pretense of righteousness on the part of these men. Jesus continues the attack to reveal that the leaders aren't able to answer certain basic questions from the Scriptures. He rebukes them as hypocrites who make an outward show of religion but inside are nothing but evil men.

Chapter 7

Why Do I Feel So Condemned?
The Sermon on the Mount

One summer when I was in the fourth grade, I opened up the family Bible; the thick volume had those praying hands on the cover and gilt-edged pages. It fell open to the New Testament, and I chanced upon a sermon preached by the Lord Jesus himself. In our particular edition of the Bible, the Sermon on the Mount had been printed on glossy pages with fancy script, and it seemed like such a religious place for me to start. I remember thinking, *What better passage can I read than this famous sermon by the Lord Jesus himself?*

But almost as soon as I began, I found myself disturbed by many of the Lord's statements. As a grade school student, I felt awed by the high standards that I read; even in the world of a 10-year-old, the recognition of my inability to live up to these commands grew stronger as I turned the pages. The more I read, the more overwhelmed I became. I can still vividly remember closing the cover of that Bible and thinking, *If this is what it takes to be a Christian, then I guess I can never be one.*

Perhaps at some point in your life you have seriously read the words of that sermon and had a similar reaction. Although it is beautiful and profound, maybe you've thought just as I did: *How on earth can I ever measure up to this?* In the first chapter of this book, I shared the difficulty Philip Yancey found in living up to the words of the Lord in this sermon. He said: "The Sermon on the Mount haunted my adolescence. . . Now that I am an adult, the crisis of the Sermon on the Mount still has not gone away."[81]

---

[81] Philip Yancey, *The Jesus I Never Knew*, Harper Collins Zondervan, 1995, p. 105.

Earlier in Chapter 1 I mentioned coming across a book put out by a respected evangelical publisher that stated that the Sermon on the Mount is "the righteous lifestyle of those who belong to the kingdom of heaven." On the back cover, the author promised: "You can be godly all the way to the core. You can become the person you long to be and live a life that pleases God." And the author claimed that this would all take place in only nine weeks!

Although the Sermon on the Mount is probably the best-known discourse that Jesus ever delivered, I'm sure it has also created more question marks in the minds of Christians than any other teaching that he ever gave. Is it the road to Christian perfection and purity, as some claim, or was the Lord's purpose different from what we normally assume?

When we think of the Sermon on the Mount, we usually picture Matthew Chapters 5, 6, and 7. But a shorter, more condensed version of the sermon is found in Luke 6:20-49. It begins with the Beatitudes and ends with the wise man building his house on the rock, just like Matthew's version. Both accounts have the same historical setting. The two passages cover the same basic essentials, and seem to be just different presentations of the same message.

I have chosen to use the Sermon on the Mount out of Luke in this chapter because it is significantly shorter than the sermon in Matthew, and it is therefore more manageable in a book format. I will be referring to Matthew where it helps to shed light. You can see by my outline that both versions break down in the same way:

1. The Beatitudes   Luke 6:20-26/Matt. 5:3-12
2. How Do We Treat Others Luke 6:27-38/Matt. 5:13-48
3. The Danger of Hypocrisy Luke 6:39-45/Matt. 6:1–7:6
4. The Call to Obedience   Luke 6:46-49/Matt. 7:7-27

The Beatitudes

Let's first examine Luke's version of the Beatitudes. Read them for yourself in Luke 6:20-26. Jesus begins by saying that it is good to be poor. He says that we're blessed if we're hungry, and we'll be happy if we weep. The Lord tells us that we are blessed when men hate us. And in Matthew's version, Jesus adds that those who hunger and thirst after righteousness are blessed. Jesus indicates that if we're well fed, we'll be hungry later; and if we laugh now, our day of mourning will surely come.

I must tell you that I didn't sign up for this program when I became a Christian. I've never really been poor (although I have been unfunded), but I must admit that I don't even like having to give a percentage of my income to the IRS every year. Perhaps if I took this passage more to heart, I would rejoice over what Uncle Sam takes, and I would receive a bigger blessing on April 15. Or I might even twist the Scriptures by insisting that Matthew's slight deviation is what Jesus meant to say: Blessed are the *"poor in spirit."* That way I might be able to justify having lots of money as long as I'm poor in spirit. Regardless of how you try to reinterpret this statement, it is certainly not one designed to entice those of us living in the comfort of the Western world.

Next, Jesus says we will be blessed if we're hungry. Now I haven't missed too many meals over the years that I didn't choose to miss, and I really can't relate to being hungry. Whenever my tummy growls, I take care of the problem. If I were to discover that my refrigerator had been padlocked, I'd probably get a screwdriver and take the door off its hinges. I'm afraid the Lord's words don't strike me as much of a blessing at all.

Jesus says that those who weep are blessed. I don't know about you, but I personally find no enjoyment in crying. In fact, I find it quite distasteful. Anything that comes into my life that might cause tears will be intensely disliked and avoided. Going to a wake is certainly not my first choice about the way I like to spend even one of my days. I would much rather spend my time laughing than weeping.

Jesus says that when men hate us and say all sorts of nasty things about us that we will be blessed. My, oh my. If there is anything which I hate, it's to be spurned and gossiped about; I hate being the butt of someone's joke. How can anyone enjoy this? Yet, the Lord claims that we'll be blessed if people treat us this way for his sake. Once again, I'm not afraid to admit that this is not what I signed up for.

A Beatitude found in Matthew's Gospel says that we are blessed if we hunger and thirst after righteousness.[82] That's another problem I have: I don't really hunger and thirst after righteousness. Certainly not in the same way I do after food and water for my stomach. Maybe as a pastor I shouldn't admit that I have only a casual desire to be righteous—but it's the truth. I just don't hunger and thirst for it like the Lord talks about here.

Jesus says if you're well fed, you're going to be hungry later. And if you laugh now, your day of mourning will surely come. If everyone tells you what a great guy you are, be wary, because you just might be like a false prophet. Frankly, I don't like any of this. None of these "blessings" ever influenced me to become a Christian. You can pretend if you want about each of these, but I'll admit straight-out that I wouldn't like to be poor, I don't enjoy being hungry, and I don't want to weep. I like to laugh, I enjoy attending nice parties, and I prefer to have a good time. I also appreciate having and spending money. I'm a carnal person.

You might be able to "spiritualize" these Beatitudes so that they don't upset you, but for me, the hard reality is that the things Jesus says are blessed are the things that I don't like or want. And the things he says are "woes" are the

---

[82] Matthew 5:6

very things that I prefer to do and have. When I honestly face what the Lord is saying here, I see I have a problem. I simply don't measure up—and I don't even want to measure up—to the standard of behavior he presents in this first part of his sermon.

This has to be one of the most difficult sections to interpret of anything found in the Gospels. One distinguished British psychologist read the Beatitudes and, following Freud's lead, he accused Jesus of both masochism and of being out of balance. After years of his own struggle with the Beatitudes, Philip Yancey stated his question bluntly: "Are the Beatitudes true? If so, why doesn't the church encourage poverty and mourning and meekness and persecution instead of striving against them?"[83]

How Do We Treat Others?

We don't fare any better in the second section of the Sermon on the Mount. Here, Jesus instructs about how we should treat other people. In Luke this passage is quite a bit shorter than in Matthew, but the instruction it offers is still just as painful. Read it for yourself in 6:27-38.

Jesus says that we are to give to those who ask of us, and never demand anything in return. He says we are to do good to those who hate us. We are to bless those who curse us and pray for those who mistreat us. The Lord suggests that we should treat others as we want them to treat us, and he takes away any credit for loving those who already love us. Jesus tells us to be kind to those who are ungrateful and evil. We're to be merciful; we're not to judge; we're to pardon so that we'll receive a pardon in return. We are to give so that it will be given to us in return.

Jesus says we are to love our enemies. Now, we usually don't go around thinking how we hate someone, but that doesn't change the fact that we don't love our enemies (or

[83] Philip Yancey, *The Jesus I Never Knew*, Harper Collins, Zondervan, 1995, p. 109.

they wouldn't be enemies). I remember a lady who told me she had no enemies. So I asked her, "What about your ex-husband?" Instantly, her face turned red as anger over-whelmed her as she thought about all of the beatings he had given her. "Oh, I guess you're right," she said, "I do hate him." Jesus tells us to love our enemies, and that can be really hard if they've done terrible things to us.

Jesus says that we should bless those who curse us and pray for those who mistreat us. I find it is easy for me to pray for my enemies—I pray that they will get what they deserve! But somehow I'm afraid that's not what the Lord had in mind. In the movie *Witness,* Harrison Ford's character goes to live in an Amish community and witnesses one of them getting beaten up by some roughnecks who want to see if the Amish man will maintain his pacifism or fight back. I remem-ber how good I felt when Harrison Ford finally beat up on the man's attackers. Perhaps you have applauded at a similar movie scene, when the bad guys get punished. That's surely a sign that we really don't love our enemies very much. We want them to receive exactly what they deserve, don't we? (Maybe you don't, but tragically I often do.)

We are to give to those who ask of us, and never de-mand anything in return. The Lord adds insult to injury by telling us, "If someone takes your coat, give him your shirt also." No way! I just won't do that. Somehow, I'll find some excuse why I simply cannot comply with this. How can the Lord ask us to give to those who are taking advantage of us?

Jesus gives what we now call the Golden Rule: "Just as you want all men to treat you, treat them in the same way." Before the time of Christ, many philosophers and relig-ious leaders had stated: "Don't treat people any way you wouldn't want them to treat you." This was sort of an an-cient "live and let live" code. Not treating others badly is sometimes difficult, but the Lord's Golden Rule goes way beyond that. It tells us to actively do good to people; to treat others just like we would like to be treated. The problem is that it's so hard to do this. When you lend something to a friend, doesn't it just burn you up when they forget to bring it back like they promised? You may smile about it, but inside, it really irritates. And that's just one of so many little things that are out of sync with what the Lord is suggesting here. How difficult is it for you to treat people nicely when you feel they are exploiting you?

Jesus even takes away the credit for loving those who already love us. That includes having the grandkids over. No credit. I get no reward for buying my wife a birthday present, because I know she'll only buy me an even nicer present for my birthday. The Lord is saying that most of these things that I do for friends and family earn no credit from God's point of view, because I know I'll get my paybacks.

Jesus tells us that God is kind to ungrateful and evil men. So if you want to measure up to God's standards, you have to treat others like he does. In other words, be kind to ungrateful and evil men. Be merciful, as God is merciful. Don't judge. Pardon, and you will be pardoned. Give, and it will be given to you.

In Matthew's account, the Lord reminds his listeners that the law taught them that they must not commit murder. But Jesus clarifies the scope of this law by saying that if we're angry and call our brother a fool, we're in danger of the fires of hell![84] Anger is tantamount to murder. Now, who hasn't been angry? Who hasn't at some point told a friend that he was a fool? These statements are so condemning. Not even the best of human beings can get past these unscathed.

But Jesus is far from being done. Among other things, he goes on to condemn those who look at a woman with lust in their hearts, and states that this is the same as committing adultery.[85] I don't think there are any red-blooded males who can completely avoid looking at a woman's body without

[84] Matthew 5:21-22
[85] Matthew 5:27-28

lusting. Not only does Jesus require complete obedience to the law, he clarifies its implications. The Lord shows that obedience to the letter of the law is simply not enough; we must live up to the law's wider ramifications.

It doesn't take too much honesty on my part to admit that I know I can't do this. The Lord's standards here are so high, that even as a boy I was overwhelmed by them. Now, as an adult, I might give lip service to doing some of this, but I know that I can't. I don't like ungrateful people; we won't even talk about those who are truly nasty. How could I ever be as merciful as God is? How could I ever pardon all of those who have hurt me? How can I give to those who just want more, and who would be totally content to take advantage of me? I'm often an angry person, and lust creeps insidiously into my heart. The answer is really simple for me: I can't do any of this!

The Danger of Hypocrisy

In the next part of the Sermon on the Mount, the Lord closes our only door of hope for feeling adequate by discussing the dangers of hypocrisy. Read it for yourself in Luke 6:39-45. Jesus gives a somewhat fragmented parable full of bizarre illustrations. A blind man, he says, is not able to guide another blind man. Why try to point out a speck that's in your brother's eye when you have a log stuck in your own? A good tree will not produce bad fruit, and figs do not come from thorn bushes, nor grapes from briar bushes. What's in your heart will come out of your mouth.

Now it's difficult to imagine one blind man ever trying to lead another blind man down the road, but that bizarre image certainly conjures up a strong mental picture. The Lord is obviously addressing the subject of hypocrisy, and this becomes increasingly clear when he talks about the stupidity of trying to remove a speck from someone else's eye when you have a log sticking out of your own. How could you even see with a log stuck in your eye? These illustrations are certainly attention grabbing and point out what most of us are so good at missing: We live hypocritically every day. We judge others while our own behavior is sometimes even worse than what we condemn in them.

As a pastor, I often counsel men to love and care for their wives. But even as I offer this important advice, my mind will often flash to some word or deed that I have inflicted upon my wife Jean. And sometimes I might feel that my church is not generous enough towards me, but at the same time I recognize my own thoughtlessness towards people in my fellowship. I can find myself disliking other pastors because they are so closed-minded; they want me to listen to them, when they should be listening *to me.* Now I share these thoughts honestly with you because I know that the same type of thoughts run through your mind toward the people with whom you live. My guess is that if you look, you'll find that you struggle with being a hypocrite.

Whenever people pretend to live up to this sermon, they must certainly end up living in hypocrisy. Some Christians try to give the *impression* that they are following the Lord's words, so no one will see just how far short they fall. Sometimes we even fool ourselves without realizing it. We want so much to obey the Lord's words that we can convince ourselves we are doing what he's asking. But the reality is that we cannot fulfill this teaching, even *after* we become true believers. And that's because this standard is just too high for us.

The Call to Obedience

The final section of the Lord's sermon is his call for our obedience, which is the last straw. Read it for yourself in Luke 6:46-49. Jesus concludes his sermon by saying, "Why do you call me Lord and don't do the things that I ask you to?" That's exactly what I see in my own life. I call him Lord, but I'm not consistently doing the things that he wants. What I do is only a limited, halfhearted version of what he wants.

The Lord gives a parable that proves how bad my situation really is. He says, "A wise man will do these things. He'll dig down to bedrock and build a strong house while a foolish man won't bother." Unfortunately, as I look at my life, I begin to see myself not as the wise man in this parable but as the fool. I'm just not doing the kind of things Jesus clearly teaches me to do. And I am doing some of the things he teaches me not to do.

Now I suppose that I could wax eloquent on the meaning of all that Jesus says in this sermon, and make a strong case for the profound and deep ethic and morality of what he presents. Of course, the ethic is so incredible, because Jesus is telling us how God views life on planet earth. He is telling us what he really wants to see in you and me, poor sinful earthlings that we are. But when this sermon was uttered, I don't believe its primary purpose for the men and women who heard it was to make them shake their heads in awe at its deep theological significance and exalted morality.

Now granted, the people did marvel at the Lord's words, especially because he did not hem and haw around as the religious "experts" of his day did. The words he spoke were straightforward and tough, because he had one major purpose in that sermon that underlies almost all of what he had to say in the synoptic Gospels. In almost every area of this sermon, Jesus puts his finger on a different character weakness. His words are like rounds being fired by an expert marksman, hitting the target over and over and leaving the listener in shock at his own pitiful condition.

This is the way these words felt when they first assaulted my youthful ten-year-old heart. Even when I was a boy, they struck me as impossible. Unless I spiritualize and soften the meaning of this sermon into something that is just not there, I can only come to the conclusion that this passage is simply not the Christianity to which I was introduced. It does not contain the grace and forgiveness that were preached to me when I first came to the Lord. This message, however deep and profound it might be, left me broken as a young boy—and it still has that same impact on me today.

There is no grace in this sermon. From beginning to end, I find myself utterly condemned and frustrated; just as those who listened that day back in Galilee must have felt. This sermon brings to mind those terrible words of the apostle Paul: "For the good that I wish to do, I do not do; but I practice the very evil that I do not wish to do."[86] I can't imagine—even with the power of the Holy Spirit in my life—that I could ever achieve the standard that the Lord introduces here. Trying to live this as a Christian standard of life is beyond my capacity for goodness.

The Roman Centurion's Reaction

After Jesus finished the sermon and descended from the mountain, he entered the seaside village of Capernaum, which was very near to the area where he delivered this message. Jesus had adopted this seaside hamlet on the edge of the Sea of Galilee as his ministry headquarters. Immediately after he arrived back in town, some of the elders from the local synagogue approached him: "Rabbi, there's a Roman centurion who has a servant he loves very much who's dying. Would you go and heal this man's servant? Even though this man is a Roman, he's a worthy man. He loves our nation and even built us our synagogue. Would you please help him?"[87]

Now when you listen to this request, it makes you wonder if these men had been up on the mountain to hear the Lord's sermon. Jesus had just said: "If you love those who love you, what credit is that to you?"[88] These Jewish elders were focusing on this Gentile's "worthiness," hoping to

---

[86] Romans 7:19
[87] This is my paraphrase of Luke 7:4-5.
[88] Luke 6:32a

arouse the Lord to action. Usually, a Jew would waste no love upon Gentiles, whom they lumped together as heathen dogs. But this soldier is different because he has used some of his money and influence to benefit the community. They see him positively disposed toward Judaism, because he's a good contributor (to say nothing of the power of his position). So his worthiness is no doubt based upon how good he has been to them.

The Lord begins walking toward the Roman's house. Apparently the centurion lived up the hill from Capernaum; he saw the Lord coming and sent a message through his friends: "Lord, do not trouble Yourself further, for I am not worthy for You to come under my roof; for this reason I did not even consider myself *worthy* to come to You..."[89] (emphasis mine). The centurion believes himself unworthy, feeling he doesn't even have the right to ask the Lord for help, so he has asked his Jewish friends to approach Jesus. The Roman indicates he understands the power and scope of authority. He knows if Jesus will just say the word, his servant will be healed.

Now the Lord marveled at his words and turned to those in his party: "I say to you, not even in Israel have I found such great faith."[90] Then he healed the man's servant from a distance, just as the man requested.

It is interesting to contrast what this Roman had to say about himself with the flattering words of his admirers. I would suggest that he was up on the mountain to hear the Lord's sermon, and that he grasped its significance. As the Roman commander in the area, he probably sent his soldiers up to patrol that gathering (crowds always made the Romans nervous, especially in Israel where rebellion was often in the air), but his interest in the Jewish religion would probably have drawn him up that hill to hear this rabbi with such a reputation.

---

[89] Luke 7:6-7
[90] Luke 7:9

Whether he heard or not, the centurion grasped the essence of the Lord's message—he had a clear awareness of his own unworthiness. His response is so much closer to what Jesus is looking for, and so the Lord commends his great faith and contrasts it with what he's seen in the rest of Israel. Here was a Roman, a heathen man, who was closer to the truth than all the religious leaders with all of their fine clothes and strict legalistic lifestyles.

I believe the story of this man is placed right after the Sermon on the Mount so that we can have a graphic illustration of the main point Jesus was teaching. When the religious leaders use the word "worthy," they are using it in a shallow and comparative fashion. They're saying, in essence: "This Roman is worthy—in comparison with other Gentiles: He's not as bad as he could be, and in fact he has actually helped us, so he's worthy of your attention." But the centurion understood how unworthy he really was from God's vantage point—he knew that he was a sinner who had completely missed the mark.

Only a Few Good Men?

In Matthew 7:13-14, Jesus tells us to "enter by the narrow gate; for the gate is wide, and the way is broad that leads to destruction, and many are those who enter by it. For the gate is small, and the way is narrow that leads to life, and few are those who find it." Many Christians have taught that the narrow way is the cross. I have no complaints with that conclusion, because no one is able to achieve salvation apart from Jesus and the cross. But I'm not convinced that this is what Jesus is saying in these verses.

In another passage in Luke the Lord says, "Strive to enter by the narrow door; for many, I tell you, will seek to enter and will not be able."[91] There is a problem if we assume that the narrow way is the same in both Matthew and Luke,

---

[91] Luke 13:24

and that it is the cross. Here in Luke's Gospel, the Lord indicates that many will seek to enter through this door and will be unable to. Now that's strange, if people will seek to enter heaven by the cross and will not be able to get in.

I believe that Jesus meant something other than the cross when he talked about a narrow way. Let me suggest that he was referring to the law of Moses. The law is a narrow and demanding path, and Jesus says that there are few that find it. The narrow way being the law is certainly consistent with the rest of the Sermon on the Mount. Those who heard this message should have asked themselves, "Am I one of the few who find this narrow way?" If they were honest, the only conclusion they would have come to was "no." Jesus' presentation of the need for a few good men is a hypothetical unreality. So "a few good men" are really none at all. Paul gives us more light when he quotes Psalm 14: "There is none righteous, no not one."[92] But Jesus allowed each man or woman in his audience to arrive at this conclusion at their own pace and in their own way.

As most Christian pastors do, I teach that salvation is not achieved through the law of Moses. According to the apostle Paul, the purpose of the law is to bring us to a place of conviction of sin. After we have reached that place and received Jesus as our Savior, we are born again and *are freed from the law*.[93] Let me suggest that while the Sermon on the Mount gives us the highest ethic, it is not the substance of the Christian life. The primary purpose of this sermon for the believer would be to help us maintain our humility and to remind us how great our need was before we were saved. But its morality is so high that it is not a reasonable text or pattern for life. To place yourself under this sermon as a rule of life is to place yourself back under a law with all the implications of the original Ten Commandments.

---

[92] Romans 3:10
[93] Romans 7:6

This sermon is like attempting to introduce a first grade student to calculus. The child does not have the background or the mental development to work with calculus. The material could be clearly presented, but the child would still not be able to learn it. In the same way, I am amazed at how many Christians I meet who are pretending to follow our Savior's teaching in this sermon. No sinner, whether he is a believer or still unregenerate, can live up to these standards.

You can go ahead if you like and try to use it as a pattern for your life, but the only hope you'll have of not being completely decimated in frustration is by living a life of hypocrisy. Jesus is not presenting a standard that we should strive to achieve. He's demanding perfection.[94] It's either pass or fail. Either you're good enough, or you're not. The ethic and morality of this sermon is similar to trying to give all your possessions to the poor, or to forgive everyone who has offended you, or to love every neighbor as much as you love yourself, or to love God with all of your heart. These tasks simply cannot be done. And that was precisely the Lord's point.

They call this the Sermon on the Mount because Jesus delivered it from a hillside, but I would suggest it should be called the Sermon on the Fault, because the Lord's purpose was to demonstrate the utter futility of ever measuring up to God's demands. Jesus graphically demonstrates over and over again how many faults we really have, and how far short we fall of God's perfect standard.

Don't Misunderstand This Sermon

The main reason Jesus uttered the Sermon on the Mount was to bring people like Tom Weaver to that place where he would admit he was entirely unworthy of being in the presence of a holy God. Like that Roman soldier, I know that I do not deserve to ask the Lord to do anything for me.

---

[94] Matthew 5:48

I'm completely without hope and merit. But fortunately, that knowledge prepares me for the marvelous message of the gospel of grace found in Christ Jesus. It prepares me without my keeping the law, without forgiving, without giving, without loving my enemies. Why? Because I'm hopelessly unable to do any of those things to ever win my salvation.

If you can accept that the teachings of the Lord before the cross were not designed to tell you how to live the Christian life but to flatten your self-righteousness, you will be right where God wants you. You will be ready to accept the work of Jesus on the cross, without which no one will ever come to the Father. This teaching is not the ultimate pattern for living. It demonstrates God's standards, and those standards are impossibly high for unworthy people. Their purpose is to bring us to the place where we fall at his feet and cry: "Lord, be gracious to me, a sinner."

Unfortunately, many have tried to sum up Jesus' teaching as the standard for what Christianity is, not realizing it is a standard that only God can keep. The failure to understand this purpose of the Lord's message has led many Christians to a tremendous burden of guilt as they have come to realize they simply don't measure up. Those who are most caring and sensitive are also the most prone to this pain. But when we reach the place of seeing ourselves as unworthy, we are finally ready for the message of the cross. The cross is more than adequate to meet our need. Our salvation is all by the grace of God, poured out through the blood of Christ on the cross.

Now, certainly as a Christian, you can look at this sermon and realize it gives a better picture of what God is like and what he would like you to be. After you have gone to the cross and become a believer, you can gaze at the impossibly high standard that the Lord presents in the Sermon on the Mount and remind yourself that you stand in God's grace. God knows your weaknesses. He knows your inability to live fully the way he lived when he walked among us as a man. So you can depend upon his grace and mercy that imputes to us his righteousness. (In other words, he *declares* you righteous, even when you are really not righteous by your behavior.)

So as a believer, walking in the grace of the Lord Jesus, you recognize that you will never be *sinless* on this side of glory. It is a reality that you actually do *sin less*, but you are still so far from the standards of the Sermon on the Mount, and your progress is slow. But the more you trust in God's grace to cover your sins, the more you will find that sin becomes distasteful, and the more you will desire to live righteously and please the Lord. But Jesus does it all. We must always depend upon his sufficiency.

A Recap of Transitionalism

Let's recap the four principles of transitionalism found in Luke 6:20-49.

1) Old Covenant. Probably no other passage in the Gospels deals more with the old covenant than the Sermon on the Mount. Yet because the church has failed to understand this, Christians have suffered much grief. From the beginning of this sermon until its completion, the Lord's focus is on interpreting the law. No real understanding of this sermon can be gained until the reader grasps that this message is a detailed presentation concerning the implications of the law. This is probably best seen in Matthew 5, but it permeates both versions of the sermon. Jesus declares emphatically that he has not come to destroy but to fulfill. His interpretation does not do away with the law; it reveals the hidden depth of God's great standard in order to let the Jews know that they are not really keeping these commandments as they thought.

2) Conviction. More than any other message of the Lord, the Sermon on the Mount is about conviction. The Beatitudes begin the process, and each new section drives the point home. Keep in mind that the Jews of Jesus' day had never heard this message. Over the years through their rigorous attention to the details of the oral traditions of the law, they had convinced themselves that God was pleased with their obedience. They failed to understand that God saw beneath the surface of their superficial obedience into their self-centered and disobedient hearts. In this message, the Lord reveals just how high God's standards really are. In no other place does the Lord pack so much conviction into one message.

3) Evocative. The Lord's ministry is like music. The first time people heard him speak, they were probably more aware of the feeling he provided than the details of what he had to say in his message. There was the excitement of the crowd, and the enthusiasm brought by his miracles. He spoke with authority and commanded attention; he used stories to conjure up strong visual images that made people smile and think. And like moody music, his words left in their hearts a sense of their great emptiness.

But as they walked the long dusty roads on the way home, I can picture their animated conversations. This message was so new and fresh and demanding. Some, I'm sure, felt the need to rise to the occasion; others scoffed at the impossible ethic this rabbi had presented. But many of those who had heard this sermon would never be the same. A painful, gaping wound had been opened in their hearts. While some would follow this teacher and become his disciples, others would turn upon him, angry at his message. But no one would leave as they had come, complacent and unmoved.

4) Interwoven Context. The sermon itself has an interwoven context that is built block by block until it calls on us to obey what we cannot obey. It is the joining of this sermon with the healing of the centurion's servant that most graphically drives home the point of the sermon; in spite of what I and others may think, we are unworthy. Matthew includes an additional miracle, the healing of a man with leprosy.[95] The leper's words have a double meaning when he replies that Jesus can make him clean. I am sure he had no idea of the significance of his own words (that Jesus can cleanse both his body and soul), but the Lord sends him to the priest as a testimony of his power.

---

[95] Matthew 8:1-4

Chapter 8

Am I Too Religious?
The Prodigal Son

The church hired Randy as their youth pastor so he could work with the troubled youth living near their facilities. Almost from the beginning, his ministry flourished, and a large number of kids trusted Jesus. Like every good pastor, he encouraged those kids to start attending church services on Sunday morning. But when they crowded into the small chapel, still dressed in their counter cultural clothes, the parishioners quickly became uncomfortable. In the end, the church let Randy go because they didn't like the "element" he was bringing into their church.

Now, it is troubling to think that a church could fire their youth pastor because he did his job too well, yet this attitude is similar to that displayed by the Pharisees when they saw all the "big sinners" flocking to Jesus. The Lord received the tax collectors, thieves, adulterers, and prostitutes with an open heart, and this led the religious leaders to reject Jesus.

When I read of the Lord's many encounters with the Pharisees, it seems only fair that these men should in turn be rejected by the Son of God. Because of their questions designed to trap him, their scathing criticism, and their outright attacks upon him, it is a wonder that Jesus gave these men any time at all. But our God isn't fair. He doesn't think as I do; he operates in the realm of grace, which is much better than being fair. Despite the open animosity between the Lord and the Pharisees, he was all the while laboring to prepare these same men for salvation. The deeper a man is entrenched in religious legalism, the more difficulty he will have responding to the grace of God. No other group of men were ever more outwardly committed to living under the law than the Pharisees.

He's Reading Their Minds

Yes, amazing as it might seem, even the hardhearted Pharisees were the object of God's love. Let me suggest that a good number of the Lord's parables in the Gospels were created primarily as tools to reach the hearts of these very men who were among Jesus' most hostile audiences. Jesus crafted the parables found in Luke 15 primarily for this purpose. I suggest that you read that chapter for yourself as we examine the events surrounding the parable of the Prodigal Son.

To understand what was happening, take a closer look at the first few verses. Luke tells us that many tax collectors and notorious sinners were coming to Jesus, and he reveals that this so upset the scribes and the Pharisees that they began to grumble. Luke actually gives us their grumbling thoughts: *What kind of man is this that accepts tax collectors and sinners, and even eats with them?*[96] These thoughts seem to be representative of many of the Pharisees. Throughout the Gospels, they constantly show offense at the company that Jesus chooses to keep. No self-respecting Pharisee would have been caught dead rubbing shoulders with the "low-lifes" with whom the Lord mingled. Even the typical citizen had a problem with tax collectors; these men had chosen to work for the Romans at the expense of their own countrymen. Jesus had many encounters with the Pharisees over the worthiness (or unworthiness) of those to whom he ministered. On one occasion, when they snubbed some in his audience, Jesus responded by saying: "It is not those who are healthy

---

[96] My paraphrase of Luke 15:2b

who need a physician, but those who are sick; I did not come to call the righteous, but sinners."[97]

On this day recorded in Luke 15, Jesus either over-heard them or sensed their attitude, because he began to teach them with a parable. He gives three parables in a row, aimed at progressively overcoming their faulty reasoning. To fully understand what was happening when Jesus spoke these words, we must grasp that the Lord was not primarily speak-ing to the notorious sinners who introduce the chapter but to the legalistic group of men standing on the edge of the crowd.

Jesus understood the powerful impact of well-crafted stories; they make a greater impression than almost any other teaching device. The Lord used them to break down his lis-teners with a wedge of truth. In this case, his purpose was to expose what was in their hearts, with the realization that the impact would be delayed.

Sometimes my wife will use a story to communicate a truth that she wants me to feel or understand from her per-spective. She claims that I often get angry when she does this, probably because her stories tend to attack my self-centered or self-righteous interests. But later I do come to a new un-derstanding of her position and seek to find a compromise. In the same way, I am not surprised that the Pharisees failed to respond positively, and instead reacted with anger. Instead of saying, "You know, Jesus, *you're right!*" their ultimate re-sponse was to seek his death. But his message would be brought home to many of them later, after the cross.

My guess is that nobody in the crowd, including the disciples, initially understood that Jesus was aiming his words at the Pharisees. Those listening that day may have walked away without realizing he had singled out this particular group as the target of his evocative message. Jesus may not

---

[97] Mark 2:17

even have looked at the Pharisees as he began telling his first parable, thus lulling them with his seemingly benign words. The Lord developed each of these stories in his typical evocative manner, which was subtle but enticing. The three stories create a natural progression designed to heighten tension and drive his listeners toward his final purpose. With these stories, Jesus presents a unified message with a surprise ending.

The Lost and Found Department

The first parable is about a man losing one of his sheep. Of the three stories, only this one is found in another Gospel.[98] Jesus tells of a shepherd who loses one of his hundred sheep and who leaves the others behind to go search for it. When he finds it, he places it upon his shoulders and gently brings the wayward animal home. Then he calls together his family and friends so they can celebrate his recovery of the lost sheep.

In the second tale, a woman loses one of her ten silver coins. Typical houses in those days had few if any windows, so the woman in the story uses a broom and a lamp to scour her home. (Most floors were made of compacted dirt, so she sweeps, hoping to move the dirt and uncover the coin from where it might be hidden.) When she finds the missing money, she too calls her friends together and invites them to rejoice because she's found her valuable lost coin.

The third parable in this trilogy is the most famous, the lost son. A son asks to obtain his inheritance from his father so he can move out on his own. He quickly uses up all his money in wild living. When a famine comes along, the only job he's able to get is feeding pigs on a farm. Realizing that he was better off working for his father, he decides to return home. When he comes down the road, his father spots him and runs to embrace him. While the son seeks to declare

---

[98] See Matthew 18:12-14. Matthew gives almost the same story, only on that occasion Jesus aims it at those who cause little ones to stumble, so the Lord's purpose here is different.

his unworthiness, his father begins to celebrate the return of his lost son.

The Lord uses the first story of the shepherd to lull the Pharisees. If you follow through logically on what Jesus is saying, the ninety-nine sheep who do not go astray could easily be interpreted as representing these dedicated religious conservatives who at least do what seems outwardly right. When Jesus gives his moral for this first parable, the Lord's purpose appears to be clarification of why he accepts repentant notorious sinners so readily. He says: "I tell you in the same way, there will be more joy in heaven over one sinner who repents, than over ninety-nine righteous persons who need no repentance."

I can picture myself as one of those Pharisees listening to that first parable. I probably would have found the parable a bit touching—at least at first. It would be easy to identify with this man who loses a sheep and cannot rest until he finds it. After all, one out of a hundred Jews falling away and then coming back is not bad. I would think, *Maybe I should rejoice in that.* But I'm afraid I still wouldn't have been able to buy the logic contained in the Lord's moral. I cannot imagine that my legal mind-set would ever allow me to think God might rejoice more over one sinner than over so many righteous, like me.

No doubt the Pharisees missed the fact that they too were lost sheep. These men considered themselves to be righteous; and because they were "not in need of repentance," the Lord's words probably dripped off them like water off the proverbial duck's back. The people who needed to repent were the notorious sinners such as the tax collectors that Jesus was welcoming—the Pharisees simply couldn't accept that the Lord was speaking about them. They couldn't imagine that God would rejoice more over sinners who repent than over those who are righteous. This parable ends with Jesus making a statement that the Pharisees probably interpreted as recognition that they were righteous. But the Lord was using this story to draw them in, like Nathan the prophet drew David in with his story of a stolen sheep.

Jesus jumps into his second parable without a pause. In this story, the woman finds her lost coin and calls her neighbors to celebrate. The Lord offers a second moral; only this time only one of the groups is given a spiritual evaluation: "In the same way, I tell you, there is joy in the presence of the angels of God over one sinner who repents." Jesus lays no implication about who the other nine coins might represent. He talks only of the one who knows he needs to repent and does so. In this second parable, the message shifts so there is no moral evaluation of the remaining nine. This is so subtle that the Pharisees would not have been offended.

If I had been a Pharisee standing there that afternoon listening to Jesus, I might have agreed—even though I may not have wanted to admit it—that there are big sinners out there who do need to repent. And I might even have conceded that I should be more accepting of those sinners who are coming into the kingdom. But I can also imagine myself questioning this "Good News Mission." *Yeah, we see these sinners coming. But how long are they gonna last? I tell you, it's only a matter of time before they run back to their sin! They're not really righteous, they're not like me.*

Note the numbers in these parables. The first presents a shepherd who loses one sheep among a hundred; this represents a loss of 1 percent of his sheep. Then the woman loses one of ten coins, which represents a larger loss—10 percent of her money. In the final parable, the father loses one son out of two—a 50 percent loss. Of course, the son is by far the most valuable item lost, and by the time Jesus gets to that final story, he has carried his audience along with him so that their defenses are lowered, and they will increasingly identify with each new loss.

The Prodigal Returns

The final story is longer and much more developed. The characters are more three-dimensional, and are therefore more compelling. This story is Jesus' destination. The other two parables are only to prepare the audience for the impact that is coming. From years of experience standing before a congregation, I can tell you that a good story always draws interest. Even people in your audience who are bored with what you have to say will instinctively perk up and lift their heads as you tell a story of any merit. The parable of the prodigal was a tale designed to hit home for many in the crowd that day. There is little doubt in my mind that when Jesus launched into this last parable, he had everyone's attention.

This tale has all of the elements of a real human drama about a restless young son who runs off and sows his wild oats. Many parents have lost a rebellious son (or daughter) to the world. If I were standing there listening to that story unfold I would have found myself identifying with either the father or the older son. As the average Pharisee was highly religious, I can't picture him identifying with this young man as his rebelliousness dissipates his inheritance. I fancy the Pharisee feeling the prodigal gets exactly what he deserves. And when a famine causes the boy to hire on to feed swine, it probably only confirmed in the Pharisee's mind that this lad was no "real" son of Abraham.

Jesus continues by sharing how the prodigal decides to humble himself and return to his father in order to plead for mercy so he can become one of his father's hired hands. I imagine a Pharisee listening to that and thinking: *Good! That's what he deserves. He should end his life working as a hired slave to pay for the wickedness he's committed.*

But then the story takes an unexpected turn. When the father spots him, he runs to receive his son; before the son can apologize, the father embraces and kisses the boy. Even when the prodigal admits that he is no longer worthy to be his father's son, the man does not accept the boy's offer to become a hired servant. Instead, he calls his slaves and has the best robe placed upon his shoulders, puts a ring (signifying authority) upon his finger, and has the servants bring out a new pair of sandals for his tired feet. He then orders the fattened calf slaughtered for a party in his son's honor.

The story has seemed pretty straightforward up until this point. In essence, Jesus is declaring that tax collectors, prostitutes, and the other notorious sinners will be allowed to come to him because of God the Father's gracious forgiving nature. If they repent, as the prodigal has done, they will be welcome.

Now a Pharisee listening to this resolution to the prodigal's problem might have been moved by the father's loving reaction towards his son, they too had sons. I'm sure that this was what the Lord desired to happen. But I imagine the Pharisee fighting off those feelings and shaking his head. *No! The boy has sinned against heaven and his father, and he should not be rewarded—he deserves to be punished!* Now the Lord begins to move in for the kill. Right at the moment the Pharisees are having those ambivalent thoughts between their appreciation of the father's mercy countered by the need to punish wrongdoing, Jesus suddenly brings the other brother back into the story as he returns from working in the field.

Over the years I have heard many sermons on this parable, but most messages seem to bog down here. It seems preachers just don't know what to make of this older brother and his animosity; his presence tends to spoil the nice neat salvation message created by the prodigal's return. Nor does the Lord conclude this parable with a moral. The only words that might qualify as a moral are uttered by the father towards the older brother: "My son . . . we had to be merry and rejoice, for this brother of yours was dead and has begun to live, and was lost and has been found." Without a resolution of the separation between the father and the older brother this story seems to end with a whimper rather than a bang. But let me make a suggestion, everything fits perfectly into the Lord's agenda for that day.

The Sins of the Older Brother

You can bet that the older brother's presence in this story was not lost on the Pharisees that afternoon. To them, he probably represented the hero. When the older son arrives home, he refuses to join the party, so his father must step outside to deal with the problem. "Son," he says in essence, "why won't you come in? Your brother, who was lost, is found. Come in and join the party." But the oldest son replies, "Father, I have served you all of my life and have never disobeyed you. But you've killed the fattened calf for this son of yours who has wasted your money on prostitutes and drunkenness. And you won't even kill a little goat for me and my friends so that we can have a good time."

As Jesus reveals the older son's offense at the father's treatment of his younger brother, I imagine the Pharisees nodding in agreement. After all, the older brother has been faithful, while his profligate younger brother has squandered the father's inheritance on prostitutes and sensuous living. *It's not fair,* they must have thought, *for the father to make his brother's return into such a big event after he has disgraced them all.* The Lord actually models the attitude of this older brother upon the Pharisees so that he can reveal at least nine sins of which they were guilty.

The first sin is that the older brother is jealous. He felt that he deserved to be honored because he had served for so many years. He claimed that the father had never so much as killed a kid so that he could celebrate with his friends. His complaint reveals his jealousy of his father's treatment of the younger brother. In the same way, the Pharisees were jealous of the way they saw Jesus treating "the sinners." So they had come to the conclusion that he could not be from God if he could reward these sinners while he ignored *their* contributions to Israel's spiritual well-being.

Second, the older brother reveals that he does not appreciate what the father has provided for him. The father answers his oldest son by saying: "All that is mine is yours." According to the custom of the day, it seems likely that a father in such a situation would have given his youngest son only a third of the inheritance, holding the rest back for the older brother. So this son stood to inherit the rest of the estate. In the same way, the Pharisees had no real sense of appreciation for all God had done for them.

Third, the older brother broke fellowship with his father. He stood outside the house and wouldn't go in because of what he considered to be his father's injustice. In just the same way, the Pharisees kept themselves outside the kingdom of God; they were jealous of the treatment received by tax collectors and sinners.

Fourth, the older brother was concerned about things that were simply none of his business. He complained to the father that his brother has "devoured your wealth with prostitutes." But his father had every right to do with his property what seemed good to him. The Pharisees busied themselves worrying about God's honor at the hands of all these sinners coming into his kingdom. But God is certainly capable of taking care of his own honor.

Fifth, the older brother loved the father's property more than he loved his own brother. He would rather have had the father's money back and his brother out of the picture. The Pharisees had little compassion for the sinners who were coming to Jesus, even though they knew these people desperately needed his help. It's hard to have compassion for anyone whom you deem to be inferior.

Sixth, the older brother found it easy to overlook his own failure. He claims that he has never disobeyed his father.

That's an interesting observation in the light of the fact that he is at the very moment disobeying his father by refusing to join the party. The Pharisees prided themselves on their religious obedience to the law, yet they were flagrantly disobeying the Son of God, who had given the law in the first place.

A seventh offense of the older brother was that he served his father with a wrong attitude. "For so many years I have been serving you," he said, but then he strongly implies that he has been working without proper compensation. It is interesting to contrast this with the younger brother's attitude. While feeding the swine, he thinks: *How many of my father's hired men have more than enough bread.* The prodigal sees his father as being generous even to the hired help. The Pharisees served God with the typical mind-set that comes with legalism; they felt God owed them because of all they had done for him.

An eighth area of the older brother's failure is how he shifted blame back onto his father. He accused his father of failing to honor him, and could not see all that his father had done. Again, this is typical of the mind-set of the Pharisees. Legalists are always tallying up accounts and "keeping score" of their good works while holding God accountable for all they perceive that he has not done for them.

Finally, the older brother fails even to acknowledge his brother. He never refers to the prodigal as his brother, only as "your son." This distancing is typical of the way the Pharisees looked at others. Even their reference to others as "sinners" implies that they were without sin themselves. By putting distance between themselves and others, they conveniently dehumanized them.

The real contrast in this final story is not between sinners and the righteous, but between "religious sinners" and "irreligious sinners." Of course, the man who is irreligious is much easier to spot; he will turn away from God and become involved in the sins of the flesh. But while the religious sinner may be more difficult to spot, he's still just as sinful. Outwardly, he's positive toward God, but inwardly his heart is really full of bitterness toward the Father.

The Coming Sequel

Jesus used these three parables to lull the Pharisees into listening, then exposed their hearts by the revelation of the older brother's attitude. While their sins are not outwardly of a sensuous nature, they are just as flagrant before God. The problem of the Pharisees is that they have used the wrong standard. As long as they measure themselves against their own standard, they may be able to appear virtuous, but once they compare themselves against God's true standard of holiness, they'll be found wanting.

Believing that Jesus Christ is the Son of God is not the first step that a man must take if he is going to come to the Lord for salvation. Nor is it to believe that Christ died on the cross for his sins. The first step that leads a man towards salvation is to believe that he himself is a sinner.

The fact that Jesus died on the cross for our sins is an important reality, but it won't drive us to repentance. Not until we first acknowledge that we are sinners and in desperate need are we ready for salvation. Jesus knew that this was the critical problem for the Pharisees: They did not see their own sin for what it was; and until they did, they would remain lost.

I find myself wondering how the message of the older brother came across to the Pharisees. Did they hear anything Jesus was trying to tell them? The outward impact of the message that afternoon was probably limited. Whenever someone's heart has become hardened, it becomes incredibly difficult to sow seeds of change and repentance within it. When you look carefully at how the Lord crafted this message of conviction for these men, you can only marvel at the Lord's sensitivity.

I remember several years ago going to see *Star Wars*. As I left the theater, I sensed that I had seen an excellent film, a story well told. Darth Vadar and Luke Skywalker had fought to an aerial climax reminiscent of so many early westerns, where the villain wore black while the hero sported a white hat. But although Luke had won the day, it was not clear that the evil Darth Vadar had actually been destroyed. As I left the theater, I sensed that one day those two characters would face each other again.

The parable of the prodigal son is similar. While the lost son has been found and his conflict is resolved by the full acceptance of his father, still the question remains: What will become of the older brother? Will he enter into the celebration with his father, or will he stay outside, pouting by himself? This really is an unfinished story. It is in the classic tradition that requires the audience to provide their own resolution to a story. Would these Pharisees be able to humble themselves and see their need?

Certainly, there had to be a sequel. Of course, there would be many sequels to this story because there were so many scribes and Pharisees listening that day. Each one had a different resolution. Even down to our day, this story will be followed by many sequels, depending upon how each person is willing to respond. Conviction is often such a elusive thing for each of us to achieve.

Who Is the Older Brother?

It is easy to sit in judgment of the Pharisees. Despite the fact they had the opportunity to sit at the feet of the Lord Jesus and hear him teach, they seemed so full of themselves. But, if I'm honest, I must admit that part of the reason I dislike these men so much is that *I'm so much like them.*

As much as I hate to admit it, every one of the nine failures that the older brother exhibited I have found within my own heart. In fact, the more I look at the older brother, the more I see of myself in his attitudes. I'm an awful lot like him. As I read this portion of Luke, I'm reminded of just how unworthy I am.

The Pharisees found that they were jealous of those sinners who had lived it up, only to repent and be accepted so readily by the Lord. How many times have I felt animosity towards other Christians and have felt that the Lord was giving them a better deal than he was giving me? When another Christian speaks behind my back, my self-centered heart can so easily write him off. I have even found myself wondering how some Christians could be accepted by the Lord into his kingdom. After the way they have treated me, they don't *deserve* to enter heaven.

If I'm honest, I am amazed at how much of myself I can see in the older brother. I'm convinced that the sin of the older brother, the sin of being religiously self-righteous, bring many to our churches today. We Christians have far more to fear from the older brother's mentality than we do from the sins of the flesh. When a believer has been within the church for any length of time, it becomes so easy to develop attitudes of self-righteousness. We must keep ourselves accountable in order to make certain we are not developing the heart of the older brother.

The Rest of the Story

It is hard to picture the religious Jews responding favorably to the Lord after the tremendous opposition they had given him. But it is significant to note that many of them later did turn to Jesus. In Acts 6:7, we're told that the word of God kept spreading "and a great many of the priests were becoming obedient to the faith."

Certainly the most noteworthy conversion of a Pharisee was that of Saul of Tarsus. In his case, his animosity was so strong that he was traveling to Damascus to arrest Christians. The Lord showed his incredible love for this fate-filled man. Saul, in his Pharisaic zeal was seeking Christians to drag them away to their deaths. With the appearance of the Messiah himself his self-righteousness quickly melting away. And so the most vehement enemy of the church became the greatest proponent of grace within its midst.

After Paul had ministered for several years, teaching the doctrine of grace, a great controversy arose within the church. Some of the believers, who became known as Judaizers, claimed that a Gentile had to be circumcised in order to be saved. Interestingly enough, we're told in Acts 15:5 that this group existed in the earliest church, and came out of the sect of the Pharisees. This group had a major negative impact upon the true message of the gospel.

When you examine them carefully, it is amazing how much of the letters of apostle Paul are devoted to combating legalistic problems. Legalism is a problem that has never really left the church. There has always been the natural tendency to corrupt Christianity into a system of do's and don'ts, rather than a relationship with the Living God. As Christians, we must guard against following in the footsteps of the older brother.

Each of us must choose whether we are going to respond to the Father's offer of salvation. I must be careful not to judge those who do not choose to follow. Their decision to walk away is not final as long as they are in this life. Someday they may choose to follow the Lord, just as many of those Pharisees did. I must make certain that I do nothing that would form a barrier and keep them away. We must live our lives in such a way that others will be drawn to the Savior.

Are We Able to Fish for Men?

One of the major messages I see in Luke 15 is that Jesus was seeking to save all sinners, not just the obvious ones. Those with obvious failure are often quick to come to the Lord because they are so overwhelmed by his offer of pardon and forgiveness for their visible sin. But in Luke 15 the Lord is actually seeking to widen his catch by opening his net to include the religious types, who also needed salvation.

What kind of a witness am I? Am I living my life in such a way that my door is open to everyone? Sometimes I must relate to the prodigal, who is losing himself in fleshly excess. At other times I must reach out to the older brother, who is caught up in self-righteousness. The gospel is a message only for those who know that they are lost, and so Jesus consistently and clearly drives that message home to everyone. Can I also communicate to these groups?

The Pharisees were not interested in seeing sinners come into God's kingdom. Legalists are never really interested in people whom they see as sinners. Why? Because when they look down on others, their sin nature makes them feel elevated. The legalist views himself as being "pretty good," and therefore he enjoys belittling those who are not outwardly on his same spiritual level.

Do you have these legalistic tendencies, so that you are repelled by conspicuous sinners? Perhaps you feel they should only get what they deserve. Does your life produce the kind of atmosphere that makes sinners want to come and be forgiven? What about your children? Do they see you as the type of person who loves them like the father loved his prodigal? Or do they see you merely putting up with their sin because, after all, they're related to you?

But let's not stop there. We may also have the same judgmental attitude towards legalists, wishing they would just stay away. The Pharisees didn't feel the big sinners deserved heaven. Could it be that we don't feel that the modern-day Pharisees deserve heaven either? Sin comes in many forms, and it is easy to do exactly what the Pharisees did by refusing to accept others; we may be rejecting legalists in the same way they spurned the carnal sinners. Even legalists need grace. How exciting that the Lord took such care to include these men in his master plan by arousing conviction in them! The Lord spent much time plowing up the fallow ground in their hearts so that many would later believe.

John Newton, the English seaman and slave trader, sank very low before he was converted. Later, he wrote the well-known hymn "Amazing Grace." Newton said he felt there would be three surprises when he reached heaven: (1) all of the people he did not expect to find there; (2) those he would find missing; and (3) the fact that he himself would be allowed in.

To be truly fishers of men, we must see ourselves, like Paul, as chief of sinners. A Christian who knows that he is saved by grace so appreciates what the Lord has done. He knows he would only be a heartbeat away from hell, were it not for the grace of God. This kind of gratefulness produces compassion for the lost, because apart from the grace of God, none of us could stand before a holy God. Praise him for his glorious grace!

A Recap of Transitionalism

1) Old Covenant. Throughout Luke 15, Jesus aims directly at the basic problem he came to solve: No one is really able to come to terms with his own sinfulness until he first sees his behavior contrasted with God's standard. The Lord's teaching here was not aimed at the church (except by way of application). It was spoken to his Jewish followers who were still under the rule of the old covenant.

2) Conviction. A comprehensive reading of Luke 15 will reveal the Lord's major purpose. Reading these three parables about something being lost, we realize that everyone is lost. All are carnal and lost; some are carnal and religious and lost. For those who heard this story, the Lord's emphasis brought them closer to feeling the need for repentance.

The Lord's major focus here is not upon those who are obviously lost and know it, but upon those who do not know they are lost. The Lord's purpose is to bring conviction to this group who are so much harder to reach. It is easy to miss this, simply because most Christians focus on carnal sinners instead of the self-righteous. Although veiled, the Lord's message is still the same. He uses parables to pound home the point that a man without conviction will never get into the kingdom of heaven.

3) Evocative. This passage is so subtle and evocative that the Pharisees would miss where Jesus was leading them. Jesus starts with the animosity of the Pharisees for the big sinners and ends up showing them that they are in an equally bad condition. His progression of 1 percent, 10 percent, 50 percent, and 100 percent being lost sneaks up on his antagonists. There is a shift from the Pharisees seemingly being as righteous as the 99 sheep to the Pharisees actually being as bad as the tax collectors. It has changed from the prodigal younger brother to the *prodigal older brother*. Jesus condemns their attitudes through the older brother, all the while wooing them into the kingdom. It is one thing to condemn someone's attitudes, but Jesus does far more than that; he offers forgiveness and reconciliation for these men who are lost in their own pride.

4) Interwoven Context. The messages of Luke 15 and 16 are both aimed directly at the Pharisees. As you will see in the next chapter, Jesus develops five parables in a row specifically for this one group. While it is easy to miss the subtle verses that show they are his target, a careful reading of these chapters reveals that the Lord is bending their minds in his own direction.

Luke 15 is part of a larger section of the Gospel that begins in Luke 9:51 and runs through Chapter 19. This section deals with Jesus' trip from Galilee to Jerusalem, and Luke demonstrates in it just how much Jesus is misunderstood. He is misunderstood by the crowds, the Pharisees, and even by his own disciples. All of Luke Chapters 14, 15 and 16 is an expansion of the Lord's comment in 13:33 that a prophet cannot perish outside of Jerusalem.

In spite of this hostility and lack of understanding on the part of his enemies, the Lord is still calling on the Pharisees to believe. We should never forget that even though we are often ungracious, the Lord is always gracious, even to his enemies. Though people are unworthy, the Lord always offers them the opportunity to be forgiven.

Chapter 9

Why Doesn't God Give Me a Sign?
Lazarus and the Rich Man

When I was attending college back in the sixties, a student on my floor of the dorm mentioned that a friend of his had proven there was no God. When I asked how he had done this, he told me that they had been driving down the road in a convertible; his friend had stood up in the back seat of the car as it was traveling, and he had shouted up at the heavens: "If there is a God, strike me dead!"

The student concluded his story by saying: "My friend wasn't struck dead, so he proved God doesn't exist."

Of course that was a foolish experiment that didn't really prove anything, but the incident does express one of the basic struggles that many have. If God wants us to believe in him, why doesn't he make himself more apparent? Why does he stay "in hiding" when it would be so easy for him to show himself to those who challenge his existence? One lightening strike at the appropriate moment would surely satisfy most people.

Anyone who has ever read the pages of the Gospels immediately notices the miracles that Jesus performed. One miraculous event after another is recorded for us to marvel over. Not only were men healed, they received immediate "therapy." Peter's mother-in-law had her fever taken away, and she immediately began to serve dinner; the lame man started to walk, and Jesus instructed him to carry away his bedroll. And whenever Jesus attended a funeral, he "ruined" it by raising the corpse from the dead.

The Lord's miracles were of such amazing quality, I

have often wondered why he doesn't use his power today so our friends would see these signs and believe. I hear people say, "If Uncle George saw a miracle like those Jesus performed in the Gospels, surely he would believe." How does God expect skeptical people to come to faith if he doesn't reveal himself in some tangible way?

Interestingly enough, Jesus was asked the same question; despite all of his miracles, he faced that same challenge during his ministry. The Jews often asked for signs to prove both his authority and his identity. Now, how could those people witness so many miracles and still ask for a sign?

When he received such a challenge, Jesus declared that the people would not receive a sign except that of the prophet Jonah; which of course was a veiled reference to his coming death and resurrection. The closer Jesus drew towards Jerusalem on that final trip, the greater the animosity of the Pharisees grew. But even in the end, he never catered to the request for a sign.

The Crafty Steward

The Pharisees often found themselves offended by Jesus because he didn't "prove" himself to them. And by the time we reach his later ministry, Jesus has more and more conflict with them. In Luke 16, the Lord gives a confusing parable about an unrighteous steward that, while spoken to the disciples, I believe was directed at the Pharisees. Read it for yourself in Luke 16:1-13.

The story is about a manager who has squandered his master's possessions. When the boss calls and gives him notice of an audit and performance review, the man realizes he's in trouble. Knowing that he will have a tough time getting another position so lucrative, he decides to contact several of those who are indebted to his master and tells them if they act quickly, he'll discount a large portion of their debt. The steward's motive in making this offer is only to buy friends who will later help him when he's out of work. The debtors are overjoyed by this deal and quickly accept the discounts.

This reminds me of a senate hearing I saw on television. A senator asked a witness if he had given a large campaign contribution to the President in part to gain access to the White House. The witness responded by saying that access to the White House was the *only* reason he had given the contribution. The people of this world know how to utilize money for their own gain.

For many the troubling part of the Lord's story is his conclusion. Jesus says that even the rich master praises this crafty fellow because he had acted so shrewdly. The Lord concludes that the sons of this age know more about dealing shrewdly among themselves than the sons of light do.

Christians often struggle to understand this story, and especially the Lord's moral. They wonder if Jesus could possibly be suggesting that they should deal deceptively with others, or if they should act shrewdly with money (even other people's money), or if they should use "unrighteous" money to buy friends and obtain the things they want.

The Lord does seem to applaud the man's shrewdness; he apparently praises the man's use of another man's money to improve his own future; and he makes little out of the fact the man was losing his job because he had squandered another's possessions. It's easy to wonder why the Lord would create such a despicable character, and then make him the hero of his story. Almost everything about this tale is difficult to reconcile with the rest of the New Testament.

The Real Audience

There are several keys to understanding this parable. The first important observation is to recognize that "mammon of unrighteousness" does not necessarily refer to ill-gotten gain. If you compare verses 9 and 11, you'll see that "mammon of unrighteousness" merely refers to the secular money system. Verse 12 even implies that the riches of this age are a stewardship that have been given to us by God. So the correct understanding would be for us to use the wealth of this age that God has entrusted to us, and lay up for ourselves true riches in heaven.

Another key is to understand the Lord's purpose is not comparison, but contrast. He is contrasting "sons of this age" with the "sons of light." The Lord states that one cannot serve both God and wealth. He has entrusted wealth to us so that it can become a conduit through which we can serve him. When a believer uses money to serve God, he is acting as a "son of light."

An interesting biblical illustration of this is found in Luke 8:1-3. It mentions Joanna, Susanna, and "many others" who were contributing financially to the Lord's ministry. These individuals were faithful with what God had given them; and by supporting Jesus, they helped the Lord and reached many souls for eternity. Jesus' primary contrast seems to be how much more deliberate and ingenious men are in terms of their use of wealth in this world (v. 8) than the children of light are, especially considering that we have an eternal reward.

Although verse 1 declares that the Lord was speaking to the disciples, immediately after Jesus is done speaking this parable, Luke tells us (in verse 14) that the Pharisees made fun of what the Lord was teaching. Sometimes when we eavesdrop on a conversation intended for someone else, we listen more intently. Jesus knew this, so while he didn't announce that this message was for them, his remarks were actually aimed at these men who were in the back of the crowd. Everything Jesus says here in Luke 16 is primarily directed at the Pharisees.

Verse 14 holds another key about what's happening in this parable. Notice that Luke tells us not only that the Pharisees were listening, but that they reacted because "they were lovers of money." I don't normally picture these men being obsessed with greed, because they made such noise about their own righteousness. But Jesus reveals their character by creating a parable designed to provoke their greed and bring it to the surface.

In this story, the unrighteous steward is a man who has been entrusted to oversee his master's great riches; he is obviously a lover of money. This man represents the Pharisees, who also love money. (It should be noted that they have also been entrusted with God's law, which they have corrupted and misused.)

Of course they reacted, as Jesus knew they would. They scoffed at the Lord's parable because they recognized its implications. The Pharisees' attitude was: *I'm better than my neighbor. I've never killed anyone or broken the Sabbath or stolen anyone's money, so I'm righteous.* They looked down their noses at the Lord; their scoffing was a form of self-defense, because his story had described them so accurately.

Jesus now directly confronts the Pharisees. He openly accuses them of hypocrisy. He points out how evil their hearts are at the very time they were glorifying themselves as righteous before men. In response to their scoffing, Jesus declares (in verse 16) that the law and the prophets were proclaimed until John (the Baptist), the last of the old covenant prophets. Now that the kingdom of God is being preached, religious men will struggle to enter that kingdom.[99]

In verse 17, the Lord points out that it will be easier for heaven and earth to pass away than for one stroke of a letter of the law to fail. If someone is going to claim to be righteous before God based upon the law, as the Pharisees were doing, they need to be able to accomplish every detail. God's standard is perfect, and it never changes.

---

[99] Matthew 11:12-19 and 23:13-39

Finally, in verse 18, the Lord deals with divorce. While on first glance this verse doesn't seem to fit the context, my suggestion is that the Lord is bringing up the subject because some of the Pharisees in the group have dealt treacherously with their wives by divorcing them and leaving them financially destitute.[100] Both the parable before and after this verse seem to be characterized by money and its use.

The Two Economies

Keep in mind that through his life, death, and resurrection, Jesus was introducing a new economy into the world. What I mean by *economy* is God's method of dealing with people. God's standard is holiness, and there are only two ways (or economies) to achieve that holiness. A man is holy by keeping the law entirely, without a single transgression. (Of course, in all of human history only one man has ever achieved that—the Lord Jesus himself.) The other way to holiness is through the cross of Christ. A man must come God's way, following his economy, or else he will be guilty of attempting to force his way into the kingdom.

People often try to approach God based upon their own merit, but they are never able to enter this way, because they cannot achieve holiness. This is the economy of law. When you try to please God by keeping his law, you find yourself in an impossible predicament. James summed it up by saying that whoever keeps the whole law and yet stumbles on one point, is guilty of all of it.[101]

Suppose a man goes out and robs a bank and then is arrested. When he is taken to court, he tells the judge: "Sure, Judge, I robbed the bank, but I've never murdered anyone. Neither have I ever beaten anyone up; and Judge, I've never committed rape. I'm only guilty of this one little crime." Do you think the judge would have mercy on him because of all the bad things that he has never done? Of course not. He will

---

[100] Malachi 2:13-14
[101] James 2:10

be judged on the basis of the crime he has actually committed. If a person is guilty of breaking one law, it means he is a
lawbreaker, and he will be punished accordingly.

The Lord's goal with these Pharisees was to show
them that they could not be saved on their own merit. But
the Pharisees were more concerned about creating the *appearance* of righteousness than actually *being* righteous. Their
entire value system reflected their own hearts and was only a
show of righteousness, rather than the genuine article.

It's a tragedy whenever a man erects a standard of
righteousness that he then declares to be God's standard. You
can accomplish that *in your mind* by lowering God's standard
so far that it is no longer his. Pascal once said that God created man in his own image, and then man returned the favor.
The Pharisees certainly created a standard of their own making, and then expected Jesus to measure up. The Jewish leaders kept demanding a sign, because Jesus condemned them
and their unbelief. Failure to accept the Lord's teaching allowed them to continue in their unbelief.

So when the Pharisees demanded a sign from Jesus, it
was merely an excuse—a way to focus on the Lord's perceived failure rather than face their own corruption. Unwilling to come God's way, they made themselves an enemy of
the Son of God and felt compelled to challenge him for
proof that he was from God. After all, they thought: *Why
doesn't he give us a sign?*

Lazarus and the Rich Man

Luke 16 continues with the Lord giving another powerful and thought-provoking parable commonly called *Lazarus and the Rich Man*. Here again, Jesus takes aim at these
religious men. This time, the Lord's purpose is to provoke
them into seeing how irrational their lack of faith is. They did
possess enough information to come to faith based upon the
law and the prophets, if they would just hear it. But because

they loved their money, their prestige, and their own self-righteousness, they demanded signs as an excuse so they wouldn't have to believe.

Read this second story for yourself in verses 16:19-31. A rich man, dressed in purple, spends his time partying. At the gate in front of his home lies a poor beggar named Lazarus, who is desperately ill and living in miserable poverty. Both men die. The rich man is buried and ends up in Hades, while Lazarus goes to Abraham's bosom, where the rich man is able to see him. The rich man is now in torment and he calls to Abraham, asking him to send Lazarus with water to cool his tongue. When Abraham refuses his request, the rich man begs that Lazarus be sent to warn his brothers about this place of torment. The man ends up arguing with Abraham about the best way to reach his five living brothers.[102] Now, what was the Lord's purpose in giving this story?

First, it's important to point out that this parable is not a condemnation of wealth, as some have taught. If you try to teach that message, you must also acknowledge that the story applauds the worst poverty. Jesus creates the dramatic financial contrast between these two characters to focus on the Pharisees' love of money.

The rich man is dressed in purple and linen every day. Purple cloth was worn only by royalty or by those with great wealth, because of the tremendous cost of purple dye.[103] This man had extravagant parties every day, while Lazarus was literally starving at his front gate. The poor man, in contrast, had nothing. He couldn't walk and had sores all over his body. His only medical attention came from the dogs that licked his sores. His one resource was to eat the crumbs that fell from the rich man's table. These two individuals are caricatures. While the rich man is a picture of the Pharisees and their pride, poor Lazarus represents how the Pharisees see the

---

[102] I have often wondered if there was a Pharisee with five brothers in the crowd.

[103] Purple clothing was a mark of prestige.

rest of the world. To them, all other men are poor and miserable, but they have no real compassion or desire to help any of them. They have just scoffed at Jesus' suggestion to help men financially in this life to receive benefit in the next life.

In the story, both men die; the rich man finds himself in Hades, while Lazarus ends up in Abraham's bosom. Many wonder about these two places. Apparently, Abraham's bosom is synonymous with paradise, and it existed during the old covenant period; it was a temporary waiting place where Old Testament saints went after they died. Paul seems to indicate that those in Abraham's bosom were raised up with the Lord and taken to heaven after the resurrection.[104] We also know from 2 Corinthians 5:8 that after Christ's resurrection, when believers die, their spirits go to be with the Lord. Today, when a believer dies, he does not go to Abraham's bosom but into the Lord's presence.

But Hades still exists. The Bible indicates that this is a place of torment, which is also a temporary "holding place" for those who do not know the Lord. They will be resurrected on the last day to stand before the Judge. Hades itself will be thrown into the lake of fire in the final judgment.[105]

The Barb in the Story

The rich man is experiencing a flame from which he can find no relief. Off in the distance he spies a place where happiness and contentment reign under Abraham's watchful care. It's interesting that he doesn't ask to be released from his torment, only that he might be comforted in it. But what's even more amazing about this man is his continued unbelief. Here he is in hell, and he still maintains an unbeliever's attitude.

The rich man has a conscious memory of his past and knows that his five living brothers are in great danger. He

---

[104] Ephesians 4:8-10
[105] Revelation 20:14

asks Abraham to send a warning to them so they won't end up coming to this place of torment. Think about that for a moment. His unbelief implies that the warning he received was not adequate to have kept him out of hell. What he's saying between the lines is: "If I had been adequately warned, I would not now be here in Hades." He's telling God, through Abraham, how he got a raw deal. These are strong statements of unbelief. It is also a strong condemnation of God for using inadequate communication. Why didn't God give him an adequate sign?

Abraham replies: "They've got Moses and the Prophets; let them hear them." Now these are the very sources the Pharisees claim to be following. But the rich man retorts: "No, Father Abraham." The word *no* is a strong expression of his unbelief. He insists on telling Abraham that he has a "better way" to reach his brothers than through Moses and the prophets.

Now here is where Jesus puts the barb into his story. The man tells Abraham, "If one comes back from the dead, then they would believe." In other words, that would be an adequate sign. Earlier in the conversation, he suggested sending Lazarus to his father's house. So the rich man believes if Lazarus returns from the dead, his family will repent.

Now his request certainly seems logical. Surely, if someone came back from the dead and warned people, they would repent. This reminds me of Dickens' famous Christmas story, and its many modern adaptations. In that story we have the return of several dead characters from the past to haunt miserly old Scrooge. In Dickens' fantasy, Scrooge changes his ways and suddenly becomes kind and giving. Unfortunately, that's just not the way things happen in real life (as we shall see.) Keep in mind that this logic is the natural man's idea, and it only reveals the depths of unbelief. God knows such suggestions are foolish. In real life, Scrooge would have quickly overcome his fear, chalked up the experience as a bad dream, and become even more cruel and heart-less.

In the case of the rich man in this parable, nothing has really changed in his self-centered heart. Even in hell he still hasn't repented. He's convinced he got a bum deal. In fact, he wants to tell God how to be God. *If only he would do things my way, I wouldn't be in this mess*, he thinks. How foolish it is when self-centered people want to give God advice.

Abraham answers the man by saying, in essence: "If they do not listen to Moses, and if they won't believe the prophets, I guarantee they still won't believe even if someone comes back from the dead." For the Pharisees, this is the Lord's blind-side punch to show the fallacy of seeking signs. Jesus has crafted this special barb just for them, so that they'll be provoked towards repentance. The reality is that *no sign is adequate for stubborn unbelief.*

Now, Why "Lazarus"?

Why did the Lord use the name *Lazarus* in this story? This is actually the only parable where Jesus gives a name to one of his characters. And there is an interesting parallel incident in the New Testament about a man by the name of Lazarus who dies and actually does come back to life. Could both of these be the same man?

In John 11, the experience of the real man named Lazarus is described. This man has some wealth and lives with his two sisters in a large home in Bethany, a couple of miles east of Jerusalem. He's able to get around, so he's not an invalid like the character in Jesus' parable. Although the real Lazarus dies, after four days in the tomb, Jesus does bring him back from the dead (in contrast to the Lazarus of the parable who doesn't come back to life). So they are clearly not the same man.

At the time Jesus gives his parable about the fictional Lazarus, we know that Jesus was on his last journey to Jerusalem.[106] That means the resurrection of the real Lazarus had already occurred only a few weeks before this story was told by the Lord. We can be certain the Pharisees knew about the real resurrection. John reveals in his Gospel that the real Lazarus had many friends who were Pharisees who told others about the miracle at his tomb.[107]

By using the name *Lazarus* in his parable, Jesus is not implying that this is the same man. He is using the same name to catch the attention of his listeners and to remind them about the real resurrection of Lazarus. Using the name *Lazarus* in conjunction with the thought of a "preacher" coming back from the dead had to elicit recognition.[108] Because the real Lazarus had just recently been brought back to life, you can bet the news of that incredible and unique miracle had spread all over Israel. Some of these same religious leaders were possibly present to witness that event, but *still they refused* to believe in Jesus. Their unbelief defies logic.

But even more amazing is what happened later. After the real Lazarus was raised from the dead, many people began to believe on Jesus because of him. Then the Pharisees conspired about how they might *put Lazarus to death!*[109] Now that's a unique response to someone returning from the dead. Instead of believing, they just decided to kill the guy again. Incredible! Unbelief always finds a way to alter reality so that the message is neutralized. These men, who claimed to keep the law, were now planning to break the law by killing an innocent man—so that they could *preserve the law*. Their logic is so twisted that they cannot see its deadly consequences.

---

[106] Luke 9:51

[107] John 11:45-46

[108] A similar idea is conveyed when we speak of someone as a "Benedict Arnold." The reality of his treason in the Revolutionary War becomes synonymous with the word *traitor*.

[109] John 12:10

No amount of signs can overcome unbelief. While curiosity and self-indulgence might for a short time draw an interested following, in the end, the greatest of signs won't produce faith. Immediately after Jesus fed the 5000 men plus women and children, we see that a great many of his followers fell away, and the Jews asked for a sign.[110] Maybe I'm a little dense, but it would seem to me that feeding 10,000 plus people with only a boy's lunch would be a pretty good sign. The fact that the leftovers filled twelve baskets should have counted for something. The logic of these individuals reminds me of a young man who grows tired of his parents telling him what to do, so he joins the Marines!

Cain and Balaam are amazing examples of unbelief in the Old Testament. Both of these men were given the opportunity to talk personally with God. They heard him answer in an audible voice, and in Balaam's case, even his donkey talked as a sign. Signs were not enough. They were not men of faith.

Examine Cain's unbelief in Genesis 4. First, he brought the wrong offering to God. The Lord gave Cain a second chance to go and make an offering of the flock; instead, he responded by killing his brother Abel. God asks Cain where his brother Abel is, and Cain could have confessed and received God's pardon. Instead, he smart-mouths God: "Am I my brother's keeper?" The Lord confronts him with the death of Abel and provides a fourth opportunity for redemption. Cain is exiled to a far country, but instead of seeing the grace of the punishment, he views God as being too harsh and unfair.

Cain's life is a good example of unbelief not being overcome by facts or signs. The problem is that unbelief in one's life makes a man unwilling to humble himself before God. (Balaam's life provides the same illustration. He had at least six opportunities to submit to God, but like the Pharisees, he loved money more than he loved God.)

---

[110] John 6:30

Why No Miracles?

People often wonder why there are all these signs in the Bible, but so few today. I would suggest that the miracles of the Bible were never intended to be the normal pattern for the life of the believer. In fact, miracles were not nearly as common in Bible times as is often thought. Sometimes we have a picture of the prophets setting up offices, almost like doctors, dispensing miracles like prescriptions. But Jesus addressed this when he mentioned that in the days of Elisha there were many people with leprosy, but only one was healed; and he was a Gentile! Jesus also stated that there were many hungry widows in Israel during the drought of Elijah's time, but only one was miraculously fed (and she was also a Gentile).

The Bible miracles took place over a period greater than 1,500 years, but they are recorded between the two covers of a relatively small book. In the 400 years between the Old and New Testaments, there appears to have been no miracles. Even John the Baptist, who Jesus called one the greatest of men, performed no miracles.

Another insight lies in understanding the purpose of the Bible miracles. I would suggest that their purpose mainly was to authenticate the messenger of God when he was bringing new revelation to the world. The miracles seem to be clumped around three periods: (1) the time of Moses and the conquest of Canaan; (2) during the ministry of the prophets; and (3) during the life of Jesus and the early ministry of the apostles. In all of these cases, new material was being revealed that needed the authentication of supernatural power. We'll talk more about faith and answers to prayer in later chapters, but it is important to emphasize that a Christian does not normally live on signs and wonders. Such a search will only lead him in the direction of putting God to the test, just as the Pharisees did.

Having Ears to Hear

For the Pharisees, the act of seeking a sign became a handy excuse for not believing. As long as Jesus did not provide the "right" sign, they would always have an excuse for unbelief. Whenever a man seeks a sign from God, as they did, he declares God's revelation as inadequate, thus freeing himself from God's claims. This was the underlying message of Luke 16. The Pharisees were discounting any of the Lord's demands on their financial resources, because they did not see Jesus as an adequate authority. But the parable of Lazarus and the rich man clearly demonstrated that nothing would satisfy their demands.

Ultimately, the complaint by unbelievers that God hasn't revealed himself through the giving of signs is only a ruse to justify being our own god. The Lord has adequately authenticated himself, but some men will still choose unbelief *even* if someone comes back from the dead—as, of course, Jesus did. So the question is not "Is God real?", but rather "Will I let him be my God?"

There is an interesting contrast that illustrates the reality of this truth in John's Gospel. In Chapter 9, a blind man receives his sight and is immediately pressured by the enemies of Jesus not to give glory to him, because they claim the Lord is a sinner. He replies, "Whether he is a sinner, I do not know; one thing I do know, that whereas I was blind, now I see." When he met Jesus later, the Lord asked, "Do you believe in the Son of Man?" The man answered, "And who is he, Lord, that I may believe in him?" So this man's heart was ready to believe in the Lord.

Yet in John 5 we read of another healing with different results. There Jesus heals a man at the Pool of Bethesda who has been sick for 38 years and is unable to walk. When the Jews asked this man who had healed him on the Sabbath, he didn't know the answer. But later Jesus came to him and said, "Behold, you have become well; do not sin any more, so

that nothing worse may befall you." The Lord's statement offended the man because Jesus had pointed out his sin. So he
continued in unbelief and went to the Jewish enemies of
Jesus out of spite. So we see two miracles: One man is healed
and believes, while the other is healed and betrays Jesus.
Clearly, signs and miracles don't, by themselves, generate belief.

Jesus loved the Pharisees and wanted them to believe.
He told this parable about this rich man to stab their conscience. He knew most of them would not respond at this
time, but the Lord was never in a hurry. He was preparing
them for a future time when some would come to faith.

The Pharisees represent the essence of religious unbelief. Unbelief is not thinking that God does not exist. At its
most basic level, it is a rebellion against God from a spirit of
ungratefulness; it is creating a god of our own imagination.
By their lifestyle and their attitudes, the religious leaders had
actually rejected God's law. Although they gave a penny's
worth of credit to the law, they reaped a pound's worth of
pride from their perverted compliance to it. When he arrived
in Jerusalem, Jesus would castigate them, comparing them
with the whitewashed tombs that are clean and beautiful on
the outside, but inside reek with corruption.

Let me ask, are you struggling with unbelief? Like the
Pharisees, you may not be able to recognize unbelief for what
it truly is. Perhaps you've been thinking to yourself: *You
know, I'm not a bad guy. I am one of the pillars in my
church. I set such a fine example.* That's exactly the mentality
of the Pharisees. Because they were convinced of their own
righteousness, they found themselves condemning the Son of
the God they claimed to love.

You can tell if you have the spirit of these Pharisees
by examining your attitudes. Unbelief will cause you to become judgmental of others while you shunt any judgment
away from yourself. "Too bad that brother is so carnal," you

might think. Or, "How can that sister wear such clothes to church!" Such thoughts could reveal that you have replaced God's standard with those of your own making to hide or excuse your own failures.

The apostle James condemns this attitude by saying: "Do not speak against one another, brethren. He who speaks against a brother, or judges his brother, speaks against the law, and judges the law; but if you judge the law, you are not a doer of the law, but a judge of it. There is only one Lawgiver and Judge, the One who is able to save and to destroy; but who are you who judge your neighbor?"[111]

How should you deal with your own self-righteous attitudes? Remember that at the heart of such an attitude is your rejection of God's standard for a lesser standard of your own making. Don't make the mistake the Pharisees made. Don't replace God's standard by pawning off one of your own. Honestly face the fact that even after you become a Christian you never are truly "good enough." As a Christian, you are always in need of the Savior; you *never* reach the point in this life where you become intrinsically good. If you deny your sinfulness, you are deceiving yourself and calling God a liar.[112] And you'll only end up judging others.

The important thing for you to do is to humble yourself and accept God's word. You must see yourself as a man or woman who is desperately in need of Christ. Mark Twain once said, "It isn't those parts of the Bible that I can't understand that bother me, it is the parts that I do understand." That's where these Pharisees were. They were bothered by what the Lord said, but they were unwilling to come to him. As we have already mentioned, many of these Pharisees would later come to faith in the Lord. That happened because of stories like these that Jesus used to prepare their hearts.

A woman recently told my wife, "If you knew the awful things that I have done, you would agree that God cannot

---
[111] James 4:11-12
[112] 1 John 1:8, 10

forgive me." I'm suggesting that this attitude is really the ideal attitude for your heart in order to become a Christian. When a person says, "I'm not good enough, I'll never please God or measure up to his standard," they are not far from the kingdom of God. That's what the law must do for us. We must let it show us God's standard so that we will be broken under its weight. Hiding behind a supposed lack of proof is only a sham argument to allow ourselves to remain our own god.

It really is a marvelous thing to be stripped of our self-righteousness by the law of God and see ourselves as entirely without merit, because then for the first time we are ready to hear the message of the cross and the glorious gospel. We are a fortunate group of people. God's Holy Spirit has worked in our hearts so that we have seen ourselves as people in need—people who cannot please God on their own merit. In the end, this produces great joy as we live under the grace Christ has bestowed upon us. We don't need more signs; we need to accept the truth that we already have.

A Recap of Transitionalism

1) Old Covenant. Throughout Luke 16, the Lord's message is aimed at the Pharisees who lived under the illusion that they were keeping the law. In his presentation of these two parables, Jesus addresses their need to understand the reality of the demands of the old covenant.

2) Conviction. Like a tape on auto-replay, Jesus continues to hammer on this same basic message. Hades awaits those who do not repent after hearing the message of the law and the prophets. A man cannot serve God if he loves money. The Pharisees are like men in our day. They were caught up with material things, yet they gave lip service to being right with God. Jesus therefore nails them to the wall with their own beliefs. He subtly points out their continued rejection of him by drawing their attention to the resurrection of Lazarus and, by extension, to his other miracles. All of this is designed to bring them under conviction.

3) Evocative. Believers will never understand the Lord's intent with these parables until they see who Jesus was addressing and what he was trying to say. Jesus began with the use of money in the first parable because he knew the Pharisees were vulnerable precisely at this point. Then he used the second parable to reveal that they were refusing to believe in Moses, the prophets, and the resurrection of Lazarus. Jesus says these things in his own subtle evocative fashion; he is not transparent.

The barb in the parable of the rich man is so needed for people today who are still seeking signs and wonders. Jesus indicated that it is an unrighteous generation that seeks signs. So he uses Lazarus' name to show these men how ineffective signs really are to those who refuse to believe.

4) Interwoven Context. In the portion of Luke in which this passage is found—from 9:51 through 19:27—you will find a series of interactions and conflicts between Jesus, the disciples, and the religious leaders while the Lord makes his way to Jerusalem. In Chapter 16, the source of the conflict had to do with the Pharisees supposed stewardship and responsibility to help others as "sons of light." These parables were designed to reveal that these religious men were truly "sons of this age," so that they would be able to see their own unbelief in the light of his undeniable miracles. Both the parable of Lazarus and the Rich Man and the parable of the Unrighteous Steward are tied together thematically.

Chapter 10

Who Will Cast the First Stone?
Church Discipline

When the preacher stood, he opened to the Book of Matthew and began to read from Chapter 18, verses 15-17. When finished, he gazed out at the congregation for a quiet moment before declaring in a calm matter-of-fact voice: "There is a problem in our church. Someone is living in sin."

What a catchy introduction! I thought to myself. He had certainly grabbed my attention. I figured this pastor could teach me a thing or two about preaching.

My wife and I had moved to Portland, Oregon, to enter Bible college in preparation for entering the ministry. We had been searching for a new church home when we visited this particular fellowship—a bustling church of about 400-500 people—and I had noticed several of the professors from my Bible school sitting in the congregation.

"We have a lady in our midst that's involved in sin," the pastor continued. "She's left her husband and her two young sons and she's living with her boyfriend. According to the passage I've just read, Jesus said that I should go and talk to this woman. So that's what I did; I went and confronted her about her adultery. She told me, 'I'm a Christian, but I don't want to go back to my husband and kids. I want to stay with my boyfriend.'"

As I sat there listening, it slowly dawned on me that this was not some hypothetical illustration that this pastor was creating to grab our attention. He was talking about a real person and a real family. He continued by telling us how he'd gone back later with two others to confront the woman again, all based on the words of Jesus. Again he related how she declined to heed their warning to repent, to leave her boyfriend, and to return to her husband and kids.

"Now, therefore, according to this passage in Matthew 18, we're bringing this woman before the church to discipline her." At that point the pastor had the husband and his two sons stand in the front row so everyone could see the family that had been betrayed. Not surprisingly, the woman was not in attendance.

Now I must confess to you as I sat there watching and listening, that a feeling of discomfort enveloped me. But as I looked around the auditorium and was struck by all these men with doctorates in theology, I thought: *Surely what the pastor is doing must be right.*

The minister projected the woman's name, address, telephone number, and place of employment up on the overhead screen and suggested, "You might want to write to this woman and tell her you're praying for her." By prior arrangement, three men in the congregation stood and prayed aloud for her, and then the congregation was dismissed. The whole service couldn't have taken more than twenty minutes.

It all seemed so strange to me. I had never seen anything like this in my thirty years of church attendance. As a brand-new student in Bible college, I walked out of that church building with an unsettling impression that this woman's sin had been handled inappropriately. While the words of Jesus were relied on as a basis of action, what I had witnessed seemed somehow alien to the tenor of Jesus' ministry. It was almost as if the Lord had said, "Let him who is without sin cast the first stone," and someone started chuckin' rocks.

Coincidentally, in the week before this service, one of my professors had assigned a chapter in our class textbook that had dealt with church discipline. I confess my mind had slept as my eyes read that chapter; now I rushed to that book and reread the material. This time the information sprang to life; in fact, the words jumped right off the page at me. Many questions formed in my mind about what I was reading. My textbook seemed to agree with what I had just witnessed. Was this what the Lord expected pastors to do? I was left with the impression that the theological experts all believed Jesus wanted pastors to chase down the "big sinners" and insist they repent on the threat of being publicly chastised.

In the following years, I watched from the sidelines as other churches inflicted public discipline on their members. In each situation, I received the distinct impression something was wrong with the way these offenses were being handled. In each case, the churches turned to Matthew 18 as the basis for their actions. While all the churches moved through the "proper steps," the process left destruction in its wake. In one case I even felt the intent was not to discipline, but to punish someone who had already repented.

It didn't seem to me that any of these examples were what the Lord had in mind when he uttered those words in Matthew 18:15-17. Although everyone seemed to see this as the "primary" passage on church discipline, the results of its use seemed only to inflame the problem, not heal it. None of the instances I saw resulted in winning anyone back to the Lord. I concluded there had to be another explanation for what Christ was saying.

The Meaning of Matthew 18

When I discovered the catalyst that made transitionalism come together—that the teaching ministry of Jesus was primarily directed to those living in the old covenant period to prepare their hearts for the transition to the new covenant—I found almost all of the "problem" passages in the Gospels were readily resolved. But a natural extension of my basic premise would be that the teachings of Jesus were never meant directly for the church; this particular passage seemed out of sync with that premise. Here, and only here, the Lord seemed to be giving instruction on how to run the church. In this passage, Jesus specifically refers to the "church." Could this passage be an exception to the Lord's main purpose in his teaching ministry?

The Greek word *ecclesia*, translated "church," appears two times in verse 17. I was surprised to learn that the word "church" only appears three times in all four Gospels, and all of those references are in Matthew. It is used twice here, and once in Matthew 16:18, where Jesus says to Peter, "Upon this rock I will build my church." In that case, it seems to me the Lord is clearly talking about the church as we know it. But does it follow that the term *church* in 18:17 also referred to the new covenant church as we use the word?

In Hebrews 2:12, this same Greek word appears. While the King James Version translated it *church*, most modern versions have chosen to translate it as *congregation*. This is because the book of Hebrews is quoting Psalm 22:22, which refers to the congregation of Israel, not the new covenant church. So the word clearly does not always refer to the church when used in the New Testament.

A parallel example of this is found in Hebrews 4:8, where the Greek word *Jeshua* is translated *Jesus* in the King James Version. Modern versions translate that name as *Joshua*, because it is clearly referring to Joshua the son of Nun. In language, the meaning of a word is established by its context, and the writer of Hebrews meant Joshua of Jericho fame. In these cases, the newer versions have correctly translated the words to clarify their meaning.

After examining Matthew 18:17, I concluded that it is highly likely that the word *church* should have been translated *congregation*. I believe that Jesus had the Jewish synagogue in mind, not the Christian church. This conclusion is supported by the immediate context. Notice that Jesus tells his listeners that if the offender does not repent, he should be treated as a "Gentile or a tax collector." These two categories are certainly not Christian, but Jewish in their outlook. Because the new covenant church ended up composed primarily of Gentiles, to treat someone as a Gentile would not make sense as a punishment. In the Lord's day, the word *Gentile* carried an impact among the Jews similar to "Yankee" when used during the reconstruction period in the South. The Jews often coupled "Gentile" with "dog."

If Jesus had been referring to the church, it seems more likely that he would have said, treat him as an "unbeliever." In fact, in 2 Thessalonians 3:14-15, when Paul warns not to associate with a believer because of his sin, he uses terms more in keeping with the church: "Do not regard him as an enemy, but admonish him as a brother." The use of the phrase *Gentile* or *tax collector* strongly suggests that the Lord was referring to casting someone out of the synagogue, not the church.

This becomes even more obvious when you notice that in verse 16 Jesus quotes from Deuteronomy 19:15. That Old Testament passage was written to provide a way for the Jews to determine the truth of a witnesses' testimony in their civil courts. Jesus was talking to the disciples about the old covenant law, because this was the religious system still in force at the time.

The All-Important Context

I am convinced we have misunderstood what Jesus was saying in Matthew 18, because we have ripped this passage out of its interwoven context. This is an important consideration, because Matthew 18 is a classic example of how the Lord's message has been interwoven with several incidents to create a particular impact. Let's examine these portions together.

The chapter begins with the disciples' question about who is the greatest in the kingdom of God. It appears that the disciples are hoping Jesus will declare his favorite among them.[113] By their focus on greatness, they reveal once again how little they understand the true nature of the kingdom of heaven. They fail to realize that their condition is pitiable, and they are lost apart from the grace which will be revealed after the cross.

Jesus answers by taking a child and placing him in front of the disciples as an object lesson. Then he begins to teach on the subject of humility—which is the exact opposite of the disciples' attitude. He tells the disciples that to get into the kingdom of heaven, they must first humble themselves like a child. Their question shows that they have obviously not done this. Then the Lord states that whoever causes a little one to stumble will be better off if a millstone is placed around his neck, and he is cast into the sea. The presence of the child certainly must have added emotional impact to this statement.

What the Lord had to say next must have stunned the disciples. Jesus tells about the danger of being a stumbling block and uses some incredibly strong symbolism about cutting off one's own offending hand or foot to avoid bringing eternal judgment on one's self. Better to enter heaven crippled or maimed than to slip into hell with all your limbs intact. Pluck out an offending eye, Jesus continues, and enter heaven with only one, rather than taking both eyes with you into hell. Such strong images dramatically make the Lord's point that being a stumbling stone is a ticket to hell.

Yet we know that plucking out an eye or cutting off a hand will never eliminate offensive behavior. This is because all offenses flow from the sinful heart. In effect, Jesus shocks his disciples to bring them to conviction; they must appreciate just how serious the sin condition really is. Again, Jesus'

---

[113] This is probably even more clear in Luke 9:46-48.

purpose is to break down their self-righteous hearts. He's showing the utter futility of attaining eternal life through works. Not even self-mutilation will accomplish it—the Lord is certainly not recommending that approach to enter the kingdom. This is another of those impossible demands designed to produce conviction.

Jesus then introduces the story of a shepherd with one hundred sheep who loses one and leaves the others to go find it.[114] The Lord concludes in verse 14 that it is not the heavenly Father's will that any of "these little ones" should perish. Within the context, it seems obvious Jesus is still referring to that child standing in their midst. If God cares so much for these little ones that anyone who causes them to stumble is destined for hell, then being great in the kingdom is not the issue. Just entering the kingdom is their more basic problem.

The Brother Who Offends

Beginning in verse 15, the Lord shifts the subject from their potential offense of children to talk of the brother who offends them. In the portion immediately following the so-called "disciplinary passage," Peter interacts with the Lord about forgiveness. In verse 21 Peter is still talking about dealing with those who have offended him. He asks Jesus how many times he must forgive such brothers. To understand this better, I invite your attention back to Chapter 4 in this book, where the subject of forgiveness is treated more thoroughly. There I attempt to show that Jesus is making an impossible demand. No one can forgive his brother in the way the Lord suggests. So his purpose is to provoke the disciples to comprehend the seriousness of their sinful condition.

In verses 15 to 17, the Lord's emphasis is on restoring the sinner who has fallen away, not on punishing those who have rankled them. But when he suggests a procedure for re-

[114] This parable has a different emphasis and purpose than the parable found in Luke 15. See Chapter 9 in *The Gospel Solution*.

storing a brother, he reveals the obvious need to forgive. For the disciples, that's the rub. Peter grasps this point and asks the Lord just how many times they must forgive. Of course the Lord reveals they must never stop forgiving.

The section on forgiveness effectively renders verses 15 to 17 useless for the disciples for any purpose that is not primarily concerned with the well-being of the offender. If they cannot forgive, they will never be able to win back a brother who has sinned against them. But this is all part of the Lord's design, because his real purpose is to probe their conscience so they can see just how vindictive and bitter they really are. If they can't forgive, neither will they be able to win back their enemies. How then can they imagine that they will ever enter the kingdom of heaven, let alone be great in it? Jesus pushes them to the point of frustration, and this is the Lord's wider message within the context of Matthew 18.

The passage also demonstrates to the disciples that God does not give up on them. They are instructed not to give up on their wandering brothers, because each individual is important, and God does not give up on them in this life. They will only comprehend this later, through grace and the power of the Holy Spirit. I believe that this view of the chapter is much more consistent with the Lord's overall ministry and the teaching of grace found in the New Testament. Jesus sought out tax collectors, prostitutes, and the other "big sinners" to offer them mercy and forgiveness—not judgment.

If we make this passage into a law or pattern for church disciplinary procedure, I believe we do a major disservice to the Lord's intent. Certainly there is need for one human being to evaluate another. Parents must do it with their children; employers pass judgment on the performance of their employees; judges send those who commit crimes to jail; and, of course, the epistles make provision for some judgment to take place within the church. But I would suggest that Matthew 18 is not the passage of primary reference for church discipline.

Misusing Matthew 18

The Lord's message here does have an application for Christians today, just as it had for the disciples. Because of our pride, we often fail to appreciate the worth of others. We are so often willing to place others under the law while bestowing grace upon ourselves. The Lord's intent was not to provide a formula for booting someone out of the church; he was showing us how we must seek lost sheep and restore them. Whenever this passage is used as a pattern for church discipline, in my experience it has inevitably resulted in the opposite impact of what the Lord intended. Rather than bringing reconciliation, it often is used to justify one man's vengeance on another.

I know of a minister who became upset when a man in his congregation criticized the ability of the pastor's wife to teach the high school Sunday school class. The pastor confronted the man according to his view of Matthew 18, and the offender replied, "Well, if I said anything to upset you, I'm sorry." The pastor reacted by saying that this wasn't a true apology. (I believe he was right about this.) He took two men for a second confrontation but received the same reply. Not satisfied, he brought the situation to his board, who encouraged him to drop the matter.

The pastor resigned, telling me later, "How could I stay in a church that would not support me in church discipline?" While the man's actions were insensitive, the pastor's actions only contributed to disharmony. My private conclusion was that the pastor was out of line in attempting to discipline this man; his board did him a favor by letting the matter slide, but he was too close to the problem to appreciate it.

In church discipline, the offending party is often dealt with *in absentia*, forcing the congregation to pass judgment on someone who has already left. How can you remove someone who is gone? "You can't kick me out! I'm already outta here!" This confrontational approach leaves lasting bitterness in those who are disciplined. It also negatively impacts those who remain. Even peripheral people are left feeling defiled and vulnerable by the open discussion of another's sin.

The overriding principles found within Matthew 18 are to humble ourselves, avoid offense, seek reconciliation, and offer forgiveness. We should look first at ourselves to see what offenses we have given. Then we must seek to resolve the problems at the lowest possible level. Sometimes it is better to look past a brother's offense than to insist upon resolution. Full resolution might be unattainable because of the different views we all have. In 1 Corinthians 6:7, Paul encourages: "Why not rather be wronged?" Care must be exercised to avoid escalating a dispute in the guise of solving it.

What about Church Discipline?

While Matthew 18 can have *an application* for church discipline, it should not be used as the central text. I believe that a more applicable text on this subject is 1 Corinthians 5. In verse 1 Paul tells of a Corinthian man who is living in sexual union with his stepmother. He declares this is a sin even the Gentiles don't accept, yet points out it has been approved within their church.[115] In verses 2 and 6, Paul indicates the Corinthians are proud of this guy, when they should have been embarrassed.

Paul declares that this man should be put out of the church. In fact, he repeats this directive four times in the chapter. Paul's first goal is to remove the impurity from the

---

[115] Those who lived in Corinth were known for being unwholesome behavior. Whenever a Corinthian was cast in a play, he was inevitably cast as a drunk. The word *Corinthian* at that time was used as a slang term for anyone who was considered a loose person.

church. (Isn't it interesting to note that the apostle neglected to use the first step of going to the man privately?[116]) Paul also suggests that this judgment is to drive the man towards repentance and that the other believers must encourage him to do this; the church is never to empower sin.

In verse 6, Paul provides an analogy for his instruction by saying, "Cast out the leaven." In the Bible leaven often stands for false teaching and sin. Paul uses this illustration to indicate that removing this man will mitigate the impact of his sin upon the church. But while the apostle says this man's behavior is like leaven, he is *not* saying the man is an unbeliever. Ironically, even the man who is excluded from the church is still a genuine part of that new batch of leaven-free dough. He too is a Christian, or he would not be in need of discipline.[117]

In verse 5, Paul instructs the Corinthians to hand this man over to Satan. Now some have suggested this shows the man was an unbeliever, but the classic example of turning someone over to Satan is when God handed Job over to Satan, and Job was clearly a man of faith. This Corinthian is given into Satan's hand so he can receive in his body the natural results of his sin. All this really means is that being removed from the church will allow sin to run its course in his life. If you sow to the flesh, you will from your own flesh reap corruption. God generally doesn't have to judge our sin in this life, because it will reap its own self-destructive consequences.[118]

In the book of Job, when God turned the Old Testament saint over to the devil, we see that it was God who brought up the subject in order to incite the events that followed. He initiated the process because he wanted to use Sa-

---

[116] This would seem to support my premise that Matthew 18:15-17 should not be seen as a primary passage in church discipline.
[117] In 1 Corinthians 5:5-13, those outside the church are explicitly left out of church judgment.
[118] Galatians 6:7-8

tan for his purposes. Satan is always God's unwilling servant. God knows how to skillfully use Satan for his own purposes, as when Satan influenced Judas' heart to betray Christ. So this Corinthian sinner was put out of the church; and the devil became God's "helper," to drive him to repentance.

The suggestion has been made that 2 Corinthians 2:5-11 and 7:8-13 are both references to this same man. Although we cannot be absolutely certain, it does seem likely that this discipline achieved its goal of bringing the man to repentance and restoration within the church.

Who Should Be Disciplined?

When you survey the book of First Corinthians, you're struck by the fact that this church is filled with a lot of problem people. Paul deals with their divisiveness; he handles squabbles over business dealings; he discusses sexual immorality with prostitutes as well as marital problems; he confronts believers who have become puffed up and proud; he addresses abuses at the communion table; he discusses the flagrant misuse of spiritual gifts; and he repeatedly addresses disunity. With so many problem people within the church, why does he only remove this one man? What makes him so unique? Many were involved in sexual sin in the Corinthian church, but Paul took aim only at this man because he met the following three criteria:

First, his sin was flagrant. Everyone in the church seems to have known about it. By bringing it up, Paul was not fanning the flames of some hidden deed; it was an in-your-face problem. Second, the man was unrepentant. In fact, it seems he's proud of himself and is not offering to change. Third, the problem was ongoing and evangelistic in nature. It's one thing to confess your sin and have it washed under the blood of Christ, but this man has taken no steps to turn away from his immorality; he's become a spokesman for his sin. I believe that each of these three conditions should be present before a church publicly disciplines one of its members:

1. The sin must be open and flagrant. In many churches today, church discipline is exacted upon people who have already left the church. When someone leaves, they are usually declaring by leaving that they feel uncomfortable within the fellowship. What good does it do to hammer someone who has already left? This only slams the door so they'll never want to come back. Discipline should only be a last resort to protect the body. It simply should not be used in an attempt to force people to perform. If the board and pastor of an average-sized church knew all of the sins within its midst, and tried to discipline them all, they would have no time for any other ministry. Just the sins of the board and its pastor alone might overload the process.

If a sin is not flagrant, be wary about dragging the offender before the entire church. This will only terrify the other sinners (which is everyone in the church), wondering when their turn will come. There's so much sin in all churches that it would be impossible to deal with it all. These type of diversions only defile the fellowship and distract it from its mission of seeking and saving the lost.

2. The offender must be unrepentant. So often discipline is laid down upon people who have already repented. That's not discipline—that's punishment. Satan is the one who is in the business of accusing the brethren.[119] Let's not become his assistant. When the goal becomes inflicting pain upon the person who has sinned, the church doesn't understand the Word of God. Discipline is meant to lead the offender towards repentance; once that has taken place, it's time for restoration.[120]

3. The sin must be ongoing and evangelistic in nature. I do not believe that this means someone who is struggling with sin should be a candidate for discipline. The person who

---

[119] Revelation 12:10
[120] 2 Corinthians 2:6-8

repents today and falls back tomorrow doesn't need discipline; he needs encouragement. Such a person hates his sin and wants to quit it. But the brother who continues openly in his sin, without any desire to repent, will soon become a problem within the church. He will be like the leaven that infects the whole lump. He will be, in effect, a salesman for evil. This man must be removed.

Don't Let the Church Go Ugly

In all of the cases when I have seen church discipline in action at the level of a public confrontation, I've found that these three conditions have not all been met. Paul apparently did not feel that the others involved in sin at Corinth needed the harsh discipline reserved for this man. The application of discipline should never be a routine matter. The Scriptures like 1 Corinthians 5; 2 Thessalonians 3:6-15; and 1 Timothy 5:19-20 (about sinning church leaders) are passages that have narrow application. Such harsh passages are clearly meant for extraordinary situations. While I recognize that my experience is limited, in my fifty years of life, I have never seen a situation where I believe public discipline was properly invoked. I have read of a few appropriate cases, several of which are notorious, but I have personally never encountered such a situation.

Joe Aldrich in his book *Life-Style Evangelism* lists four things that make the church ugly: (1) hypocrisy, (2) rationalism, (3) impurity and (4) legalism.[121] I would suggest that whenever you marry hypocrisy and legalism—which is what I believe so often happens when judgment is meted out in the church—that you create a "double ugly." When churches or individual Christians attempt to use Matthew 18 and 1 Corinthians 5 to justify inflicting their personal judgment, they often create an "ugliness" that is baptized by their misapplication of these Scriptures.

---

[121] Joe Aldrich, *Life-Style Evangelism*, Multnomah Press, 1981, p. 123.

A few years ago, a man in my church told me he had been involved in a business dealing that had gone sour with people in his previous church. Mike admitted his deeds and told me that his previous church had confronted him. He claimed to have apologized and attempted to make the situation right as best he could, but this had not satisfied the leadership of his previous church. They returned with two others, in typical Matthew 18 fashion, and confronted him a second time. Again, he freely confessed and expressed sorrow, but they remained unhappy and demanded he appear before the entire church board. Because Mike was no longer attending the church, I suggested he skip the meeting. It seemed unnecessary for him to bear another punishment session at their hands. But he had given his word, so I decided to go with him.

At the meeting, the first thing one of the men said was: "I don't care what he says; I'm never going to forgive him!" No one on the board responded to this statement, as if his attitude was acceptable. When they laid out the charges against Mike, I was surprised to hear that they were exactly what he had told me. My experience with people is that they generally whitewash their own actions, omitting the most condemning details. But Mike had taken full responsibility. Again, he apologized for his actions. As far as I could see, he had made all possible restitution. But once again, these Christians harshly condemned him.

After hearing both sides, I'm convinced Mike did everything he should have done to make the offense right, but the motives of that church board were wrong. They wanted to inflict pain upon him, while receiving self-gratification as spiritual men. They had not brought him in with the desire to heal, and they certainly refused to forgive. Mike openly apologized in front of them; but they turned him away, only adding to his pain. What I saw was ugly, and it troubled me.

Let me suggest to you that when we come to the Lord Jesus Christ and are born again, we receive salvation and become children of God. The Bible says: "Those whom the Lord loves He disciplines."[122] Now that's a wonderful truth. When my daughter and son were growing up, my wife and I disciplined them, but we did this because we loved them. That's an example of the new covenant, which believers are under. God disciplines our lives when we do poorly, but he does not judge us. And his discipline merely brings us to a place of a richer walk in Christ.

The Redemptive Lifestyle

I am convinced that there is a much better passage to be used for dealing with the sin of believers. I believe Galatians 6:1 should be considered *the primary reference* for dealing with those in the church who are found in sin. While the church discipline passages used above should have narrow application, Galatians 6:1 should have a much broader application. Paul says: "Brethren, even if a man is caught in any trespass, you who are spiritual, restore such a one in a spirit of gentleness, each one looking to yourself, lest you too be tempted." It's my estimation that this is the answer to the vast majority of sin problems within the church.

Galatians is a letter in which Paul concentrates on attacking legalism. His antidote to this problem is to show us how to live and walk in the Spirit. In 6:1, he charges the church to live what I would call a "redemptive lifestyle." This lifestyle can effectively bring beauty to the church. Paul is saying that we are to live in such a way that we are restoring one another in all gentleness and humility.

In Romans 12:18, the apostle summarizes this lifestyle by saying, "If possible, as far as it depends on you, be at peace with all men." This lifestyle helps to overcome divisions and misunderstandings. Instead of judging those who have offended us or who have fallen into some sin, we must ask

[122] Hebrews 12:6

how we can be reconciled. This will often mean we must suffer an offense in silence, allowing ourselves to be wronged and defrauded.

I read of a woman who purchased a package of cookies, a magazine, and a cup of coffee in a crowded airport lounge while awaiting her flight. As she started to reach for a cookie, a man seated at her table reached over and also helped himself to one of them without asking. His rude action startled her into speechlessness. When she glared at him, he only smiled back. She could feel her face turning red, and she found it difficult to concentrate on her magazine. Then he smiled and *took another cookie!* Quickly, she grabbed a second herself, leaving only one on the table between them. To her astonishment, the man picked up the last cookie and broke it in two; he took half for himself and shoved the other piece toward her! At this last indignity, she seized the piece of cookie, stuffed it into her mouth, and stood up, flushed with anger. Snatching up her purse, she stuck her magazine inside it, only to discover the package of cookies that she had purchased—unopened.

I believe that woman responded like many Christians do when they see someone ensnared in some grievous sin. They don't realize they are just as guilty, and perhaps more so, when they become indignant with self-righteous anger. This behavior is similar to King David's, when he was told of his own actions by Nathan the prophet. Nathan used a story to disguise the facts of the case. When the king heard the story, the facts were less condemning than his own sin, yet still he declared to the prophet: "The man deserves to die!" He did not realize that he was condemning himself. Instead of being judgmental toward our brothers, we should learn to practice a redemptive lifestyle in all situations. God gives us grace for our sin; can we in good conscience deny grace to other believers? If we do not forgive others, we will inevitably find their sin later on our own face.

Paul indicates in this verse that our response should be *active*. He calls us to take the initiative. Remember that we will never be able to remove sin from anyone's life by an act of judgment; but by our actions *we can establish an atmosphere* where it is possible and likely that a transgressor will be restored.

One of the best places where this is taught is in the parable of the prodigal son. The son had chosen to reject his father by moving a great distance away and consuming his inheritance. But the father had created an atmosphere of redemption within his home that he still remembered. The prodigal knew from experience that his father was a kind man who treated his workers well. It was this knowledge that encouraged him to return home, knowing his father would not reject him.

True to form, when the father saw the son, he ran and embraced him, kissing him on the neck. He never required his son to get down on his knees and apologize. The act of his return signaled repentance and reconciliation. This parable is an illustration of the redemptive lifestyle that God ultimately shares with us through Christ. Let me ask you, would sinners feel they are welcome in your home? This parable demonstrates the active response you should have toward other sinners.

In Galatians 6:1, the word translated as "restore" comes from the Greek word from which we get our English word *artisan*. Paul is suggesting that we become skilled craftsman in our efforts to restore others. It is interesting that we regularly see this characteristic in God. When Adam first sinned, God did not rush into the garden with accusations and immediately punish him. He appeared quietly, opening the door for Adam to confess, even though he was met by excuses and denial.

If you search throughout the Scriptures, you'll discover that God is skilled in his response to sinning people. He leaves the door open for their repentance. In the same way, we must learn to become skilled in our response to those who are involved in sin around us. It's probably not necessary to preach to others. Instead, we must win them back by our attitude of grace.

Finally, restoration demands a *spirit of gentleness*. Paul warns us, in effect, to be careful how we deal with others, lest we too fall to the same temptation. John 8 provides an excellent illustration of this. The Pharisees bring a woman to Jesus who has been found in the very act of adultery. Recognizing the motives of the men who brought the woman, the Lord responds to her accusers by writing on the ground. We don't know what he wrote. In the silent film version of *King of Kings*, Jesus is depicted as writing the Ten Commandments. It has also been suggested that the Lord wrote the sins of those waiting for his response. But my favorite suggestion is that he wrote the names of those Pharisees who had committed adultery with the woman.

When they pressed him to condemn her, Jesus uttered those famous words: "Let him who is without sin cast the first stone." Then one by one, each of the accusers left "in order," beginning with the oldest. When only the woman remained, Jesus approached her with kindness and tact, calling her to righteous living. You can clearly see in this illustration that the Lord was *active, skillful,* and *gentle* in his dealings both with this woman and her accusers.

If you attempt to restore a person caught in a trespass, you have made a bold statement. As soon as you have begun to restore someone, you proclaim by your actions that you are a spiritual person. That's a pretty bold statement. In other words, those who are spiritual are the type of people who will restore others.

A great danger we face in seeking to restore another person is our own spiritual pride. Richard Lenski said, "Those who are filled with unholy ambition are glad to see a brother blemished by some transgression." The people I've seen who have misapplied Matthew 18 are generally glad to see their brother tragically fail. Lenski goes on to say: "Yet they do not see that their spiritual pride is the worst blemish yet."[123]

Sometimes we are so blinded by our own ambitions that we cannot see the big picture. I don't know whether it is true, but it has been suggested that when General Custer caught up with the Indians at the Little Big Horn he said: "Good news, boys, we've caught 'em." We often misinterpret the events of other people's trespasses because we're blinded by our own selfish ambition. Nothing is more difficult than to acknowledge our own weaknesses when we would rather scold others for theirs.

We are all vulnerable. The church is really not a pure people; instead we are a redeemed community. Any church that concentrates on casting out all the sinners will end up extremely legalistic and empty. On the surface, it will give the impression of purity; but under the surface, it will be a church full of people who do not dare reveal any of their imperfections for fear they will become the next "stoning" victim. (On the other hand, this approach will certainly solve any parking problems.) But the church that proclaims the precious gift of God's love will become a place where sinners flock for healing. By establishing an atmosphere of grace and mercy, we proclaim to the world that the church is a sanctuary where transgressors can be restored. Keep in mind that such a fellowship, just like the Corinthian church, will be filled with people with sin problems. But somehow, I believe that is the kind of church that the Lord wanted us to have.

---

[123] R. C. H. Lenski, *The Interpretation of St. Paul's Epistles to the Galatians, Ephesians and Philippians,* assigned to Augsburg, p. 296.

A Recap of Transitionalism

1) Old Covenant. In Matthew 18 Jesus speaks to his disciples living under the old covenant and still trapped in the legal mind-set that assumes the only way one can please God is through works. Because of their question about greatness, he begins where they are at, slowly provoking them toward conviction. To please God, they must meet his standard, humble themselves, not be a stumbling block, and forgive from the heart. The use of the categories *Gentiles* and *tax collectors* would also indicate strongly that Jesus was talking in old covenant terms.

2) Conviction. The Lord meant to convict the disciples about how unable they are to meet the standards of a holy God. When they realize how difficult true greatness will be, they are left in despair. All of this comes with those terrifying illustrations about chopping off body parts. The entire chapter reeks with the pride of the apostles. Peter seeks to justify himself by sounding like he is a forgiver, but once again Jesus gives the ramifications of trying to please God by our own efforts, and Peter is left with only his empty boasting.

The Lord's words in this chapter were never really meant to show the disciples how they could avoid offense, or how they could restore other sinners, or how they might forgive as a means of earning their way into the kingdom of heaven. Nice as it might have been for them to upgrade their character, heaven can never be reached by such works. So the Lord's purpose was certainly not to introduce an even harder path into the kingdom; it was to show the futility of attaining eternal life through being good.

3) Evocative. The evocative nature of the Lord's approach here is subtly revealed by the disciples' inability to humble themselves. This teaching is another step that leads them to recognize their inability to be men of forgiveness, and that realization can lead only to frustration. The self-mutilation portion was also designed to cause introspection. The Lord's words here were meant to provoke a greater sense of urgency on the part of these men to get right with God.

4) Interwoven Context. This so-called discipline passage is woven into the larger context of a major section that begins in Matthew 16:13 and continues on through the preparations for Palm Sunday.[124] To understand this section (which is so often taken out of context and applied to the church), it is necessary to see that it is part of a larger portion of the Scriptures where Jesus begins to reveal his plan of the coming cross. But the disciples did not comprehend what Jesus was saying. Their lack of understanding was part of his plan to reveal to them how sinful they really were.

This chapter shows that God demands perfection. As the Lord gets closer to the end of his earthly ministry, we find him pushing the disciples harder toward conviction. The teaching in Matthew 18 is designed to frustrate them with the law. They are being made ready for God to wash away their sin with the blood of the cross, an act of grace without any merit on their part. Until they experience the cross and the coming of the Holy Spirit, they'll never be able to measure up.

Now if you have been carefully working through Matthew 18, you might have noted that I have neglected to comment on verses 18 to 20. Because these verses deal primarily with prayer, I have left most of my comments on that subject to Chapter 12, where I'll examine the Lord's bold prayer promises in much greater detail. But here it's important to clarify what these three verses *do not* say.

---

[124] See the notes for the Recap at the end of Chapter 4.

What was Jesus' intent when he declared in verse 18 that what the disciples would bind on earth would be bound in heaven? It certainly cannot be a statement about their spiritual maturity at that time. James and John had recently asked the Lord about calling down fire from heaven on the Samaritans.[125] This leads me to believe that this verse is primarily meant to provoke their swelling pride, as well as being a prophecy about their future ministry after Pentecost.[126]

Next, the Lord gives a short vignette in verses 19 and 20 that would appear to be out of place. Again, the meaning is best determined by examining the context in which it's found. Before and after these verses, the Lord talks about forgiveness, so it appears that this is one of the Lord's more subtle evocative statements. This time, Jesus utters an apparent prayer promise by declaring that if the disciples ask for anything in his name, it will be given.

The Greek word translated "name" (*onoma*) not only refers to what someone is called, but it also speaks of a person's authority and character. So when Jesus mentions praying in his name, he's referring to acting with the Lord's authority. Yet this is a difficult statement, when the reality of unanswered prayer is examined (again, see Chapter 12). Why does the Lord offer such a promise, considering that most Christians quickly figure out that using these words is not a guarantee to get their prayers answered?

I often receive junk mail disguised to look like a payroll check or some official government correspondence. Once the letter is opened and the contents are seen, the advertiser's intentions quickly become obvious; despite the creative packaging, it's still just a piece of junk mail. In the same way, whenever someone tacks on "in the name of Jesus" to their prayers they may actually be attempting to disguise their real self-centered intentions with this "formula."

---

[125] Luke 9:51-56

[126] By the time the disciples reach Acts 5, we see the spiritual discernment of the apostles growing to this level.

Peter reveals in verse 21 that he sees himself as worthy of God's praise and special blessing. After all, look how forgiving Peter is. But in reality, the disciples are at this point limited in their spiritual maturity, like a child who's playing dress-up. They claim to be following the Lord, but they don't really have a clue where this is all leading. In fact, Peter tells Jesus that he will simply not allow him to go to the cross.

So it seems likely that Jesus utters these verses, which seem so out of context, to provoke the disciples to think. They will quickly realize that saying "in Jesus' name" is no guarantee—just like when they attempted and failed to cast out some demons. This will cause them to come to the end of their own resources and be ready for the message of grace.

Chapter 11

Why Don't I Have Enough Faith?
Mustard Seed Faith

Eleven-year-old Wesley Parker listened with great interest as the visiting evangelist told the congregation about his own recent healing from a painful spinal condition. The boy had been diagnosed with diabetes at age six and had been hospitalized for the condition the previous year. Now at the Sunday service in the First Assembly of God Church in Barstow, California, the evangelist invited anyone who needed a miracle to come to the altar, where they would receive prayer. Wesley glanced at his parents and then the family stepped forward. The date was August 21, 1973.

"Do you understand what we are going to pray for now?" asked the evangelist as the Parkers knelt before him.

"Yes," replied Wesley, "I want to be healed of diabetes."

"I believe God is going to heal you, Wesley. Do you believe it?"

"Uh-huh," he answered.

Wesley believed. In fact, after the service he started telling his friends that he'd been healed. The next morning, the Parkers took their son's insulin away. The boy asked if he could have sugar on his cereal, and his mother agreed. But over the next two days, he showed all the signs of rising blood sugar and diabetic decline, including vomiting, headaches, excessive urination, and stomach pain. The Parkers responded with fervent prayer, trying to persuade themselves that doubt was the real enemy.

By Tuesday, Wesley's discomfort had grown to the point that the Parkers almost caved in and bought insulin. But three members of Mrs. Parker's prayer group encouraged them to stay "in faith." By early Wednesday, the child's breathing had become labored. When Gary Nash, their pastor, kneeled to pray at Wesley's bedside, the rasping seemed to ease, and father Larry Parker's faith was strengthened. Later that morning, Nash returned to the Parkers' home and recommended that Wesley be taken to a doctor. But the parents had convinced themselves that to give up now would be to reject the Lord.

Early that afternoon, the boy lapsed into a coma. A few hours later, while his friends and parents prayed at his bedside, Wesley Parker suffered a final diabetic convulsion and died. Even then, the parents did not give up. The Parkers conducted a "resurrection service" at the funeral home, but when their prayers failed to bring him back, they were arrested for involuntary manslaughter and child abuse.[127]

Why did God allow this experiment in faith to end in tragedy? Although this family audaciously took their faith to the limit, they are certainly not alone in their attempts to believe the promises of the Lord. Over a 15-year period, at least 126 children died because medical treatment was withheld based upon the parents' doctrinal conviction. You can imagine the frustration that results when God responds to such bold prayers with silence.

In the Gospels, Jesus seemed to indicate that if we had faith, we could perform miracles. I have some faith, yet I see no miracles, so what's wrong with me? When we see no miracles, we either conclude they are no longer possible today, or that our faith is to too weak to produce results. This

---

[127] *People* Magazine, 1988. Wesley's parents, Larry and Lucky Parker, wrote a book on the tragedy entitled *We Let Our Son Die*. A few years ago, a CBS TV movie called *Promised a Miracle* dramatized the story. The parents have renounced their error and allowed the drama to be produced so others might learn from their tragic mistake.

is the dilemma of the faith-healing movement. Whenever a believer attempts to produce miracles and fails, he ends up doubting that he has "the right stuff." He may even doubt his salvation. Another approach is to blame the person who seeks a healing for their lack of faith.

I mentioned a woman in the opening chapter whose mother contracted cancer. The church that the family attended encouraged the girl that if she prayed and believed, her mother would get well. She prayed and believed, but her mother died. This incident became the defining moment of her unbelief. She reasoned that if this was the best God could do, she no longer needed him in her life.

Now I suppose one could say that this woman's response to her mother's death showed that she did not really have faith. But I find this approach to be a "catch-22." If a person doesn't obtain what he has requested, the issue can always be resolved by concluding there was insufficient belief. But does anyone have enough faith to see such miraculous results? In this situation, the entire church had prayed for her mother. Didn't even one person have adequate faith?

The Mustard Seed Faith Passages

There are two main Gospel passages in which Jesus talked about faith-inspired miracles. The first is in Matthew, where the disciples are unable to cast a demon out of a young man. When they ask the Lord in private why they cannot perform the exorcism, he replies: "Because of the littleness of your faith, for truly I say to you, if you have faith as a mustard seed, you shall say to this mountain, 'Move from here to there,' and it shall move; and nothing shall be impossible to you."[128] Jesus says that their faith is too little, yet if it is only the size of a mustard seed, they will be able to move mountains and *nothing shall be impossible for them.* Luke quotes Jesus making a similar statement: "If you had faith like a

---

[128] Matthew 17:20

mustard seed, you would say to this mulberry tree, 'Be uprooted and be planted in the sea'; and it would obey."[129]

These two passages offer essentially the same bold promise. Jesus declares that proper faith can uproot trees and move mountains. The key question seems to be, what is this "mustard seed faith"? Whatever it is, it doesn't appear to be common. I'm afraid I know of no one who is performing miracles like this. If no one can move mountains or trees, we are either misunderstanding what the Lord is saying, or we must figure out how to get this faith. Either way, something is wrong with our understanding of these verses.

To fully comprehend this promise, we must examine it within its context. Whenever the words of the Lord are separated and isolated like individual proverbs, we inevitably miss the Lord's intent. Although context is always important in the Gospels, with these two passages it is *essential* to our understanding. Even though these statements are similar, I will focus on the passage in Luke, because I find it to be the clearer of the two.

The Root of the Problem

The exchange in Luke 17 contains one of those intriguingly evocative series of events that characterizes Jesus' ministry. The Lord first instructs the disciples that they must avoid causing others to stumble. He finishes his mini-message by stating they must forgive others up to seven times a day. This teaching could be summed up as *give no offense and take no offense.*

The disciples were quick to grasp that they could not measure up to his instruction. This blunt teaching must have hit them hard; the reaction of the disciples was to see their inability to obey, and this caused them to ask for more faith. Jesus had indicated that anyone who is a stumbling block would be better off having a millstone hung around his neck

---

[129] Luke 17:6

and be thrown into the sea. And now the Lord describes such offenses as "inevitable." He also includes an additional demand for his disciples to forgive.

Now, certainly the Lord is not saying that his followers should never offend anyone by living godly lives of faith. The Lord indicated elsewhere that a true believer can be sure that he will offend others. Here he is saying that the disciples should not lead others astray through the sin in their lives.

It seems that most people never comprehend the extent of the pain they cause. In a survey of divorced people, each was asked to explain what contributed to the breakup of their marriages. Well over 80 percent of these people felt their spouse's adultery was a major contributing factor in the divorce, yet less than 5 percent felt that *their* adultery could have had any significant impact upon ending their marriage. People so often delude themselves into believing that they do not offend others, yet others certainly would not agree with that assessment.

The second emphasis of the Lord's short teaching session was that the disciples needed to forgive one another. As we discussed in Chapter 4, this is an impossible challenge for real people. Most of us are filled with many grievances against parents, former spouses, and friends; and I imagine that these words made the disciples quite uncomfortable.

The desire to get even with those who have offended us is an almost universal response. I read about some market researchers who struggled to determine why many low-income women would not switch to a new and better roach killer delivered in a tray. Trying to understand their refusal to switch, the researchers had these women draw pictures of roaches, writing stories about them in hopes of probing their subconscious feelings. The research revealed that many of these women viewed roaches as males, symbolizing their ex-husbands and boyfriends who had left them poor and powerless. Even though the poison bait trays were more effective against the insects, they were seen as too passive. Killing roaches directly with a bug spray allowed these women to watch the insects squirm and die, thus venting their hostility. The sin nature expresses itself in many subtle ways.

Jesus hopes to bring the disciples to a self awareness of sin's subtlety by raising the standard hopelessly out of their reach; to forgive up to seven times a day must have seemed to them like an impossible dream. Again, the Lord demonstrates to the disciples his basic message: *You are sinners, hopelessly unable to meet God's standard.* He meant to provoke conviction in the disciples. When they perceived their need, they pleaded for more faith.

The Desire for a Magic Solution

The Lord's response to the request of the disciples is enlightening. They're asking for faith, and Jesus launches into a discussion on the supernatural removal of trees. I believe Jesus gives this answer because he knows the disciples' inner thoughts better than they do themselves. By addressing the unspoken request within their hearts, Jesus tailors his message for maximum impact. His reply is our clue to understanding what the disciples were feeling.

By blaming their shortcomings on a lack of faith, they were attempting to shift the blame for their failure to forgive from themselves back onto God. Adam was the first to use this approach. In the Garden, he defended his sin by saying: "It's the woman that *you* gave me." He implied: "Lord, if it weren't for you and this woman, I wouldn't be in this mess!" I believe the disciples are unconsciously doing the same thing. They're saying: "Lord, if we can't forgive, it's because you haven't given us the faith to do the job!"

It is far easier to pray, "Give me patience," than it is to control our temper. When we pray for patience (in the shadow of a temper tantrum), what we may be saying is that our temper is really God's fault. After all, if he would just answer my prayer, my rotten temper would go away.

I'm acquainted with a man who, as near as I can recollect, had never done a single kind act toward me. He developed a serious family relationship crisis and suddenly performed a good deed for me without any prompting. When this happened, I wondered to myself, *Why is he doing this?* I would suggest that because I am a pastor, he may have viewed me as God's representative and reasoned that by pleasing me he could strike a bargain with God. Often there is a hidden reason under the surface that controls our behavior. So when the disciples ask for more faith, Jesus subtly reveals their hidden agenda. They wanted power to perform miracles[130] more than to change their own behavior. And the Lord indicates that even a small faith is more than adequate.

Now most people want power. Even though we might ask for more faith (because that's the acceptable religious thing to do), what we really want is power and influence over others. We hope people will notice us and acknowledge how important we are. Think of how impressed your friends and loved ones would be if your faith could bring about miracles at will. You could be a humble miracle worker and drive around in a little red sports car.

The Lord's statement about miracles was not meant as a formula for tree removal; it merely addressed what was on the disciples' minds. Their question, and the Lord's evocative answer, appears to have contributed to many of our modern misconceptions about the use of faith. We would have preferred the Lord to give a straight answer on this subject. If he had just provided three simple steps for increasing faith, then we'd all know exactly what we should do. But the Lord's response left the question up in the air.

We know that we cannot please God without faith,[131]

---

[130] This can be seen more clearly in the companion passage in Matthew 17:20, where the disciples do not have enough faith to cast out a demon.
[131] Hebrews 11:6

but how can we use the Lord's answer to increase our belief? And if we think we have succeeded in increasing it, how can we ever measure its growth? Over the years, Christians have tried all sorts of ineffective methods to supercharge their faith into the kind that can call down miracles.

I like to call one of those methods the "put God to the test" approach. I know a lady who tried to heal her eyesight by smashing her only set of contact lenses with a hammer. She did this, believing God would recognize her faith and grant her wish. But apparently this didn't do the trick, because God did not heal her vision. With considerable embarrassment, she had to cycle to work on a bicycle until she replaced those contacts. When a believer misunderstands this faith passage, he may find spiritual confusion developing in his life.

Another method is the "grit your teeth" approach. You pray and quote Scripture that seems to promise an answer back to God. When the answer does not come, you can pray harder, gritting your teeth and making your hands into fists while you say something like: "Lord, you know I believe you and your Word. Lord, give me the answer I desire!" I have had personal experience with both these methods—without success.

The Mustard Seed Mystery

To determine how to increase our faith, we must first know what mustard seed faith is all about. Why is it that no one seems to have developed enough of it to bounce mulberry trees around? This could be so useful for those in the logging business. A logger could say: "Tree, be cut down, bucked up and limbed, and then load yourself on that truck over there." This would certainly make life safer and simpler for some of those in dangerous professions.

The key to making sense of this passage is to understand what Jesus meant by "mustard seed faith." Some have pointed to another passage in Matthew, where Jesus used the mustard seed to illustrate the kingdom of God; in that passage, the Lord indicated that although it is the smallest of all seeds, like the kingdom of God, it grows up into a large bush.[132] I've heard it suggested that mustard seed faith is therefore a growing faith. Preachers sometimes claim that the roots of the mustard bush are hardy and will grow up under blacktop, so that mustard seed faith must be tenacious. This interpretation implies that if our faith grows strong enough, we will be able to uproot trees.

If this is true, why haven't any Christian loggers learned how to move trees? Is the problem that none of them have ever increased their faith to this level? And why can't any of my Christian friends transplant trees in their yard? Now you might suggest that we don't live in a mulberry tree region, but I don't see anyone moving rhododendrons or rose bushes. Most of us would be elated if our faith would just remove a little ice off our windshields in winter. None of this happens.

When I preached on this subject, I dug up an alder tree and brought it into the church in a bucket. I asked rhetorically, "Does anyone think that they can move this tree by their faith?" One fellow actually raised his hand; he thought he could do it. Of course, what he was saying was that he had faith in the words of Jesus. But he didn't move it, and the reality I saw was much simpler. His faith, as sincere and meaningful as it was, couldn't move the tree.

The problem of this "growing faith" interpretation is that no one ever achieves the level to be able to call down miracles. I don't have this kind of faith, and I've never met anyone who does. Besides, growth and tenaciousness come only after the seed is planted and sprouts. I don't believe this is what Jesus was saying in Luke 17. In that passage, the Lord compares faith to a mustard *seed,* not a mustard *plant.* This "growing faith" is another way we test God (or we simply grit

---

[132] Matthew 13:31-32

our teeth), and it produces Christians who struggle in vain to raise their level of faith.

A Simple Faith

Let me suggest a different answer. I believe what Jesus meant by "faith like a mustard seed" was actually just small faith. Nothing more. The disciples already had faith, or they wouldn't have asked for an increase; and Jesus said that their faith was small, but if it was just the size of a mustard seed it would be big enough to do the job. Jesus' answer in verse 6 might be paraphrased to read: "Your faith is small, but you don't need more faith because the smallest amount can perform miracles, even uprooting trees. You already have enough faith. What you need to do is to use what you have."

I don't believe this verse is meant to be a promise about faith. Instead, the Lord merely gives an illustration about faith's great potential. Christians have wasted too much energy attempting to generate this special miracle-working quality when Jesus indicates that even small faith is adequate. The Lord's focus was not on miracles but on showing that a little faith is enough. So verse 6 was not a miracle-working formula; it is an illustration.

Because of what you've been taught in the past, your emotions might tend to struggle with this conclusion. If you find yourself in this situation, I challenge you to answer why no one achieves the results. I'm not saying that miracles are never performed, but certainly no believer can create them on a regular basis, as the common misinterpretation of this passage would seem to indicate. I would love this passage to be a formula for creating miracles, but this was not the Lord's intent.

Misunderstanding what Jesus was saying can lead a believer into doctrinal problems. After Wesley Parker's death, his father stated: "Many times we've prayed, 'Lord why couldn't we have learned another way that this kind of faith is wrong, that it's not really faith at all, but presumption?'"

Some faith teachers actually claim that God must provide whatever they request, because they believe this passage places him under obligation to do as their faith demands. Not only is this unscriptural, it defies logic. If God can be controlled by a faith formula, he is no longer God but an impotent lackey, a spiritual butler. This heretical teaching takes the disciple's desire for power to its ultimate carnal extreme.

The Lord's message was much more far reaching. The disciples would only fully understand it after the coming of the new covenant and the message of grace. When a man becomes a Christian, God removes his guilt by Christ's death on the cross. While no believer becomes sinless, he is forgiven because of his faith in Christ's sacrifice. His faith, small as it might be, is capable of imparting the righteousness of Christ.

What About That Slave?

People struggle in part with Jesus' answer because they stop after verse 6 and cut off the rest of the Lord's answer. Read for yourself through verse 10. Here Jesus explains how a slave must do what he is told, because it is his duty. Slaves had to serve their masters in ways that were often tedious. There was nothing unusual about this (it is the same for employees today), but the Lord finishes his illustration by saying: "And you too, when you do all the things which are commanded you, say, 'We are unworthy slaves; we have done only that which we ought to have done.'"[133]

The Lord's teaching suggests that the task of treating others properly involves no special merit. It is what the disciples are supposed to do. We might paraphrase Jesus by say-

---

[133] You should understand that the phrase *we are unworthy slaves* is an oriental expression. We often think of the Bible as a Western book, when it's cultural setting is actually Eastern. In the movie *The Good Earth* (about China), someone would bring over tea and call it *unworthy tea* or they would describe their home as *their unworthy house*. The tea and home were actually good; it was only a matter of self-deprecation. So *we are unworthy slaves* is really the same type of phrase; it is an Eastern statement of humility.

ing: "You claim to need more faith, but what you need is more faithfulness." This message is certainly one that the church can apply today. We don't need more faith to perform our tasks, we need more obedience. The disciples were making excuses for themselves, and we should be careful not to make that same mistake. You should do your duty as the Lord reveals it to you in the Scriptures, but we must be careful not to bring the conditional elements found under the old covenant and apply them as if they were part of the new covenant.

Many want a miracle, and they're upset that God has not touched their situation with a magic wand. But God is asking us to be faithful in hard situations; he is not teaching us how to bring about magical changes. God wants faithfulness, because it glorifies him and will increase our faith. This is why activities like attending church, praying regularly, and reading your Bible are so important for growth. As we obey the Lord, he is glorified, and we bask in that glow. In the end, the Lord was showing the disciples their need for being faithful.

The Obedient Leper

But Luke is not finished with this subject. The next event that he records in the chapter is an incident that he uses to illustrate what Jesus has just been teaching. Read about the ten lepers for yourself in verses 11 through 19.

This is an unusual miracle.[134] Jesus doesn't touch these ten men or heal them directly. Neither does he restore them with a word. Instead, he encourages them to go to the priest, where (according to the law of Moses), they would make an offering of thanksgiving for their healing. This offering is commanded only after a healing has taken place,[135] but

---

[134]Of course, an *unusual miracle* is an oxymoron. All miracles are unusual. I use the term *unusual* here to point out that this miracle had distinctive aspects for teaching purposes.

[135] Leviticus 14:1-32

these men are not actually healed until they head off toward the temple. They were healed as they were going.

The location where this encounter takes place is between Samaria and Galilee; and so Jesus was asking these men to travel all the way to Jerusalem, because the temple was the only location where this offering could be given. The journey was long, and they had not yet been healed.

One of those lepers who began the journey faced an impossible problem. As a Samaritan, he would not have been permitted to enter the temple to make the offering that Moses required. In fact, within the temple complex, there was a sign which read: "Any foreigner who goes beyond this wall will have only himself to blame for his ensuing death." If that Samaritan attempted to make the offering which Jesus commanded, he would have been put to death. For him, following the Lord's command was an impossibility. Yet he began the trip to Jerusalem like the others, and as he walked, he was healed. When he returned to thank Jesus, the Lord indicated that his faith had made him well.

Most comments I have read on this passage declare that the moral of this story is gratitude. If that's true, what's the lesson? Only one out of ten individuals express gratitude? Samaritans are the only ones who are thankful? Are outcasts more thankful than the culturally dominant? What is the lesson on thankfulness? Let me suggest that the message in this passage is not primarily about gratitude, but about faithfulness.

The man attempted to do what the Lord asked, *even when it was impossible.* Even though he would never have been able to complete the mission, God blessed his faithfulness. The Samaritan was rewarded just by the act of attempting the journey. The man's faithfulness allowed the Lord to work in his life in a miraculous manner.

Do you want to see God perform great feats in your life? Do you want to see an occasional mulberry tree uprooted and planted in the sea? Do you want to see miracles that can change your situation? Then you must exercise both your faith and your *faithfulness*. First, believe in the Lord for your salvation. Then faithfully do what Jesus asks you to do out of gratitude. By fulfilling your duty humbly and without complaint, God will transform your life. Do this even when the task seems impossible—because God is asking you to.

If you do this, and then when you subsequently encounter a barrier in your path—and there is no way around that barrier either to the right or to the left—you will have the confidence to speak to it based upon the power of God's Word. In some way, the Lord will pluck up that barrier for you and cast it aside. It may not be the way you expect, but he will deal with it for you or through you or provide the grace for you to bear it. Jesus is asking you to faithfully do your duty; and when you do, I believe he will remove the barrier or empower you through it to ultimate victory.

My problem isn't that a mulberry tree is in my way; it's that I don't like doing the humble things God has called me to do. My problem is not a lack of faith; it is a lack of obedience. When I obey, I see God work in remarkable ways. Although I have never been able to move a literal tree, God has shown me paths around trees, and I have experienced the Lord's power in my life. The skeptic might call this a coincidence, but I've found that the Lord has opened my path in ways beyond my expectation or plan.

Are You Doing Your Duty?

The first thing Jesus taught in this passage was that the disciples should not cause others to stumble by the way they lived their lives. Although we too may have many excuses for why we can't do what the Lord asks, ultimately we become a stumbling stone to others if we fail to live out our faith. Let me ask you, are you being faithful in the things that God has called you to do?

As a husband, are you following through on those responsibilities that God requires in your position as a husband and father? For example, are you providing for your family financially? Now, this might seem like an obvious responsibility, yet I've met men who are not meeting the financial needs of their families, and they often have weak excuses why they fail to do so. Some of their reasons are even religious in nature. If this is your situation, I believe the Lord wants you to do your duty. By contrast, don't allow your faithful financial provision for your family to become an excuse for neglecting other duties.

As a wife, do you fulfill your appointed tasks as a homemaker? Are you meeting your family's needs by fulfilling your responsibilities within the home? If you are a woman who works outside the home, are you balancing the responsibilities in an effective Christian fashion? Often I hear of women who are so busy that their families are suffering. Don't make excuses for yourself; accomplish the tasks to which God has called you. Even working in the church to the detriment of your family can be a form of disobedience to the Lord. (I have known several adults who were angry at the church because they had felt neglected by mothers who had dedicated themselves to the work of the church.)

As a parent, are you giving the hours you should to your children? Sometimes parents offer the excuse that while they don't spend *much time* with their kids, they spend *quality time*. Now what exactly is "quality time"? It often takes a lot of quantity to achieve quality in the lives of our children. Craftsmanship cannot be hurried in any endeavor. Jesus calls us to fulfill our duty toward our kids.

Many Christians live in open sin, cohabiting without the benefit of marriage. Now most of these believers know the Lord is displeased with this practice, but they continue anyway. If you are in this situation, God wants you to repent and turn away from this lifestyle to walk in faithfulness.

Some Christians are involved in ministry within the church, but they seem to be constantly in need of extra encouragement to keep going. A wise pastor will encourage his church workers, but a faithful Christian should be able to perform his tasks for at least a few days without encouragement. He should be able to do his ministry for the Lord rather than for the applause of men. We should say to ourselves: *I am an unworthy servant. I've only done what I ought to have done.* As you do your duty, you will see God work in your life. This is the kind faith that uproots trees and moves mountains.

Do We Have Enough Faith?

Another interesting passage to consider is when Jesus promised in the Gospel of John that the disciples would do greater works than he did himself.[136] What are these greater works? Because the miracles of Jesus were never exceeded by the apostles, I doubt that the works of which the Lord was referring were signs and wonders. Let me suggest that these greater works are introducing others to eternal life where they are indwelt by the Spirit. If this is not the meaning, I can think of no other. Bringing a man to eternal life is certainly far greater than any other short-lived miracle would be in a man's life. When the disciples began to preach, the Good News burst upon the world with the incredible power of the Holy Spirit and spread to the entire world.

Christianity was born and authenticated amidst a display of supernatural power. But often in our carnality, we find it easy to focus on the overtly miraculous, losing sight of the greater miracle of the new birth and the changed life that salvation brings with it. In our passage in Luke, it was not the Lord's purpose to instruct the disciples how to perform mira-

---

[136] John 14:12 says, "Truly, truly, I say to you, he who believes in Me, the works that I do shall he do also; and greater works than these shall he do: because I go to the Father."

cles. His main teaching emphasis was to point out their inability to meet God's standard through their own efforts; his secondary goal was to encourage them to faithfulness.

Jesus evaluated the quality of the faith he saw in his encounters with many different people. About the Roman centurion he declared, "not even in Israel have I found such great faith."[137] By contrast, Jesus labeled his own disciples as: "Ones of little faith."

How much faith do we need? In this passage, Jesus is offering a measuring stick. He states that the smallest possible amount of faith, even so small that it can only be compared with a little mustard seed, is large enough to bring incredible results. But the foundational and most important accomplishment of faith is when we first believe Christ wants to save us from our sin. It really doesn't take much to believe on Jesus. We may not have the faith of a spiritual giant, but the Lord assures us just a little bit is enough.

Once we have accepted his sacrifice in faith, we can begin to grow towards spiritual maturity. The most important point that the Lord makes to his disciples—and ultimately by application to the church—is that he wants us to exercise the faith that we have. No matter how small your faith, he wants you to use it to trust him. Commit yourself to be faithful to Christ, and you'll experience the tremendous joy that comes from serving the Lord. And as Jesus pointed out, your faithfulness will cause your Christian life to blossom like a rose in the desert.

---

[137] Luke 7:9

A Recap of Transitionalism

1) Old Covenant. Throughout Luke 17:1-10, Jesus again aims directly at the basic problem he came to solve: No one is really able to come to terms with their own sinfulness until he first sees his behavior contrasted with God's holiness. The Lord's teaching here was not aimed at the church (except by way of application). It was spoken to his Jewish followers who were under the bondage of the old covenant.

2) Conviction. When the Lord instructs his followers not to offend or to be offended, he again reveals the impossibility of keeping God's laws. This short message was designed to heap conviction upon the disciples, because he knew they would never be able to perform it. By their request for more faith, the disciples reveal they are feeling the heat of the Lord's high demands.

3) Evocative. This passage is so subtle that many Christians have completely missed what it is teaching. Jesus' message is often misunderstood, because of our carnality. Most Christians fail to see that his focus is on faithfulness because of their own latent desire for power and miracles. Jesus also teaches here that a man's faith does not have to be great in order to experience God's great blessing, but that faithfulness will bear great blessings.

4) Interwoven Context. Understanding the interwoven context is particularly helpful in Luke 17. Jesus' short teaching session leads the disciples to conviction, which causes them to shift the blame for their failure onto the Lord by asking for more faith. He responds to their request by teaching on faithfulness. It is only through the interrelationship of these different incidents that we are fully able to comprehend the Lord's focus on personal responsibility

Chapter 12

Why Doesn't the Lord Answer Me?
Unanswered Prayer

Some years ago, a little girl in my church contracted leukemia. After a lot of prayer and a protracted medical struggle to save her life, her Christian parents sought out a religious leader who was known for his healing ministry. They took their daughter and flew to where the man was preaching.

During the service, the preacher claimed he had a message from God that there was a little girl in the congregation on her mother's lap who had leukemia. Their hearts jumped. The preacher said that God had told him he was healing the girl at that time. But the girl wasn't healed. In fact, she died a year later. When she died, the father cried out in pain: "Why didn't God answer our prayer?"

Sooner or later, it seems that almost every Christian will call out to God about some life crisis only to encounter the Lord's silence. But unanswered prayer is so much more puzzling because of the dramatic promises that Jesus made. He boldly says that we should pray and expect to receive what we ask for.

As I was growing up, I longed to see without glasses. At the age of 14, I prayed that God would heal my eyes and make my vision 20/20. Just in case he had forgotten, I even repeated the Scriptures back to God: "Lord, you say whatever I ask for believing, I will have it. Lord, I believe, now please heal my eyesight." I felt my faith was strong in the Lord's promise, and I remember opening my eyes to see how good God had made my vision. But my eyesight did not change, and I had to live with those glasses and this unanswered prayer for the next thirty years (until I was able to afford laser surgery to correct the problem).

An Embarrassing Promise?

C. S. Lewis, who was no stranger to unanswered prayer, stated that: "The New Testament contains embarrassing promises that what we pray for with faith we shall receive. Mark 11:24 is the most staggering. Whatever we ask for, believing that we'll get it, we'll get. No question, it seems, of confining it to spiritual gifts; *whatever* we ask for. How is this astonishing promise to be reconciled?"

Lewis viewed the Lord's promise in his own words as being downright "embarrassing." Even with his great intellect, he could not reconcile this staggering statement, especially in the shadow of his own wife's untimely death from cancer.[138] He stated: "I have no answer to my problem, though I have taken it to about every Christian I know, learned or simple, lay or clerical, within my own Communion or without."[139]

In *The Gospel Solution*, we have reexamined the words of Jesus so that we could better understand him, but to question the Lord's promises on prayer almost seems like questioning Jesus himself. If we can't believe his promises, what can we believe? Yet something must be wrong with our understanding, simply because so many Christians cannot reconcile these promises with their experience. While some believers may bubble over with outspoken confidence at the Lord's answer to their prayers, many are quietly frustrated because they feel ignored by him.

---

[138] See the illustration at the beginning of Chapter 1.

[139] C. S. Lewis, *Christian Reflections*, "Petitionary Prayer: A Problem Without An Answer," Eerdmans, Grand Rapids, 1967, p. 150.

Lewis claimed that the Lord's most staggering prayer promise was found in Mark's Gospel: "Truly I say to you, whoever says to this mountain, 'Be taken up and cast into the sea,' and does not doubt in his heart, but believes that what he says is going to happen, it shall be granted him. Therefore I say to you, all things for which you pray and ask, believe that you have received them, and they shall be granted you."[140]

If a group of Christians were asked by a show of hands if they believe this promise of the Lord is true, I imagine every hand would go up. Although some like myself would raise their hand reluctantly, still all hands would rise. Yet if the same group were asked: "Have you ever prayed in such a way that you felt you fulfilled the Lord's conditions, but your prayer wasn't answered?" many arms would be meekly lifted. We want to believe the Lord's promise, but our experience often contradicts it. To an outsider, the inconsistent experience between our faith and our results on this matter would seem to be a farce, a pie-in-the-sky fantasy.

Over the years, I have met many Christians who were encouraged by this promise to pray for the removal of some mountain from their path. Using all the faith they possessed, they nonetheless found that the mountain remained. The experience can shake a person's faith, causing them to doubt Jesus or themselves. *Is he playing some kind of cruel joke on me? Am I doing something wrong? Is there sin or unbelief in my life? Does he really care how I feel?* Such experiences can shatter a believer's confidence.

I have studied this passage over the years, trying to make sense of this promise in the light of my own failure in prayer. I remained stymied until I began to look at this passage within its interwoven context. The fourth principle of transitionalism points to the Gospel writer editorially choosing elements of Jesus' earthly ministry. He interweaves his

---

[140] Mark 11:23-24

message with several of these incidents so that the message is enhanced by the interrelationships. Although context is always an important consideration in the Bible, in this particular passage, it is particularly fruitful.

At least two commentators I have read think that Mark hooks together these separate incidents for his editorial purposes.[141] If this is the case, to understand this passage means we must examine the larger interwoven context and see why these stories were grouped together.

I suggest that you should read the entire passage for yourself in Mark 11:12-26. You will see that the Lord's prayer promise came in the middle of some strange doings. He curses a fig tree and then casts out those who were buying and selling merchandise in the temple before uttering his promise on prayer.

The Cursing of the Fig Tree

The incident of the fig tree seems so unlike Jesus' other miracles. Our image of the Lord is more the gentle God/man who picks up little children and blesses them; this seems so different from cursing a poor tree.

We know what season of the year it was when this event took place, because Passover arrives near the same time each spring. The Jews are on a lunar calendar and their month Nisan begins on the new moon after March 6 each year. This places Passover between March 21 and April 18 (inclusive) of any given year. If Jesus was crucified in A.D. 30, as many believe, we can be even more specific about the date. He would have arrived in Jerusalem around the second or the third of April, so when he passes by this fig tree, it would still be about six or seven weeks before anyone could reasonably ex-

---

[141] Mark does this at least seven times. You can find the other six in 3:20-35; 4:1-20; 5:21-43; 14:1-14; 14:53-72; and 15:40—16:8. See James A. Brooks, *Mark*, Broadman, 1991, p. 73. See also J. R. Edwards, "Markan Sandwiches: The Significance of Interpolations in Markan Narratives," *Novum Testamentum*, 31 (1989), p. 193-216.

pect to find figs. Yet Jesus approaches this poor tree and then curses it, killing it.

Now why did he do that? To my mind it would have been more appropriate if Jesus had approached the tree and said: "Although figs are out of season, I'm hungry. Watch as the Father supplies all of our needs." And reaching up, Jesus pulled down huge clusters of figs—table-ready. Now that just sounds more "Jesus-like" to me. But instead, he curses the tree, and it dies.

I'm not alone in my discomfort with this incident. A cursing miracle bothers many. There is only one other place in the Gospels where Jesus performs an action that could loosely be considered a cursing miracle.[142] The story here is unique. We can only speculate that this tree is growing wild by the roadside, so that no owner would be financially impacted by the Lord's action.[143] Because the results are destructive and seem so counter to our image of Jesus, it's reasonable to believe that there must be some spiritual message that solves the enigma this incident creates.

Fig trees are occasionally used in the Scriptures for symbolic purposes. And in fact, the Lord gives an interesting parable in Luke about an unproductive fig tree. In the story, a man plants a tree in his vineyard and comes looking for fruit for three years. Finding none, he instructs the keeper of the vineyard to cut the tree down. But the vine-keeper suggests that the owner should wait another year. He will dig around the tree and fertilize it; if it still fails to bear fruit by the next season, then he will cut it down as ordered.[144]

Many Bible scholars believe the fig tree in this parable represents the nation of Israel. Because of Israel's rejection both of the prophets and now of Jesus, I believe that the

[142] Luke 8:26-39. Jesus casts a legion of demons out of a man and then gives permission for them to possess a large herd of pigs, which run off a cliff and drown in the sea.

[143] Note my capitalist bent.

[144] Luke 13:6-9

Lord is declaring here that Israel will be cut down, at least for a while. This would happen at the hands of the Romans in just forty years, and Jesus predicts these events on another occasion.[145]

When the Lord cursed this fig tree because it had no fruit, we are clearly told that it wasn't the season for figs. I believe Mark points this out so that we'll understand how strange this event is. It is precisely because this incident seems so unreasonable that we are drawn to dig deeper for the real intent. This tree is an object lesson, and the Lord's words are meant to be provocative, to elicit a reaction on the part of the disciples, and ultimately, us.

God sometimes creates "living parables," illustrating his message more vividly. He did this at various times in the Old Testament. For example, God told Jeremiah to take some underwear to Babylon and bury it beside the Euphrates River. Later, Jeremiah is instructed to dig up his BVDs and bring them back to Judah. The incident was an acted-out parable that the Lord used to illustrate to the Jews how they would be deported to Babylon for a time of captivity before being returned to the promised land.[146]

I believe that when Jesus cursed this fig tree, he was acting out his own parable found in Luke 13. He was declaring that God would soon chop Israel down, just like the vineyard owner in his parable. After Jesus curses this tree beside the road, it begins to wither. The next day, his disciples notice that it has shriveled and died. What a strong image the Lord created in the minds of his followers with this incident. During their lifetime, a number of the disciples would witness the fulfillment of this and other prophecies when the Romans sacked Jerusalem and carted most of the surviving Jews off into slavery.

---

[145] Luke 21:5-7, 20-24
[146] The story is found in Jeremiah 13.

The Cleansing of the Temple

The second passage in this section is the cleansing of the temple courtyard. Earlier in his ministry, Jesus had confronted the businessmen in the temple courts,[147] but now Mark records a second encounter.

Each year, every Jewish man had to give a half-shekel offering for the temple tax. The money for this tax could not be paid with Roman coins, because each carried the image of Caesar (which the Jews considered to be idolatrous, based upon the second commandment). These Roman coins needed to be traded for temple money, and the moneychangers performed this transaction for a fee.

Whenever the Scriptures talk about the temple, they are often referring to the courtyards surrounding the actual structure itself. These included the court of the Gentiles, the court of the women, the court of Israel, and the court of the priests. Composed of an area of about 22 acres, the largest portion was taken up by the court of the Gentiles.

On the east wall of the courtyard there was a gate that led to the Kidron Valley and the Mount of Olives; many found it convenient to use this route to reach the city of Jerusalem, and apparently it had become a shortcut.[148] Josephus indicates that in A.D. 65, the lambs sacrificed at Passover numbered 250,000. We can surmise that in A.D. 30, when Jesus arrived in the courtyard, the number of lambs being sacrificed would have been roughly the same. Because each lamb represented at least one family visiting the city of Jerusalem, it has been estimated that the number of people in Jerusalem for Passover would have been several million. While many raised their own lambs for the Passover sacrifice, some came from great distances and would have entered the temple seeking a good buy on a sacrificial lamb.

---

[147] John 2:13-22

[148] Today there is still a gate in the wall, but it has been blocked off so no one can take this shortcut through the courtyard surrounding the Dome of the Rock.

As Jesus entered the courtyard, the atmosphere must have resembled a bazaar with loud price haggling. When he lifted his whip to cleanse the area, the crowd must have been charged with emotion as the animals fled before him, tables were turned over, coins bounced off stones, and traders yelled in anger and frustration. In the midst of this turmoil, Jesus cried out at these men, declaring they had transformed his Father's house into a den of robbers.

Now, how were these men robbers? It has been suggested that many carried on unethical business dealings, gouging those who had come to buy in an obvious seller's market, but that view condemns all the merchants, both the innocent and the guilty. Jesus also stopped those who were using the grounds as a shortcut to carry their merchandise into the city.[149] But how are they robbers?

In the Old Testament, God spoke through Malachi to accuse Israel of robbing him. When they asked what they had done, God declared they had withheld their tithes and offerings that belonged in his temple. Malachi also indicated that Israel had profaned the temple with faulty sacrifices.

Let me suggest that the Lord's use of the word *robbers* is a general charge laid against all of Israel. It speaks of disobedience and a wrong attitude. I do not believe that the transgressors are merely these businessmen in the courtyard; rather, Jesus is crying out against the state of mind in Israel of which this is but one visible example. A shortcut was more important to them than reverence.

The Lord quotes Jeremiah about turning God's temple into a den of thieves.[150] If you look at the context of that prophecy, you will see that the prophet predicts the destruction of Israel and the temple. This incident illustrates the judgment that would soon be coming.

---

[149] Mark 11:16
[150] See all of Jeremiah 7 and especially verses 11; 21-34.

How Big Is This Promise?

The final part of this threefold passage in Mark is the Lord's promise on prayer. The next day, Jesus and his followers passed by the fig tree, and the disciples discover it has withered. Christ used their interest in the fig tree's demise to illustrate the power of prayer. Then he presents a second, almost whimsical, illustration about someone casting a mountain into the sea. The disciples are encouraged to expect similar results.

Does the Lord mean for us to take all of this literally? Certainly, we are not to plop hills into lakes and kill trees that will not bear fruit upon demand. I can imagine some latching onto these illustrations and uttering curses disguised as prayers against their opponents, while others might make requests like a child on Santa's knee. It seems highly unlikely that the Lord ever meant to encourage such capricious requests. If the Lord's illustrations were not meant to be taken literally, what is meant? Is the Lord's prayer promise what it appears to be?

Some not only take Christ's promise here as completely literal, they find in it a carte blanche promise for believers. I met a man once who told me that Jesus would give him anything he asked for. "Then why don't you pray for $1,000,000?" I challenged. He assured me that if he requested it, God would surely give it to him, but in his own time. I encouraged him to specifically ask God to provide the money *right now*. (I also suggested that it would be fair for him to share any windfall with me, since the request was my idea.) Perhaps realizing the ridiculousness of his claim, he did not ask, and therefore did not receive his million. I suppose that was his way of eliminating the potential for doubt which certainly would have arisen had he put his naive, albeit genuine, belief to the test.

Someone might suggest that we don't always ask for what is good, and so God withholds those things that might hurt us. This is certainly good theology, and it has often been suggested that "no" is still an answer. But in Mark 11, Jesus doesn't just promise "an answer," he boldly offers "all things for which you pray."

If you see the Lord's promise here as a guarantee, and follow it through to its logical conclusion, you might conclude that we should be able to put an end to problems like war and crime. Some Christians actually feel we have power over disease and even death through our prayers. Many believe that God is under an obligation to give them whatever they "claim" when they use the proper prayer/faith formula.

But this defies logic, experience, and biblical examples. Christians support many different causes; their sports teams and nations are often at odds with each other. At times when a believer prays for God to bless his cause, he pits himself against the prayers of other Christians. One man needs rain, and another needs the sun. Even if a believer invokes a guarantee from the Lord, it would be obviously impossible for God to grant every request, since many of our desires are in conflict with the prayers of other true believers. Magnify this problem by the countless millions of requests God hears each day, and you realize Jesus could not possibly have been speaking carte blanche in Mark 11. Such a promise is fundamentally impossible.

C. S. Lewis pointed out: "Every war, every famine or plague, almost every deathbed, is the monument to a petition that was not granted."[151] That is a disturbing but true insight. Every tragedy that takes place flies in the face of what Jesus has promised, because many are praying for God's intervention but so often it doesn't materialize. Logic declares that Jesus couldn't be answering all of our prayers as we pray them or he would be giving us unlimited power.

---

[151] C. S. Lewis, *Letters to Malcolm: Chiefly on Prayer,* A Harvest/HBJ Book, 1963, p. 58. (This quote was also used in Chapter 1.)

Is This a Living Parable?

So much is strange in this passage that it appears one of the Lord's primary motives was to evoke in the disciples some deeper truth. Jesus meant to arouse interest in the larger message under the surface, even if they did not understand it all until later. Although he uses strong language to stimulate thought, he is not trying to be clear. This is probably one of the hardest things for us to realize, that Jesus often *meant* to be unclear. His prayer promise has other purposes than just to give us whatever we want.

Why are these three stories interwoven together? I believe that this is done because the message of each is related. Notice the order in the development of the passage: The cursing of the fig tree, the cleansing of the temple as a profaned house of prayer, followed by the dead fig tree as an example of answered prayer. The subject matter can be summarized as fig tree/temple/prayer/fig tree/prayer. Both prayer and judgment are woven throughout the section.

With the cursing of the fig tree, the message was the destruction coming upon Israel following the charge of fruitlessness. The temple cleansing also emphasized judgment upon Israel because she had transformed God's house of prayer into a den of thieves. These two passages illustrate God's judgment upon Israel.

Perhaps one reason the Lord illustrates his prayer promise with the cursing of the fig tree and the casting of a mountain into the sea is because he knows the church will later be prone to the same failures as Israel. We ask for things selfishly. Even when we do pray for the well-being of others, our motives are so often tainted. But this prayer promise is tied to these two symbolic illustrations of judgment.

Do You Have Faith?

Jesus promises we will receive what we pray for in verses 22-24: "Have faith in God." When the petitioner "does not doubt in his heart, but believes that what he says is going to happen, it shall be granted." Therefore, the Lord instructs him to "believe that he has received" his requests, and it shall be granted.

These statements have been used to spawn a prayer theology of "claiming" that teaches that if a Christian does not doubt, he can "speak his wishes into existence." As we discussed in the last chapter, Jesus never meant to teach faith as a means by which we could force God to do our bidding. This was certainly not the Lord's intent here in Mark. Despite their claims, I would suggest that those who practice this "positive confession" theology are no more successful in receiving answers than other Christians.

Practical experience tells us that mere faith, without doubting, is not the "key" to this prayer promise. In fact, this view can be detrimental to faith. When Christians use this magical sort of faith, they come to believe their prayers must be answered, and the power lies in their faith. But when answers don't come, the blame for that failure is shifted back onto the one who prays. He fears that he doesn't possess enough faith, and this creates an unnecessary guilt trip, especially considering that Jesus made it plain elsewhere that even the smallest faith is enough.[152]

I would suggest that unanswered petitionary prayer is the norm, not the exception. Does this mean that true faith is the exception rather than the rule? Interestingly, no one seems to question if they have adequate faith for salvation. If our faith is inadequate for petitionary prayer, why do we suppose it is enough to deal with redemption and regeneration? Could it be because unanswered petitionary prayer is easily demonstrated, while salvation is a subjective experience?

---

[152] Luke 17:6

An Interesting Inclusion

Just as the Lord's action with the fig tree and the temple cleansing are designed to communicate God's dissatisfaction with his chosen people, so we Christians should see the similarities between the way we live our lives and the Jews of the Lord's day. They were living spiritually unfruitful and self-centered lives, but are we any better? Our prayers so often focus only upon what we demand, with little room for humility.

The Lord then includes a statement about forgiveness in verses 25-26. Jesus says: "And whenever you stand praying, forgive, if you have anything against anyone; so that your Father also who is in heaven may forgive you your transgressions. But if you do not forgive, neither will your Father who is in heaven forgive your transgressions."[153]

Isn't it interesting how often the Lord talks about the need to forgive? As much as we might desire to forgive, we are not capable of forgiving *all* those who have offended us. Why then does the Lord add this pronouncement at the time of his prayer promise?

The introduction of this statement would seem to indicate that the Lord's primary message is far greater than just the subject of prayer. He is provoking the disciples to comprehend their own spiritual poverty. If they cannot completely forgive—and who can—isn't it possible that they too might be a den of thieves? The Lord declares if they do forgive, their heavenly Father will forgive them. The tone of this condition is clearly old covenant law; it is not grace at all. On the surface, this prayer promise seems so bold, yet in reality it was aimed at stimulating self-examination as well as confidence in God's power to answer prayer.

---

[153] While verse 26 is not in many of the best and oldest manuscripts, the message spoken here on forgiveness is very similar to that given by the Lord in other passages. Its inclusion is not unreasonable, nor would its exclusion alter our discussion on prayer.

This section of Mark is actually an acted-out parable. When a Christian attempts to act on this promise, he will often end up frustrated because his problem is the same as Israel's: outwardly religious, but inwardly carnal. I believe that the Lord often does not answer petitionary requests because they are crass expressions of our own self-centeredness. They may be requests made in a religious manner, but they are not prayer.

This reminds me of the story, "The Monkey's Paw," which tells about a paw (similar to a rabbit's foot), that had the power to grant three wishes. In the story, a woman obtains the paw but doesn't really believe it will work, so she flippantly wishes for a large sum of money. Soon an insurance adjuster arrives at her door with a cash settlement resulting from an industrial accident in which her son has been terribly mangled and killed. This greatly distresses the woman, so she makes a second wish to have the money taken away and her son restored to life. He comes back, but now he is only a breathing, mangled body. The woman makes her third and final wish that her son would die so he would be out of pain. All three of her wishes are granted, but her life has been devastated. In a similar way, a Christian's life would be diminished if his shallow and self-serving prayers were invariably answered as he prayed them.

By focusing on faith, over which we have no control, we blind ourselves to the bitterness and treachery that lurks within our hearts. I have had extended conversations with others about this prayer passage but have found few who are interested in dwelling on their failure to forgive others.

In my own life, I was quick to jump to the portion of the Lord's promise about getting "whatever I asked," but slow in noticing the portion about "forgiving." The question we should all ask ourselves is: *If I fail to forgive others, how am I any different than a thief?*

Our Real Motives

Do you remember the parable about the Pharisee and the tax collector? Jesus spoke it to those who "trusted in themselves that they were righteous, and despised others." Jesus states that this Pharisee "prayed thus *with himself*" implying that his prayer didn't rise above the ceiling. The man thanked God that he was not like others who were extortioners, adulterers, and tax collectors. This religious man praised himself for fasting twice a week and tithing of all he possessed. (I wish he had been in my church; we would have made him a deacon.) He felt proud of his religious behavior because he was doing all of those things good Jews felt God wanted. In contrast, the tax collector in the Lord's parable was too embarrassed by his own sin even to look up to heaven. He beat his breast and asked God for mercy, because he knew that he was a transgressor.[154] How often when I pray am I praying with myself rather than to God?

Jesus concluded that the tax collector, rather than the Pharisee, went home justified, even though he had no religious works and much obvious sin in his life. The difference between these two men is conviction. While one man built up his "self-image," the other cried out for mercy. In the same way, one element of the Lord's teaching on prayer was designed to show our pride.

New Covenant Balance

The parallel new covenant portion that corresponds to what Jesus was teaching is found in James: "You do not have because you do not ask. You ask and do not receive, because you ask with wrong motives, so that you may spend it on your pleasures."[155] This portion of the New Testament provides the correct balance to counter what Jesus is saying in Mark 11. On one hand, it emphasizes the great power and

---

[154] This parable is found only in Luke 18:9-14.

[155] James 4:2b-3

resource of prayer, declaring that prayer can and does bring great answers. On the other hand, it reveals our problem is that we often ask with wrong motives, which God in his mercy does not grant. I am deeply, passionately burdened that my prayer isn't answered as I prayed it, yet I am only casually concerned that I can't forgive, or that my prayers are so self-serving.

Many of our prayers are the prayers of a thief. Often we throw up blackmail letters or ransom notes. "God, if you give me what I want, I'll *really* serve you." "Lord, get me out of this mess, and I'll never do this again." "Jesus, heal my daughter, or I'll never talk to you again." "Father, tell the pastor to do what I want, or I'll stop going to church." "Lord, make this congregation be nice to me, or I'll run away and pastor some other church." (I have too much investment in my education to leave the ministry altogether.) Although we may not pray these exact words, the intention of our hearts is to hold God hostage and to manipulate him. Is it any wonder that so many of my prayers go unanswered?

The Lord's Goals

I believe the Lord had three goals when he spoke the promise in Mark 11. First, and foremost, his purpose was to demonstrate the true nature of the old covenant. By the call to forgive, he was showing once again that his people were under condemnation and that they had a great need. Right up to the moment Jesus is nailed to the cross, he never deviates from this central focus of his message. The entire direction of this section in Mark 11, from the fig tree to the passage on prayer, is designed to bring conviction of sin.

Second, the Lord is stressing that God does hear and answers prayer. Prayer has unlimited power with God; even something as bizarre as cursing a fig tree for not having figs out of season doesn't exhaust the potential of prayer. But that does not mean it makes us God's master. I must always focus upon being a humble but expectant petitioner, realizing God always has the final say.

Third, it was the Lord's purpose to stimulate our understanding of just how self-centered most of our prayers are. Jesus wants us to evaluate if our prayers are genuine, or if we are a den of thieves. The Lord uses his promise to reveal our attempts to manipulate God.

One of the things that made the early church so dynamic was the power of its prayers. In the book of Acts, you see the disciples had a compelling sense of urgency in their prayers. Not only did they pray, but they received great answers. But they certainly did not receive all of their requests, as witnessed by the epistles. Prayer has always been dependent upon God's grace and his thoughtful intervention.

When you understand the Lord's purposes, you can be at peace, because you realize that your faith is really adequate after all. Your confidence in Jesus grows stronger because now you know that the alarming boldness of his promise serves to illuminate our carnality, and in no way diminishes the great power of the God we serve. He still hears and responds to prayer, giving supernatural answers according to his will. But what is even better, our God forgives sin and wisely answers our prayers in the way that is best, despite the fact that we are still unable to fully forgive.

Some Final Thoughts on Prayer

Before I leave the subject of prayer, I would remind you that Paul told us we really don't know how to pray as we should. The apostle then informs us of the wonderful truth that the Holy Spirit prays on our behalf.[156] Over the years I have had a great number of my prayers answered, but many have remained mercifully unanswered (in the form I asked). Knowing my sinful heart and my tendency to pray against my own best interests, I prefer the Spirit's wishes in my life

---

[156] Romans 8:26

rather than my own desires. As Jesus said in Gethsemane, "Not my will, but thine be done."

There are other portions given in the rest of the New Testament to teach us about prayer. These are generally more conditional in their promises and cause less misunderstanding than these words of the Lord, simply because his purpose was intentionally to be less clear and direct. The prayer passages in the epistles are much more to the point.

Two of the strongest promises are found in 1 John. In both places answered prayer is conditional. In 1 John 5:14-15, the apostle tells us we can receive what we ask for if we know we are praying according to God's will. Once we pray according to his will, we will be heard, and that guarantees that our prayers will be answered. That's a strong promise, but the key in the passage is understanding the will of God. We can only pray humbly, searching to comprehend his will.

In 1 John 3:19-22, the apostle gives another condition, which is that our "hearts do not condemn us." Perhaps this means that the Holy Spirit will convict us when our requests are out of line with the will of God (or give us peace if they are in line, whichever the case may be). The Lord will use our conscience to prod our hearts when something is wrong with our motives. Either way, with both of these New Testament passages, the results are conditional. Jesus' teaching in Mark 11 is clearly for purposes of introspection, to evoke conviction and humility, and is not designed to be open ended on prayer.

A Recap of Transitionalism

1) Old Covenant. Throughout Mark 11:12-26, Jesus is dealing in terms that people under the old covenant would understand. When the Lord cleanses the temple, he is confronting a legalistic religious society. His living parable of the cursed fig tree is aimed at providing a message about the approaching end to the old covenant period. The conditional nature of forgiveness is typical of the old covenant.

2) Conviction. This passage is ripe with conviction. From the clear statements in the temple to the implied judgment of the cursed fig tree, the message is bent toward arousing conviction or anger. The final injunction to forgive so that God can forgive you is another encouragement to frustration that will drive honest seekers to their knees. Even the church must ask, "How are we doing, compared to Israel? Do we make the church a den of thieves?"

3) Evocative. The Lord's approach in this section is highly evocative, and that is the reason his actions have been so misunderstood. He does not spell out his purpose in cursing the fig tree, and so the reader is mystified by this miracle. Only when we realize how out of character this event is do we probe deeper to find the Lord's hidden intent. Even the cleansing of the temple is not obvious, although Jesus does quote Jeremiah from a passage that predicts the destruction both of the temple and of the nation of Israel. Truth is present, but it is clouded by these emotionally charged events.

More difficult for us to grasp is the bold promise at the end of this section. Here the Lord mixes what appear to be clear statements about answered prayer with these two capricious and bizarre illustrations, trees dying and mountains being moved. He drops in this apparently unrelated phrase about forgiveness. When we analyze what the Lord is saying, it becomes apparent that Jesus does not offer us the power to play God as some have taught. The Lord's purpose is as much to demonstrate character as it is to instruct about prayer. Jesus remains true to form with his other teaching throughout the Gospels; he is consistently striving to convict his audience of the desperate condition of their hearts.

4) Interwoven Context. This is the key to understanding this difficult portion of Scripture. It is because the results of my analysis dovetail so perfectly with the teaching on prayer in the epistles that I am confident that this portion is an evocative presentation of James 4:2b-3. Transitionalism in general and interwoven context in particular become the key to unlocking the intent of this section.

Chapter 13

Is Divorce the Unforgivable Sin?
Jesus' Divorce Teachings

One morning, I taught an adult Sunday school class on the subject of divorce. As I shared my views, a lively discussion followed, but after class I was struck by the conflicting responses of two individuals. One man declared to me that I had been too easy on divorce; according to him, I had failed because I had not come down hard enough. But the other individual was a divorced lady who expressed profound discouragement because she felt she must be living in sin. Despite my encouragement, the words of Jesus had convinced her that she didn't belong in the church.

One of the most difficult problems I have faced as a pastor is the struggle to interpret the words of Jesus on divorce. His teaching on this subject is incredibly hard to reconcile with the gospel of grace. For years, I didn't find it difficult—I found it impossible. Since so many of my own church members have suffered a broken marriage, I agonized over how best to interpret the Lord's words. If most pastors *really* teach what they believe Jesus was saying on this subject, they would probably find it necessary to disfellowship those who are divorced and remarried within their churches. But such action seems so inconsistent with the gospel of grace and the Lord's sensitive ministry to those who were lost in sin. Because of this, many churches deal with the Lord's teaching on divorce simply by overlooking the actions of their people.

Do We Follow the Lord?

I know of a minister whose wife died; he was a leader at the district level in a church-planting organization. After he remarried another Christian woman, the leadership in the organization in which he ministered discovered that his new wife had a divorce in her background. Because of the position of the organization, and the view of many of their parish pastors on the subject, they felt he had compromised. Although the man himself had not been divorced, it seemed to them that Jesus might now condemn him for adultery.

I suppose if they took the Lord's words at face value, this Christian organization might have fired him as an adulterer and encouraged him to end his adulterous marriage. (But such strong measures would only have compounded the problem further, making him into a divorcee as well.) The organization "solved" the problem by promoting him to a position where he no longer had direct contact with other pastors. This approach is typical, because while Christians don't want to disobey the teaching of the Lord, they do not find his words compatible with the gospel of grace.

When I was in Bible school, one of the students wrote a paper on divorce. He took the classic position that while divorce may be acceptable in certain situations, remarriage is a sin.

"Suppose you become a pastor," asked the teacher, "and a man comes to you and says, 'I'm divorced and I would like to marry this Christian lady. What do you think, Pastor?' What would you tell this man?"

"Well, I'd advise him not to get married," replied the student.

"Would you tell him that to remarry would make him guilty of adultery?"

The student paused for a moment and said, "Yes. I think I would."

"Okay," continued the teacher, "but let's say that the

man ignores your advice and gets married anyway. What would you do when he returned to your church with his new wife?"

"Well . . . I suppose . . . " the student stammered, "I guess I wouldn't do anything."

That's been the practice in every church I've ever been involved with. Pastors speak against divorce and remarriage, saying it is wrong, but when people who are actually divorced and remarried come into their churches, they inevitably accept them into the church. But if divorce and remarriage causes ongoing adultery, and if the Lord was giving instructions for the church, then aren't we at odds with what Jesus taught?

Please take a moment to read the passages where Jesus talks on the subject of divorce and remarriage. Matthew 19:1-12 (and the companion passage found in Mark 10:1-12) give details of a confrontation the Lord had with the Pharisees that resulted in his most definitive teaching on the subject. Luke 16:18 contains a single troubling statement about remarriage. Then in Matthew 5:32, in the Sermon on the Mount, the Lord repeats this same message but softens it somewhat by adding *the exception clause* (which implies that Christ will not view divorce and remarriage as adultery if one's spouse was first involved in adultery).[157] The Lord's stand is so different from that of the culture in which we live; in our day, "no-fault" legal action makes divorce more socially acceptable, much easier to obtain, and incredibly common.

What's Your Position?

The words of the Lord remain controversial. I've read many books on divorce, and all of the authors claim that they are letting the Bible speak for itself—yet the authors arrive at such diverse conclusions. This is certainly odd, considering

---

[157] This exception clause is also found in Matthew 19:9.

these writers use the same Bible and most begin from the
same theological predisposition. It's amazing that the words
of Christ can create such a variety of opinion.

In addition to adultery, some of these teachers accept
desertion by the unbelieving mate as an acceptable basis for
divorce and remarriage based upon 1 Corinthians 7. Others
consider any divorce prior to conversion as being nonexist-
ent.[158] Many teachers hold that there are different grounds
for divorce than for remarriage, so that while a believer may
be allowed to divorce, he may not be permitted to remarry.
Some believe if an ex-spouse remarries, then the divorced
Christian is free to marry. Still others feel that a divorced
person cannot remarry until the death of the ex-partner.

Unfortunately, no matter what position a pastor embraces, he is inevitably forced into the role of Bible lawyer in
order to determine if a parishioner has had a "valid" divorce.
He might have to ask, for example: "Did your previous
spouse commit adultery? And did that adultery cause the
breakup of your marriage?" Or, "Was the mate who deserted
you an unbeliever?"

I've heard people define a former spouse as an unbeliever when I suspected that they were individuals of faith.
I've also seen believers place pressure upon nonbelieving
mates to file for divorce, knowing that the believer could
then claim "desertion" and be free to remarry. I've even heard
of believers who pray for God to put their ex-spouse to death
so that they will be free to remarry and get on with their
lives.

Divorce has become such a hot issue, especially for
those who have been impacted by it. A few years ago, an article in *Leadership*, a journal for Christian clergy, noted that
many pastors alter their views on divorce the moment it
strikes their daughters. In that article, one pastor states: "For
thirty years of ministry I had Matthew 19 down to a T, and

---

[158] The logic for this is that the cross eliminates all of a person's past sins.

then my daughter got divorced. I sat in my study for days and cried, remembering what I'd said to hundreds of people over the years. Those faces kept coming back to me, and I couldn't help thinking, *My God, what will I do if somebody says all those things to my daughter?*"[159]

I suspect you will find that your own personal experiences will have a great bearing upon your receptivity to the conclusions found in this chapter. I also expect that some will wonder if this chapter is the result of a divorce in my past. Let me set the record straight that I have never been divorced and neither has my wife Jean. The conclusions I have come to here are based purely upon the application of the principals of *transitionalism* to the passages found in the Gospels.

Those Hardhearted Pharisees

As I attempt to interpret what the Lord was saying about divorce I will concentrate on one major passage, the encounter with the Pharisees. This was followed immediately by his interaction with the disciples, found in Matthew 19:1-12. Again, let me suggest that you open your Bible to that Scripture so you can examine it as we go along. The question the Lord fielded that day was whether or not it was lawful for a man to divorce his wife for any reason at all.

When the Pharisees asked this question, they certainly did not expect Jesus to settle the debate. Matthew and Mark inform us that they were testing Jesus. The primary Old Testament passage permitting divorce was found in Deuteronomy 24.[160] I'm sure they had already come to their own conclusions about its meaning.

[159] "Request to Remarry: The Pastor's Catch-22," *Leadership*, a journal for Christian Clergy. Summer 1983, Vol. 4 no. 3, p. 118. The article claimed that a pastor's view isn't impacted by the divorce of his son, but it is significantly altered when his daughter is divorced. (By the way, my daughter hasn't been divorced.)

[160] Deuteronomy 24:1. See also verses 2-4. The religious leaders quoted it to Jesus in verse 7.

This Scripture established that a man could divorce his wife if he found an indecency in her. A great controversy developed over what would constitute this "indecency." A rabbi by the name of Shammai maintained that the only legitimate grounds for divorce was adultery. Rabbi Hillel taught that anything which displeased the husband—even poor cooking—would be adequate justification for divorcing her. This was the controversy the leaders presented to Jesus.

On every occasion when the Pharisees confronted the Lord with some sticky question, they were motivated by a hidden, self-serving agenda. These men spent so much energy condemning others that they could not see their own transgressions. From the Lord's answer to their question, my guess is that many of these men had embraced Hillel's view and had divorced their wives to marry younger women.

Jesus asked if they had ever read how God ordained that a man should leave his father and mother and cleave to his wife, becoming one flesh with her. They would have been well acquainted with these words from Genesis 2. The Lord concluded if God causes a married couple to become one flesh, what business did any man have trying to break it up? Although Jesus does not answer the question directly, he draws them to the proper conclusion.

But his answer did not satisfy them, so they asked why Moses had allowed divorce. Jesus responded by saying that Moses permitted divorce because of the hardness of their hearts, but that this was not what God had intended.

In these statements, Jesus did not offer much that was really new. Malachi had already revealed that God hated divorce. In fact, the prophet showed that God abhorred their practice of putting away older wives to marry younger women.[161] So Jesus is merely confirming what God has already stated. Hillel is wrong. They were not to divorce their wives for trivial self-centered reasons.

---

[161] Malachi 2:10-16

But then Jesus utters a final dramatic statement that goes beyond anything the Scriptures had said before: "And I say to you, whoever divorces his wife, except for immorality, and marries another woman, commits adultery."

This statement is meant to be provocative; I would suggest it was designed to stun them. The pronouncement is so difficult that I'm confident the Lord's purpose was not to develop a point of doctrine in contrast to the Mosaic Law. In one between-your-eyes moment, Jesus splashes conviction all over the Pharisees. It is interesting that even the disciples react by saying if the relationship with a man and his wife is like this, it would be better never to get married. Now why did the disciples react this way? It is easy to inflict our Christian point of view on the disciples and miss the fact that they, too, were hardhearted; they could not conceive of remaining in a marriage that didn't please them.

Skilled as they were in the law, the Pharisees certainly understood the ramifications of the Lord's statement, but even the disciples grasped the significance of this declaration. If what Jesus said was true, when a man married, he would be taking the chance that his relationship might end in divorce. If he were then to remarry, it would cause God to view him as an adulterer. And that, of course, would have doomed him to eternal destruction.

If a man couldn't dispose of his wife when she no longer pleased him, then maybe it was best just to live with a woman. Now the disciples could not say that aloud, so they left it at not being married. Jesus responded to their statement by saying, "Yes, there are even some who will not marry for the kingdom's sake." This must have been difficult for the disciples to accept at the time. Keep in mind that the disciples did not walk away from this discussion with a new respect for marriage, but they revealed that they only saw women as objects to meet the whims and pleasures of men.

Christ was zeroing in on the essential message these men needed to hear. Because he knew that old platitudes and formula solutions were not enough to reach them, Jesus threw out a statement intended to provoke. Because the Pharisees were masters at warping the law to justify their behavior, the Lord forced them to peer into God's mind. Again, he pulled back the curtain so they could see their self-serving behavior contrasted with God's holiness. Jesus clearly blamed their failure on hardheartedness.

"Let me show you how God views your behavior," Jesus is saying. "If you leave your wife and marry another woman without just cause, God sees you as an adulterer."

In each of the passages where the Lord talks about divorce, Jesus delivers his message with this same startling impact.[162] The Pharisees were so convinced of their religious superiority that the Lord needed to rip out the mat from beneath their sandals. His purpose is not to write a new doctrine; his purpose is to give insight into God's view of things in order to provoke a reaction that would lead them toward repentance.

New Rules for the Church?

Now what has become of this statement that was designed to convict these Jews of their sin? Unfortunately, it has been accepted as the new law on divorce for the church. Christians have taken these words of Jesus and interpreted them to be part of the new covenant, believing they supersede the old covenant given by Moses. But as we have shown, the Lord does not introduce the new covenant in his earthly teaching ministry. The gospel of grace comes only after the Lord's death. While there are some veiled references (which

---

[162] In the companion passage in Mark 10:12 Jesus adds that if a wife divorces her husband, she also commits adultery. Luke 16:18 declares that when a man divorces and remarries he causes his former spouse to commit adultery if she remarries. The cumulative effect of all three passages is quite strong.

are clear to us today in retrospect), the disciples did not understand much of the Lord's teaching until after the resurrection. Therefore, if we interpret the words of Jesus on divorce as a direct message for the church, we will completely misunderstand his purpose, and we will succeed only in creating another form of legalism.

If a man is involved in ongoing adultery because he has been divorced and remarried, how can he ever repent of that sin? Even if he were to divorce his new wife and remarry his first wife, he would only be compounding the problem. And if a man was to divorce his second wife and remarry the first, he would be violating the clear teaching of Moses.[163] Nothing he does can alter his status, short of divorcing again and remaining single for life. Such a harsh law would leave him no remedy for full repentance, and this is certainly in conflict with grace.

Christians believe that grace covers sin committed before conversion, but what about those transgressions which take place after salvation? If grace does not cover them, you can be assured that no believer will make it into heaven. So, if a man is divorced and remarried after he has become a Christian, and this act is determined to be something for which he cannot repent and therefore becomes ongoing adultery, how can he ever enter heaven?[164] This teaching makes divorce and remarriage into an unpardonable sin. Can you see that if the Lord's statements are seen as church law, we effectively neutralize the power of grace?

Jesus also indicated that if a man looks at a woman to lust after her, he has committed adultery already in his heart.[165] Now if this pronouncement was meant to be the rule for the church, and if a Christian man is guilty of adultery because he looks lustfully upon a woman, then the one

---

[163] Deuteronomy 24:4
[164] 1 Corinthians 6:9-10 tells us that adulterers will not inherit the kingdom of God.
[165] Matthew 5:28

who lusts is under an equal burden of guilt as the one who is divorced and remarried. If he does not (or cannot) stop lusting, he would be doomed to hell. The church has limited the activity of divorced people, based upon the concept of ongoing adultery; if this is true, should we not also include those who have lust in their hearts?

By taking these tough statements of Jesus, which were designed to arouse conviction, and making them into church law, we have produced incredible bondage. Ultimately, every believer will find himself under condemnation. The Lord's teaching, as it is recorded in the first three Gospels, was designed to reveal the full ramifications of the Old Testament law. It was never designed to replace it with an even more difficult burden.

Is Divorce and Remarriage Ongoing Adultery?

So often remarried Christians read the words of the Lord and cringe, wondering if they are in the state of ongoing adultery. I do not believe Jesus' intent was to say that a divorced person who remarries is continuing in adultery; the Lord never meant to pronounce that divorce and remarriage are unforgivable acts that cannot be undone. His purpose was not to condemn but to convict.

The tense of the language Jesus used agrees with this conclusion. Both in Matthew 19:9 and Mark 10:11-12, the Greek should be translated "he is made adulterous" rather than "he commits adultery," according to Greek scholar Richard Lenski, because of the tense used and the fact that Jesus is dealing primarily with the man's action as it affects himself.[166] It follows that Jesus could not have been teaching that a new legitimate marriage produces the ongoing sin of adultery but is rather a single act of adultery against the former spouse.

---

[166] R. C. H. Lenski, *St. Mark's Gospel*, Augsburg Publishing House, 1946, p. 421.

If the Lord was actually telling us that remarriage invokes a permanent state of adultery, then Jesus must not recognize divorce, for if remarriage constitutes adultery against the first spouse, then we can only conclude that the first marriage has not been truly severed. On the other hand, if God does recognize divorce, the remarriage must also be valid, even if it makes God unhappy. It cannot be considered adultery but is only a sin against the former spouse, on the same level as all others.

When the Lord declares that Moses permitted divorce and remarriage, he is indicating that God allowed divorce, for God gave the Law to Moses. Everywhere Moses is spoken of by Jesus, it is with the utmost respect. To attribute something to Moses was to attribute it to God. The Lord was certainly not saying that Moses made a mistake or went beyond his authority.

Jesus gives another interesting clue to understanding this issue by his attitude toward the Samaritan woman in John 4. When the Lord asked her to call her husband, she answered that she had no husband. He replied: "You know, you've answered correctly. You've actually had five husbands, and the man you're living with now is not your husband."[167] By making this statement, Jesus recognized all five of her marriages as being legitimate. He also acknowledged all five of her divorces. If they weren't valid, he most certainly would have told her that she was still tied to her first husband. The Lord even acknowledges a distinction between being married and living together.

Now if ever someone needed to hear from the Lord about divorce, it would have been this woman. Yet Jesus presents a completely different message to her. Why does he use such kid gloves with this multi-divorced woman? Why doesn't he lay on her the same message that he dropped on the Pharisees and the disciples? The difference seems to be

---

[167] This is my paraphrase of John 4:17b-18.

the condition of her heart. This woman would quickly come under conviction, while the self-righteous Pharisees were so hardened they needed an artillery barrage for softening. So the message Jesus gives to the Pharisees is not meant to eliminate divorce and remarriage, because like Moses, the Lord recognized both divorce and remarriage.

Marriage is a God-given union much older than the church. It is also regulated in our society by the God-ordained institution of the state. This means that a marriage outside of the church and one before Christian salvation is just as real as a marriage in the church after salvation. It also holds true that a divorce before a man's conversion is as valid as one afterward. If Jesus recognizes divorce and remarriage, then we must be careful not to condemn any union as one of ongoing adultery.

Can God Ever Approve of a Divorce?

I've met Christians who are weighed down under one or more divorces who wonder if God will ever approve of them. There are at least four times in the Bible where divorce is put in a positive light. Matthew reveals that when Joseph found Mary to be pregnant, he decided to divorce her. He could have humiliated her publicly and perhaps even had her stoned to death, but instead he chose to divorce her privately. The Scriptures tell us that his choice only to divorce her was indicative of him being a righteous man.[168]

Now I suppose someone might say, "That wouldn't have been a divorce, because they weren't *really* married. Their union hadn't even been consummated." Although that would be true in our society, in the society of Jesus' day, Joseph and Mary were married. Even though it had not been consummated, it was considered a "done deal" that could only be ended by a divorce. (If we wish to discuss biblical issues, we must see them from a biblical perspective; the Jews

---

[168] Matthew 1:19

of Jesus' day considered them to be married.) Of course, God sent an angel to inform Joseph that the child Mary carried had been conceived by the Holy Spirit, but the passage seems to indicate that God would have approved of Joseph's action to privately divorce his wife had the child been from another man.

Divorce is also accepted at face value in Exodus.[169] In this passage, the Jews were told that if a man who was a servant received his freedom, any wife and the children she had borne him during his servanthood would remain with his master. This is clearly a divorce, and the obvious implication in this passage is that property rights superseded marriage rites.

A third place where divorce is approved of is found in Ezra 10. The Jews had just come back from the Babylonian captivity, and many brought back foreign wives. This was a great travesty for Israel to embrace these idolatrous wives. So we find the people promising Ezra that they would put away their foreign wives, and the children born to them.

In Ezra 9 and 10, you see that the sin of marrying these foreign wives is dealt with through fasting, prayer, and repentance, which resulted in the divorces. What they did was considered a blessing, and nowhere in the Bible do we find this conclusion contradicted. The Scriptures present divorce as being appropriate in this case, because these men had displayed hard hearts by marrying against God's will. (Now please, don't quote me as saying that I'm recommending that Christians should be divorced if they have married the "wrong person" or an unbeliever. My purpose here is merely to show what has happened in the past.)

The fourth illustration involves Abraham, who divorced his wife Hagar. The Bible tells us that Sarah came to him after Ishmael mocked Isaac at the celebration following his weaning. Sarah told Abraham to get rid of Hagar and her

---

[169] Exodus 21:1-6

son. This grieved the patriarch, and he seems to have done what husbands often do when they don't like their wife's advice—he stonewalled (probably hoping Sarah would cool down and forget about it). But God intervened and told Abraham to listen to Sarah; he was to cast out both Hagar and Ishmael.[170]

Let me suggest to you that here is a divorce God not only condoned, but that he actually commanded. Now you may be thinking: *Hagar and Abraham weren't married; she was only his concubine.* But Hagar is called his "wife" in Genesis.[171] In the Scriptures, a concubine is a genuine wife, though of lower status.[172]

The prophet Malachi even made a reference to Abraham's divorce. When he berates the Jews for divorcing their wives to marry younger women, he says, "And what did that one do while he was seeking a godly offspring?"[173] Instead of divorcing his older first wife, like the Jews of Malachi's day, Abraham obeyed God's command and divorced his younger wife. Even Paul refers to Abraham's divorce as a Bible type.[174] Paul's reference clearly affirms the correctness of Abraham's divorce.

Now let's not overemphasize these four examples. Just because God has, in fact, approved of divorce in the past does not mean that he likes it. God will always hate divorce, because it always causes great suffering and pain for someone. But there are times when it is the best course in a hardhearted world. That doesn't make it good; just a necessary evil. It is God's desire that husbands and wives stay together for life, yet divorce will always be a reality for many of God's people

[170] Genesis 21:8-14
[171] Genesis 16:3
[172] The significance of a concubine's status seems most important with respect to rights of inheritance of her children.
[173] Malachi 2:15
[174] Galatians 4:21-25; 28-31

because of sin. Sometimes divorce happens despite all of our best efforts to stop it. The Scriptures make it plain that God knew and understood this reality for the nation of Israel, and he also understands it for the church.

Do You Hate Divorce?

Let's stop playing Bible lawyer to determine which divorces are good and which are bad. We should conclude that all divorces are bad. They all cause pain for someone. That was the point Jesus was driving home to the Pharisees and the disciples. Don't make excuses for yourselves. Divorce is outside of God's original plan, and even if there is justification, it should always be avoided, if at all possible.

In most congregations, the people who hate divorce the most are not the theologians, but those who have experienced one or more divorces themselves. Probably only one other group could contend for hating them more, and that would be the children of divorced people. Those of us who have not had divorces don't hate it nearly as much as those who've actually experienced it.

Think of some of the problems that come packaged with a divorce. There is the breakdown in communication within the family, the emotional pain, and the feelings of rejection. Guilt sometimes turns into hostility. Those coming through a divorce are often in emotional shambles. Then there are the problems of the bedroom: The thought that someone else is sleeping with a former partner can present a haunting specter, and sexual comparison can soil any new relationship.

Think about the pain inflicted upon the children; they may have tremendous animosity toward their parents and stepparents, who are often hated irrationally. (Children often hold the new mate responsible, even if they had nothing to do with the breakup.) Some children irrationally blame themselves for the divorce of their parents, and adult logic will often not change their perception. Then there are custody fights, alimony, unpaid child support, and squabbling over visitation. The problems of divorce never seem to end. I know people who have been divorced for thirty years, yet the event still powerfully impacts them. Even splitting the estate among one's heirs can be a traumatic issue.

Someone has said that there is no such thing as a final decree. No one hates divorce more than those who have experienced it. Divorce is a tragedy. It is *prima facie* evidence that people are sinners. It has great ramifications; and although by itself it is only a symptom of the sin, it usually comes out of many offenses, and certainly can lead to many more transgressions.

What Is God's Plan?

Jesus repeats God's plan for marriage in Matthew 19. God created Adam and Eve to be sexual beings. So when they are united together in the marriage bed, they become "one flesh." God also said in Genesis, "It is not good for the man to be alone."[175] So his plan clearly calls for a married man and woman to remain together for life. This is his plan concerning marriage, and it began before the Fall in the Garden. After sin entered the world, people became hardened, and divorce became an unavoidable reality. It is a reality of sin that the church must accept, just as God instructed Israel through Moses.

When the disciples reacted to the Lord's statement, Jesus replied: "Not all men can accept this statement, but only those to whom it has been given." He then proceeded to say that some have made themselves into eunuchs for the sake of the kingdom of heaven. Jesus said that he who was able to accept this should accept it. In other words, not everyone is able to remain unmarried. Even though it would be best for divorced people to remain single, most are unable to

---

[175] Genesis 2:18

do this. I believe Jesus understood that to demand a divorced person remain unmarried is a burden that is impossible for many to bear. Christians should avoid inflicting any more pain upon those who have already been through the trauma of divorce by laying another burden upon them. But unfortunately, this is often done by well-meaning believers.

To gain a little perspective, let's remember an event that happened in the early history of the church. In the book of Acts, the Christian leaders convened a conference in Jerusalem because some were insisting that Gentile converts needed to keep the Law in order to be saved. It was Peter who said: "Now therefore why do you put God to the test by placing upon the neck of the disciples a yoke which neither our fathers nor we have been able to bear?"[176] He pointed out the futility of keeping the Mosaic law. As a result of that conference, it was determined that Gentiles were full believers on the basis of grace alone.

Our modern church has done what the Christians in the Jerusalem conference refused to do. While the Old Testament permitted both divorce and remarriage, the church claims it won't allow either. This is a direct contradiction to what Peter told the infant church. Can you imagine if the Jerusalem council had decided to adopt an even stricter set of laws than what was delivered by the hand of Moses? That would have been ludicrous. Yet that is what we've done in this area by misapplying what Jesus said about divorce, placing it as a burden upon the church.

The concept of making a new law for the church, which is so much more difficult than the Old Testament Mosaic Law, is pure foolishness. Because of their needs, people will get remarried—whether the church gives permission or not. Ireland experienced the reality of a state without divorce and remarriage for many years. In 1996, the voters finally allowed divorce, realizing that prohibiting divorce does not

---

[176] Acts 15:10

eliminate the problems brought on by the hard heart of men—it only pushes sin underground. The first divorce Ireland granted was given by a court several months before the law was to go into effect so that a man could marry the mother of his child before he died of cancer. Without that divorce, the child would have remained illegitimate.

God created us as sexual beings, so let's get past this harmful teaching that Christians should not get remarried after a divorce. The goal of the church is to produce a redeemed people who are willing to live their lives as close as they can to God's ideal, with the full knowledge that they will often fall short of God's standard.

What about 1 Corinthians 7?

Now I'm sure some are wondering about the teaching of 1 Corinthians 7:10-11, which reads: "But to the married I give instructions, not I, but the Lord, that the wife should not leave her husband (but if she does leave, let her remain unmarried, or else be reconciled to her husband), and that the husband should not send his wife away."

When Paul refers to the Lord giving this teaching, he is talking about Christ's teaching in passages like Matthew 19 and Mark 10, where he indicates that it is God's design that divorce should not be a part of our lives. You might wonder then if Paul is forbidding divorce and remarriage. When you carefully examine the overall message of 1 Corinthians 7, you will see that one of Paul's recurring themes is to encourage believers to remain single. Twelve times in this chapter he recommends that Christians stay unmarried.[177] In verse 11, he says that a Christian woman should remain unmarried if she has been divorced from her husband; but let me suggest that this is another of those optional recommendations the apostle gives to remain single.

---

[177] See verses 1, 7-8, 11, 26-28, 32-34, 38, and 40.

Earlier in the chapter he gives an important adjunct message: "because of immoralities, let each man have his own wife, and let each woman have her own husband."[178] He calls this a concession to the sexual desires that most men and women possess (and which apparently he did not, having been given the gift of celibacy).[179] Paul also says the unmarried should be allowed to marry if they do not have self-control.[180]

Later in the chapter he says, "Are you released from a wife? Do not seek a wife. But if you should marry, you have not sinned; and if a virgin should marry, she has not sinned."[181] So while Paul was encouraging all Christians to remain single so that they could dedicate themselves to the Lord, he made it quite plain that if they got married, they would not be sinning. He tells this to the church for its benefit, "not to put a restraint upon you."[182] So I believe that Paul is saying throughout the chapter that it is best to remain single, but if we do marry, *we have not sinned*. Paul is certainly not making a law for the church that prohibits remarriage (as the rest of the chapter clearly shows).

In verse 15, believers who have been deserted by an unbelieving mate are told that they are "not under bondage." I have heard it suggested that this means the believer is no longer bound to the marriage but is still not free to remarry. This is a weak argument, because when someone has been deserted, they certainly don't need anyone to tell them they are free of their mate. I feel comfortable that this phrase "not under bondage" can only mean the believer is free to marry someone else.

---

[178] Verse 2
[179] Verses 6-7
[180] Verse 9
[181] Verses 27-28
[182] Verse 35

How Can We Apply This?

It is a serious mistake for the church not to permit remarriage. The vast majority of people are sexually driven, and to prohibit remarriage will inevitably push many believers into immorality and then often right out of the church. The proper expression of our sexuality is within the bonds of marriage, and when someone is not allowed to remarry, it will merely drive their sexual expression underground. Even if divorce and remarriage are prohibited, people will still find a way to fulfill their sexual desires.

Divorce reflects the sinfulness of mankind. But, as Christians, we believe that when we repent of sin, it is covered; it goes under the blood of Jesus, just like all other sin. And we must let it remain there so we do not become like Satan, who lives to accuse the brethren and haunt them with their past deeds.[183]

Now please don't misunderstand what I'm saying. I am not encouraging easy divorces so people can remarry. That's exactly what Jesus was condemning. We understand that divorce should never be entered into for trivial reasons, and that it is a great evil. A believer always needs to seek the Lord's counsel about how to build up a relationship and keep it alive. Several passages of Scripture were even written to encourage believers to work on winning over unbelieving husbands or wives to the Lord.[184] I want to suggest to you that all of us have to live out our lives in a less than ideal way. We do not, and will not, achieve all of the things God wants for us in this life. But don't make excuses for yourself and rush into a quick divorce simply because God will allow it. Divorces are still alien to God's plan, even if he does allow them.

If you are single, let me suggest that you live your life in the way that will enable you to best match up with God's standard of one woman and one man, married for life. Be

---

[183] Revelation 12:9-11
[184] 1 Corinthians 7:10-16 and 1 Peter 3:1-7

wise in your choice of a spouse. Refuse to let your hormones run your life or make your decision for a mate. For the divorced person, the best thing you can do is to live as close as possible to the standards God has established. Live your life in purity and holiness, waiting for God to provide for you the right person to marry. If you are divorced, I would like to make several suggestions for your life.

First, repent of past sin that led to divorce. Ask for God's forgiveness and cleansing.[185] With the Lord's help, forgive those who have defrauded you in past relationships, including any past partners. This may need to be done internally, without direct contact, because of past problems. (Sometimes when you forgive someone, they conceive of it as a personal attack, and they feel that you think they were the only one at fault.) But it is important for you to work at forgiveness, so that you will not be consumed by bitterness.

Second, when you become involved in the courtship process, you should consider only believers. Christians are called to marry believers, so they should avoid developing romantic relationships with non-Christians that may inevitably lead to marriage.[186]

Third, keep yourself sexually pure before your wedding. I know that this may be difficult because of your past sexual experience, but it is not unreasonable. If you want your next marriage to be a success, you are better off entering into it God's way. Playing around sexually before you marry someone will only create guilt and negative emotions that may surface later in your marriage. If you are now involved sexually, break it off so that you can have a time of purity together before you wed.

Fourth, make a commitment to the new marriage as if it were your first. Second marriages are just as real as first marriages. God recognizes both your past divorce and your

---

[185] 1 John 1:9
[186] 2 Corinthians 6:14-18 and 1 Corinthians 7:39

new marriage. So enter into this relationship as a lifetime commitment—until the two of you are parted by death.

Fifth, fulfill all of the obligations of any past marriages. By that, I mean pay your child support, observe visitation with your kids, and perform any other commitments that you might have. You should make certain that your new spouse understands your need to fulfill past obligations.

I have heard that in this country over 50 percent of all marriages will end in divorce and 40 percent of those that remain married will be unhappy. So what can make your marriage happy and fulfilling? Just because you are a Christian is certainly no guarantee of happiness. When you follow through on fulfilling God's plan in your marriage (as it is presented in the Scriptures), the chances become much greater that your marriage will thrive.

Learn to love as God instructs us. Love is not a feeling; it is a way of living life. Jesus did not feel like going to the cross, but love drove him to it. You should be more concerned about what's good for your mate than what you want for yourself. Live your life from today onward as closely to God's ideal as possible. Don't dwell on the failures of the past, but look with hope on your God and Savior, the Lord Jesus Christ, who loves you and who has forgiven you.

A Recap of Transitionalism

1) Old Covenant. In Matthew 19:1-12, Jesus is asked a question about the law on divorce that was prompted by Deuteronomy 24:1. The Lord's answer is clearly directed towards the problems that the Jews encountered in their attempts to keep this old covenant law. No matter how much Christians might want to interpret the Lord's teaching as being for the church, he was directing his message for those who were living under the Mosaic law.

2) Conviction. It is clear from the tone of the Lord's answer to the Pharisees that his intention was to bring these men to conviction. But the reaction of the disciples to his statement that divorce and remarriage cause adultery indicated that the disciples were also convicted by what the Lord had to say.

3) Evocative. When the Lord speaks about divorce and remarriage, he utters this harsh statement, which is plainly designed to provoke a response. His sentence about remarriage causing adultery caused a strong reaction. The disciples considered this too difficult, claiming that it meant a man was better off never getting married. Even the disciples couldn't imagine remaining in a marriage that didn't please them. Jesus meant to arouse these men so that they could see their hard hearts more clearly. He provoked their emotions to bring their sinful attitudes to the surface.

4) Interwoven Context. The context that Matthew gives us around this passage shows that his primary purpose is to reveal the rising conflict between Jesus and the Jewish leadership. This is just another incident within this large section of Matthew where the tension between Jesus and the religious leaders grows. The passage is also meant to demonstrate how little the disciples understand. This teaching must have been a real challenge to his followers, because they, too, saw women as merely playthings for the whims of men. All of the interaction that we find in the surrounding context tends to show that the disciples fail to understand or measure up to the Lord's standards.

Chapter 14

Does *Transitionalism* Work?

As I conclude this book and my introduction of transitionalism, I believe that it is important to think about the impact this method of interpretation might have upon Christians who embrace it. Because this approach reinterprets so much of what the Lord was saying and puts it into a different perspective, it will inevitably cause many Christians to rethink some of their beliefs. This rethinking is likely to have a dramatic impact upon their spiritual lives.

Will Transitionalism Help You?

I'm sure the ultimate question is, will this approach help you live the Christian life, or will it give you an excuse to sin? It is my belief that you will find this approach solves conflicts you might have had with the Scriptures, and it will make living for the Lord a more joyous experience, compared to the traditional approaches that so many have promoted.

Transitionalism's contention is that the Lord did not introduce the good news of salvation through the cross, nor did he ever intend to provide a set of regulations for the church. Instead, he came to reveal fully the ramifications of the law, and by doing that, crush the hope of the self-righteous so that their hearts would be prepared to receive salvation through grace.

This means that the majority of the Lord's words were *not* aimed directly at the church. Because he was not instructing Christians, we should only make applications of his teaching by extension. As believers, we must therefore establish our doctrine from the epistles, making certain that any teaching from the Gospels is supported and initiated in the New Testament letters. If all of this is true, then the doctrine of grace will be allowed to fully take center stage (as it was always meant to). No longer will we need to reconcile the Lord's words of conviction with the post-resurrection ministry of the apostles. We can now focus upon walking in grace, not on reconciling a mixture of grace plus the Lord's presentation of the old covenant law. I believe this outlook will bring incredible freedom and spiritual healing to many believers.

Some pastors will inevitably fear that this approach might lead Christians to become flippant towards evil and fall into sin. For example, if we take away the Lord's tough restraints, won't believers rush into the sin of divorce? Won't Christians feel that they can sin with impunity and remain within the church? Might we even refuse to forgive others, harboring bitterness in our hearts simply because our salvation is no longer dependent upon forgiving others?

A pastor may resist transitionalism when he realizes that it will free believers from striving to measure up to the high standard presented in the Gospels. He may wonder: *Will Christians stop attending church and tithing? Will they continue to resist sin if they are under pure grace?* This fear will strike hardest with those who least understand the nature of grace as it is taught in the New Testament.

All of these fears neglect the reality that transitionalism offers no more license than grace has ever offered. All this interpretation does is free Christians to allow grace to be grace as it is clearly taught within the epistles. After all, what motivates a Christian to live righteously? Under the old covenant, a sinner received judgment for his disobedience; but under the new covenant, we receive mercy and forgiveness as well as eternal life, simply because we believe. The old motivation for being good was fear, while the new motivation for good behavior is gratitude. A Christian living under grace desires to be righteous, because he wants to please the Lord who has bought him and given him a place of honor in God's family.

The teaching of grace is really counter intuitive. Something is "counter intuitive" when the results seem to be the opposite of what our logic would predict. A few years ago, I knew a mother whose son was in the sixth grade. His school work was so poor that she began to push him, setting aside a time for him to do his homework each evening. But every night was a battle, and still his grades did not improve. Her son had so many problems at school she was on a first-name basis with the principal. When he advised the woman to let the boy worry about his own homework and face the consequences, the woman was aghast at the principal's suggestion. But she had already tried everything else, so she decided to back off and allow her son to become responsible for his own actions. To her surprise, he picked up the responsibility and raised his grades. That was counter intuitive.

In the same way, when a believer comes to recognize the awesome love God showers on him, despite his performance, he will experience a new freedom that produces radical changes in his life. The apostle Paul tells us that God loved us so much, even when we were his enemy, that he sent his son to die for our sins. Paul then makes an amazing statement: "For if while we were enemies, we were reconciled to God through the death of His Son, much more, having been reconciled, we shall be saved by His life."[187] When a believer grasps the extent of God's love, it will do more to change his life than all the rules or threats of judgment could ever bring. This is counter intuitive.

This same principle can be seen in the behavior of children in homes where there is an insecure environment.

---

[187] Romans 5:10

Intuition might suggest that insecurity would make children behave better, because they must strive to attain status and then keep from losing it. Yet children whose environments are insecure generally have more behavior problems than those who live within homes offering a strong sense of security. Employers often try to use insecurity to motivate their employees to better performance. While this might appear effective in the short run, such success will be short lived. Secure, loving freedom will generally produce better behavior than rules and judgment.[188]

What Makes Us "Good"?

The Christian life is not just morality. Although Christians do practice a morality, this is not what ultimately defines Christianity. Becoming a Christian is a supernatural event that takes place when a person receives Christ through faith. This could be called the "born again" or conversion experience, which is a common belief in virtually all denominational expressions of the Christian faith. This "born again" phrase is used by the apostles John, Peter, and Paul.[189] When a Christian receives the new birth, he also receives the Holy Spirit, who places the nature of the holy God within his heart.

In contrast, all of us receive the spirit of Adam—the sin nature—when we're born into the world. So when we attempt to control believers by using rules and prohibitions, we are not taking into consideration the reality of the new nature. We are attempting to control the sin nature, rather than

---

[188] I say *generally*, because there are always people who will not respond to grace. The world is full of men like Cain, Balaam, Ananias (and his wife Sapphira) and Judas. Because some people will abuse the grace of God does not eliminate the reality that grace is the best way to produce godly results in men.

[189] Some people recoil from the phrase *born again*. In using it, I do not want to imply that only those groups that use the phrase are truly Christian, but that all Christians must have had a conversion experience. See John 3:7; Titus 3:5 (the term here is regeneration); and 1 Peter 1:23.

directing the spiritual man. I would suggest that this is a mistake, because it is the spiritual life that makes a man a Christian, and it is this new nature that becomes the driving factor in all the behavioral changes in his life.

It is illegal for parents to mistreat and abuse their children, but while such laws are enforced, there is not one parent in a hundred who considers them when he instructs his children. Most parents would never dream of doing anything to abuse their offspring. They may not always do what is best, acting out of anger or ignorance, but almost universally, their actions are motivated by love. These laws don't change their behavior one bit; they only punish gross parental misbehavior.

In the same way, the apostle Paul makes it clear that the old covenant law is not made for the righteous man, but for the lawbreaker.[190] It seeks to regulate those who are living within the motivations of that lower sinful nature. So why do we think that laying down rules upon a believer will make him into a better person? Such an approach only caters to his old nature, and it is doomed to fail.

When you came to faith in Christ, you received the Holy Spirit and gained this new nature. You may not always act in accord with that nature, and at times you may fall considerably short, but the reality of all that you are as a Christian is summed up in that new nature. Paul uses an analogy of marriage and widowhood; he says that a wife is bound to her husband as long as he lives, but when he dies, she is free of him. In the same way, because you have died to self in the new birth, you are no longer under that law that was designed for the sinful nature.[191]

This truth is clearly taught in the epistles. Paul tells us in Galatians that the law no longer has a place in the life of

---

[190] 1 Timothy 1:9-10
[191] Romans 7:2-6. This analogy is not perfect, because the wrong person has to die to make it work.

the believer;[192] you now serve God in the newness of the Spirit. So to attempt to control believers with a list of legal expectations designed to keep them attending church, giving of their money, or serving in ministry will in the end turn out to be counterproductive for their spiritual lives.

How New is *Transitionalism?*

I have been asked if anyone has previously taught the ideas of transitionalism (the implication being that if it hasn't been taught in the past, it can't be true). That may not be a valid issue, considering that such a criteria would have eliminated some of the strides taken by the Christian church over the years. Even the doctrine of grace was questioned during the apostle Paul's lifetime, and the Protestant Reformation certainly appeared to be a new wind of doctrine to the majority of church theologians during Luther's day. The principles of transitionalism do not contain any new doctrine that many others have not stated at some point in the past. This teaching is only a *system of interpretation* that allows the Scriptures to be seen in harmony, making greater sense. We have also discovered that many believers have found this approach to be quite easy to embrace, because it reaffirms what they have traditionally believed.

I must admit that I am not aware of this system of interpretation in any literature I have read, although it may exist, but I have seen fits and starts for each of the four principles individually. My contribution is only in the systemization of the principles. Transitionalism is the result of my search to harmonize the ministries of Jesus and Paul within the Scriptures. The apparent conflict between the synoptic Gospels and the letters of Paul which this book addresses has been broadly recognized in theological circles. From Catholic to evangelical Protestant, it has been noted and discussed.

---

[192] Galatians 4:21-31

Hans Kung, in his book *Justification,* said: "Luther and the younger Melanchthon exaggerated when they saw in Paul nothing other than a teacher of justification. And none of the Gospels, nor any of the other New Testament writings are easy to harmonize with Pauline teaching on justification; the problem is not only with the Letter of James."[193]

Douglas Moo, commenting on Romans 3:21, tells us: "'But now' marks the shift in Paul's focus from the old era of sin's domination to the new era of salvation. This contrast between two eras in salvation history is one of Paul's most basic theological conceptions, providing the framework for many of his key ideas." Moo then states in his footnote, "Paul here views the transition from the standpoint of history, with the cross as the point of transition between old era and new. He can also apply this basic salvation-historical concept at the level of the individual, with conversion as the point of transition."[194]

James Montgomery Boice doesn't make a radical distinction between the teaching and passion ministry of Jesus as I have done, but he says: "When the tax collector prayed, 'God, have mercy on me, a sinner,' he was thinking of the animal sacrifices because, although Jesus was then present, He had not yet died."[195]

But probably the man who came closest to verbalizing the nature of this problem as I see it was C. S. Lewis. He stated:

"A most astonishing misconception has long dominated the modern mind on the subject of St. Paul. It is to this effect: that Jesus preached a kindly and simple religion found in the Gospels, and that St. Paul afterwards corrupted it into a cruel and complicated religion (found in the Epistles). This is real-

[193] Hans Kung, *Justification,* Thomas Nelson & Sons, 1964, p. 11.
[194] Douglas Moo, *The Epistle to the Romans,* The New International Commentary on the New Testament, Wm. B. Eerdmans, 1996, p. 221.
[195] James Montgomery Boice, *The Parables of Jesus,* Moody Press, 1989, p. 91.

ly quite untenable. All the most terrifying texts come from the mouth of Our Lord; all the texts on which we can base such warrant as we have for hoping that all men will be saved come from St. Paul.

"If it could be proved that St. Paul altered the teaching of his Master in any way, he altered it in exactly the opposite way to that which is popularly supposed. But there is no real evidence for a pre-Pauline doctrine different from St. Paul's. The Epistles are, for the most part, the earliest Christian documents we possess. The Gospels come later. They are not 'the gospel,' the statement of the Christian belief. They were written for those who had already been converted, who had already accepted 'the gospel.'"[196]

Lewis clearly recognized the inconsistencies between Paul and the harshness of the Lord's words found in the Gospels, although he did not seem to have an adequate answer for it. He also understood that frightening words were contained in Matthew, Mark, and Luke. This, of course, is because the gospel message could not be fully proclaimed until after the crucifixion and resurrection had taken place.

Why Do We Have the Synoptics?

You might be wondering if Jesus' teachings are not the rule for the church, what are they for? Why do we have so much material in these books if it wasn't written directly for the church? First, a parallel can be drawn between how the Lord's earthly ministry prepared us for the new covenant to the way Genesis and the first half of Exodus set the historical stage for the coming of the old covenant. In each case, the passages were necessary to establish the historical context of the respective covenants. Because the Bible is a historical document, it requires a setting in real time and place.

Without the Gospels, Christ's life and death might

[196] C. S. Lewis; *God in the Dock*, William B. Eerdmans, 1970, p. 232.

have taken on the character of a myth. Without the synoptic Gospels, we would never know about the supernatural birth of the Lord and the fact that he is God in human flesh. We would not see the incredible variety of his miracles that clearly demonstrate his divine mission. Without this setting, we would also not understand the reaction Jesus received from his enemies, and the events which led to his crucifixion.

One-third of the four Gospels take place in the eight-day period from Palm Sunday to Easter Sunday. Twenty-nine of the 89 chapters in the four Gospels are devoted to the last week of Jesus' life. The fact that so much space is dedicated to the passion ministry of Jesus indicates its great significance. Certainly because the new covenant is sealed by the Lord's death and resurrection, God wanted us to have an adequate record of this period so that we would know for certain that the Lord's death and resurrection are true historical events.

The Gospels also open up for us how the Lord thinks. Most obvious is his reinterpretation of the old covenant law; here we see the incredible depth of God's holiness and our absolute inability to ever measure up to this standard, which requires the cross and God's grace to bring us to salvation.

When we examine the way in which Jesus approached his people, our love for him can only grow. As I have studied the Lord's parables and many of his messages through this transitional perspective, I am amazed at the new appreciation I have developed for the Lord and his genius. I think you'll find as you view the Synoptics on your own, using this transitional lens, that you'll discover many insights and details that you had never noticed before.

Through the Gospels, we come to know our Savior. One element that has particularly struck me is how we can glimpse Jesus' person by his interaction with individuals he encounters. I think particularly of the times they came to trap Jesus. The Lord answered the unanswerable questions;

he overwhelmed the intelligentsia of his day, as well as readers of all time, with his profound answers. The Lord's dinner at the home of Simon the Pharisee stands out in my mind. Simon was aghast when a loose woman washed the Lord's feet; so Jesus crushed Simon's self-righteousness with a parable. And who hasn't marveled at the way Jesus dealt with the question of paying tribute to Caesar?

To try to understand the rest of the New Testament without the Gospels would be a little like trying to understand the U.S. Constitution without a knowledge of the colonial period, the Revolutionary War, and the Articles of Confederation. Certainly much can be known from the Constitution alone, but the reasons behind our bicameral system and the Bill of Rights cannot be fully grasped without their historical setting. But we would never attempt to govern ourselves today using the Articles of Confederation; as important as that document is to shed valuable light upon the Constitution, we leave it where it belongs, in the realm of background information.

In a similar way, the teaching ministry of Jesus helps us understand the new covenant, but it is not itself the new covenant. The Gospels prepare us to see our own need for the Savior, and indeed, the words of Jesus are incredibly effective in producing conviction. But if we fail to understand the Lord's purpose in uttering them, they can lead us into bondage. Because the words of Jesus found in Matthew, Mark, and Luke were not spoken to the church and fall under the old covenant period, we know that the Lord was speaking primarily to the Jews of his day. While much of what the Lord says can certainly be applied to the church, the church must be careful to not take the Lord's teachings in the Synoptics and use them as a rule for Christian conduct. To do that is to put believers under a taskmaster both severe and harsh, which may lead to spiritual grief, as many Christians have discovered.

When they are properly presented, the Gospels can also be an incredibly powerful means of preparing an unbeliever for the good news of salvation by grace. The Lord's parables and messages are like cannons that take aim at a man's heart, bringing him to conviction. A wise preacher will use the Gospels in the same way the Lord did, to reveal the utter sinfulness and inability of men to achieve the righteousness of God apart from the Lord's marvelous forgiveness. No one is ready for grace until he has first been broken under the Lord's holy standard. This makes these documents incredibly valuable for winning the lost to Jesus.

What about John's Gospel?

As we indicated earlier in this book, John's Gospel is different from the Synoptics. He wrote it from the perspective of grace, looking back at the Lord's ministry. John composed his Gospel after the others had been written. Eusebius, a church historian in the fourth century, revealed that when John wrote, he had the other three Gospels available to him; so unless his purposes required it, he apparently chose other events and messages from the Lord's ministry to accomplish his purpose, editorially commenting upon them to teach that salvation was by grace through faith.

When you read John Chapter 3, for example, you see a clear presentation of how to be born again. But I would suggest that the section beginning at verse 16 and continuing to verse 21 has been added by John as editorial comment. He does this because his purpose is to clarify the gospel of grace within the context of the Lord's life. He uses this approach quite often, because his purpose is different than that of the synoptic writers. John says in 1:17: "For the Law was given through Moses," but "grace and truth were realized through Jesus Christ." And later he proclaims his purpose in 20:31, where he writes, "that you may believe that Jesus is the Christ, the Son of God; and that believing you may have life in His name." So his Gospel is a presentation of the good news of our salvation, presented through the editorial comments he has chosen to clarify the message.

It is important to understand this difference between John's Gospel and the Synoptics, so that you will know how to interpret them. John editorializes and explains the Lord's ministry from the perspective of grace. The book deals with the same historical period as in the other three Gospels, but this common time frame does not mean a common message. His purpose is to emphasize how the Lord's ministry relates to our salvation. The synoptics emphasize how the Lord's ministry relates to Law.

The apostle John focuses upon subject matter within *his* Gospel that will emphasize the gospel of grace. He uses many one-on-one encounters that the Lord had because they suit his purpose. Nicodemus' nighttime visit in John 3, the woman at the well in John 4, and the healing of a blind man in John 9 all present a message that is consistent with grace. But the reader must keep in mind that John is selecting his material and editorializing with the view to present the gospel of grace While the Lord's purpose during his lifetime was much more limited. Because Jesus lived in a transitional period, he chose not to present the gospel of grace. His major purpose was still to bring sinners under conviction, *not* to present the message of salvation.

I should mention that the instruction in the Upper Room Discourse as found in John Chapters 13 through 17 seems to have a different focus from Jesus' other messages. On the night before his crucifixion, the Lord begins to clearly address the needs of his coming church. Towards the end of this discourse, the disciples comment that Jesus was speaking 'plainly,' without using figures of speech.[197] (I should point out that they still didn't understand. The women went to the tomb on Easter to finish the burial, not to see the empty

---

[197] John 16:29-30

tomb. And when the women told the disciples he had risen, they didn't believe the women.) It certainly seems that Jesus had begun to clarify his teachings and to give his followers the new commandments that are aimed directly to the church, to believe on the Son and to love the brethren. But it remained for after the resurrection for the disciples to truly begin to understand.

So the Gospel of John presents a different interpretive situation for believers. Because the teachings of Jesus are filtered through John's editorial comments, a teacher must endeavor to determine what is editorial in nature and what was actually spoken by the Lord himself. In contrast, whenever a Christian preaches from any of the synoptic Gospels, it becomes his task to *supply* those editorial comments (as John did) that will interpret what the Lord had to say from the new covenant perspective of grace. Knowing the Lord's purpose and the limits of his ministry to the Jews, it becomes the job of the pastor/teacher to interpret in the light of new covenant theology as taught in the epistles. (We do the same thing when we preach from the old covenant teachings like those in the book of Deuteronomy.)

What Makes a Teacher "Great"?

A case could be made that Jesus was an ineffective teacher. Jesus was not ashamed to declare that he used parables to confuse people.[198] If my children had a school teacher who made a statement that one of his goals was to confuse his students, I would not consider him great. Any teacher who has the power to heal the sick and raise the dead, but who can only generate a few hundred disciples would certainly seem to be a limited success. This lack of results (when compared to our twentieth century point of view) seems somewhat mysterious. Naturally, we assume that he should have been the most successful evangelist that ever lived. Here

---

[198] Matthew 13:13

he was, God in human flesh, and yet he alienated so many individuals.

We are told that the Lord's own brothers chided him
saying, "'For no one does anything in secret, when he himself
seeks to be known publicly.' If You do these things, show
Yourself to the world. For not even His brothers were believing in Him."[199] They had a point. In all of the Gospel accounts, Jerusalem is the only major city in which we find the
Lord ministering. Apparently he did not teach in Tiberius,
Caesarea, or even Sepphoris, the capitol of Galilee during this
era. This is surprising because we normally think a great
teacher needs to be heard in order to communicate his message.

Yet Jesus really was the greatest teacher that ever
lived, if we use the right criteria. If we think that good teaching leads the audience to adopt the exact same view, we'll
miss the point. The Lord's teaching led to confusion and soul
searching, because that best served his purpose. He did not
want to fill his listeners with information; instead, he sought
to antagonize and polarize his audiences. He intended that
his teaching would lead to guilt and hopelessness—he did
provide hope for the hopeless, but brought the self-reliant to
despair.

While the Lord's miracles certainly attracted large
crowds, he once fled from their grasp, knowing that his free
lunch program was the cause of their desire to anoint him as
their king. Jesus had no illusions that this temporary popular-
ity would ever accomplish his mission. He avoided the larger
population centers, and he never sought out the Gentiles, because his mission was restricted to fulfilling the Law and the
Prophets for his chosen people, the Jews.

Neither did he seek showy conversions. In fact,
whenever we see an inquirer coming to Jesus, we often watch
the seeker being turned away, troubled and disappointed by

---

[199] John 7:1-5

the Lord's requirements. His calling of the disciples is juxta-posed with the way he repelled many of those who sought him out. And the answers he gave to questions often baffle us, because he so seldom answered a question directly. His keen understanding of human nature always led him to the appropriate response to drive a man toward conviction.

The Lord accomplished his mission through evoking a feeling, or building a foundation for belief that would later bring about the new birth. He was far more interested in im-parting troubling new insights rather than in obtaining instant conversions. Today, we miss so much of what Jesus was doing because we miss the mood he created even with his silences. When people communicate on a deeply intimate level, what they don't say is often more powerful than what they say, and the Lord was a master at this.

Jesus was the greatest teacher who ever lived, not be-cause people came to accept his teaching, but because he ab-solutely achieved his purpose. He was so great that he didn't need the acclaim of the crowd. His goal was to send people searching for something that was still unavailable, and which had yet to be revealed. And he achieved his goal to prepare people for the cross and brought them from the place of say-ing: "So what?" to the place of saying: "Oh! What can I do?" In fact, that is exactly what the crowds asked Peter on the day of Pentecost: "What can we do?"

What about Theology?

The goal of this book has not been to change your theology. It has been to help you harmonize your theology with the teaching of Jesus. I have noticed in talking to Chris-tians from many different backgrounds that they can often accept the ideas presented in this book without changing their theology. In fact, I hear repeatedly that now, for the first time, people have harmonized their theology with the teachings of Jesus and that many of their "problems" have been cleared up.

A pastor friend of mine modified his ideas on the place of divorced people in the church after being introduced to this material. He claimed he changed his theology on divorce, but I suggest that he did not change his theology; he reconciled his views on the place of divorced people in the church with the doctrine of grace that he already believed. Transitionalism brought consistency to his views.

Another important problem that I believe transitionalism will combat is that of hypocrisy. Good theology has a tendency to be an antidote for hypocrisy. Because many are trying to live up to the principles Jesus taught, they end up frustrated at their inability to measure up, even though they have had a genuine conversion experience. These Christians often begin to put on a front and pretend to have attained to the Lord's standard of holiness. But this makes them feel like hypocrites. In reality, they are only believers saved by grace who are trying to "fake it 'til they make it."

We can compare this to my desire to own a Ferrari. I would like to own one, but alas, I drive a Ford. Now I could paint my Ford *Rubio Rosa*, but it will not transform it into a Ferrari. In the same way, pretending to be good doesn't make me good, it only makes me an actor. Bad theology creates the need for me to carry on a charade, while good theology allows me to readily admit my failures and still see my acceptance in Christ. Once I can accept my failures, I can accept the failures of others. Hypocrisy is claiming to be doing one thing while actually doing another, and the need for it vanishes once we can honestly face reality.

Three Areas of Practical Growth

I believe that transitionalism should lead you towards three areas of growth. These fall into a natural progression: transparency, confidence, and finally peace.

(1)**Transparency.** No longer must you pretend that you are a truly good person. As you grow in grace, you should be able to share your trials and failures with others in the church. Now I am not suggesting that you should indiscriminately confess your sins in public, but you can admit failure in general, and failure in particular, when appropriate. One of the things I hear over and over again in my ministry is that people are encouraged when I admit my failures from the pulpit. (Others are concerned that I may overdo it.)

But within all of us, I think there is the hope that someone, somewhere, is fully living up to the standards taught by Jesus—even when we know that no one could. This is one of the reasons why many ministers keep a little distance from their congregations. They know that people want to see them as "the example of Christianity in action," and so they keep themselves hidden, lest they burst everyone's bubble. No pastor is able to live up to this standard. Let's face it, we probably wouldn't really like anyone who could actually achieve the Lord's standard of perfection, they would make us feel totally inadequate.

J. Grant Howard says that sin causes people to hide and to hurl (cast blame). We hide from and then hurl at God, at others, and even at ourselves. I want to be perfect, but I'm not, so I hide. I want others to be perfect, but they're not, so I hurl. But when I learn to accept myself and others as being sinners, it breaks the power of this destructive cycle in my life.[200]

Even as I write this, I can hear some thinking: *Doesn't sin matter at all?* Of course it does. But when we come to Christ, he forgives all of our sin: Past, present *and future.* If this is not the case, we would have to go back to the cross and receive salvation each time we sinned. Probably the clearest passage on this is 1 John 1:5-10. Verse 9 says: "If we confess our sins, He is faithful and righteous to forgive us

---

[200] J. Grant Howard, *The Trauma of Transparency,* Multnomah Press, 1979, Chapters 2 and 3.

our sins and to cleanse us from all unrighteousness." 1 John was written to Christians so that they might know that they had eternal life, yet it teaches that confession is to be an ongoing part of the Christian life.

Verses 8 and 10 in the same chapter indicate that if we claim that we don't a sin, we're making God out to be a liar. Christians continue to sin, but as 1 John 1:6 indicates, we sin *in the light* (while unbelievers sin in the darkness). In other words, as believers, we can see our sin for what it is, and so we constantly make the choice to confess it and move on. Our sin was dealt with at the cross in a vital and powerful way, and we don't have to punish ourselves over and over for it—it is under the blood. The cross deals with sin in a powerful fashion.

G. K. Chesterton stated this powerfully for me when he said: "The real problem is—Can the lion lie down with the lamb and still retain his royal ferocity? That is the problem the Church attempted: That is the miracle she achieves. Those underrate Christianity who say that it discovered mercy; anyone might discover mercy. If fact, everyone did. But to discover a plan for being merciful and also severe—that was to anticipate a strange need of human nature."[201] The cross of Christ was so royally ferocious, miraculous, and severe in anticipation of my sinful needs, that I can afford to be transparent because all of my sin is now covered under the blood of Christ.

(2)Transparency leads to confidence. When we are able to become transparent about our inability to measure up to God's standards, it leads to a greater confidence in our salvation. It is our fear of our past deeds that leads to a destruction of our confidence in our salvation.

There was an interesting illustration of this concept found in the movie *The Firm*. Tom Cruise plays a young and

---

[201] G. K. Chesterton, *Orthodoxy*, Doubleday, New York, 1990, p. 98.

happily married law school graduate who receives the job offer of a lifetime. But the law firm that hires him turns out to have underworld connections. They send him to the Caribbean and while he's there, the firm manipulates him into an adulterous situation; they photograph his involvement with a young woman and use the pictures to blackmail him into cooperating with their illegal activities. If he doesn't cooperate, they threaten to mail the explicit pictures to his wife. It is not until Cruise finally takes the initiative to tell his wife about the infidelity and the pictures that their hold over him is broken.

When you lose confidence, you will not stand up for what you believe to be right. But when you are able to deal with your feelings of guilt and the fear of exposure, you can develop a new confidence in your salvation and in your relationship with other believers. It is no longer necessary to put on the facade of perfection. Transparency should lead to a confidence that will allow you to live your life more honestly.

(3) Confidence leads to peace. Finally, there is a peace which comes from a recognition of being fully known and fully accepted by God, and even possibly by yourself. Great peace certainly comes from knowing that another shoe is not about to drop. When you are able to become truly transparent, not only will your confidence grow, but you will no longer have the disabling fear and guilt that result from feeling that you are not good enough for God. You will also lose that slow burning anger towards God, caused by feeling he has not come through for you. Confidence in the Lord and our relationship with him allows us to begin to accept our lot in life—as well as being able to accept the failures and weaknesses of both ourselves and others around us. We come to peace with God and his ways, because we finally begin to understand them.

Let me close with an illustration I read from St. Therese of Lisieux. We are a lot like the small child who is only beginning to stand, and doesn't yet know how to walk, but who wants to join his mother at the top of a set of stairs. We lift our little foot to conquer that first step, only to discover how futile our effort is as we fall back without any advancement at all. We Christians are little spiritual children climbing up to God. We are not even able to reach that first step, but fortunately, the Lord knows this. When our futile efforts to achieve his presence are finally exhausted, then he will descend to take us up to his kingdom.[202]

In the same way, when you stop striving to be what you can never be, you will find that the Lord will fill your heart with great peace as you rely completely upon him to live this lifestyle that we call Christianity. May God bless you as you apply these truths to your life.

---

[202] St. Therese of Lisieux, *Histoire d'une ame* (Story of a Soul), 1953, p. 205.

Appendix

The Second Great Commandment

As we indicated in Chapter 6, the first great commandment is a summary of the first table of the Ten Commandments, and it instructs us to love God with all of our heart, mind, soul, and strength. It is a standard that is impossible for the believer to live up to—even after experiencing the new birth. We pointed out in that chapter that if our contention is correct, this command will not be given to the church in the epistles as a rule of life for those under the new covenant. And, of course, it isn't presented at all after Luke's Gospel.

But the same should also be true for the Lord's second great summary commandment, which was a statement taken from Leviticus that told the Jews to love their neighbor as much as they loved themselves. This second great commandment summarizes the second table of the law, which deals with a man's relationship with others. Most Christians take it for granted that this commandment applies to them, yet I believe that this concept *is not taught* in the rest of the New Testament as a law.

While this commandment is quoted three times after the Gospel of Luke,[203] I want to suggest that it is never given as a law for the church. It is merely used to demonstrate the contrast between the old and the new, between law and grace. Let's look at each of these three quotations in the epistles.

---

[203] Galatians 5:14; Romans 13:9; and James 2:8

1. **Galatians 5:14.** Please read the verse and its context. You'll notice that Paul earlier writes: "I testify again to every man who receives circumcision, that he is under obligation to keep the *whole Law*. You have been severed from Christ, you who are seeking to be justified by Law; you have fallen from grace."[204] The apostle clearly states that the Law was not given to save us, but to convict us. But if we're going to try to follow it as a way of life, we need to follow the *whole Law*. And if we attempt to keep the *whole Law*, we'll actually end up falling from grace; the Law, once it has done its job of convicting us of our sin and bringing us to the cross, is excluded by grace. So the apostle makes the point that we can't keep the whole Law.

Then, just ten verses later, in Galatians 5:14, Paul says, "For the *whole Law* is fulfilled in one word, in the statement, 'You shall love your neighbor as yourself.'" Now Paul is using this summary commandment as a contrast between law and grace. Here he's saying that just because we are freed from the law, does not mean we have a license to mistreat one another. In fact, that's what verse 13 says: "For you were called to freedom, brethren; only do not turn your freedom into an opportunity for the flesh, but through love serve one another." So Paul's intent in quoting the second summary commandment here is not to make it a standard of life for Christians, but to show how it contrasts with the New Testament principle of loving one another.

2. **Romans 13:9.** The next reference to the second great commandment also comes from Paul and is found in the book of Romans. The apostle begins by saying: "Owe nothing to anyone except to love one another, for he who loves his neighbor has fulfilled the law."[205] He then quotes four of the ten commandments (from the second table of the law) before saying: "It is summed up in this saying, 'You shall

---

[204] Galatians 5:3-4
[205] Romans 13:8

love your neighbor as yourself.' Love does no wrong to a neighbor; love therefore is the fulfillment of the law."[206]

Now we know that Paul clearly teaches in both Romans and Galatians that no one can keep the law. So when he again uses this phrase and says that love is the fulfillment of the law, he is demonstrating that we can never fulfill this debt. He has already made it plain that this is impossible, by use of the word 'except' in Romans 13:8. We will always owe this because we can never fully pay it.

Paul indicates that our debt can never be paid by any of our works. Earlier, in Romans, Paul states that believers are set free from the law of sin and death, but that *the law is fulfilled in us through Christ.*[207] It is Christ's love that fulfills the law—not ours. The apostle only presents the second commandment as the unreachable ideal that is set before us as the ultimate standard.

3. James 2:8. The third quote is found in the book of James. Here we are told if "you are fulfilling the royal law, according to the Scripture, 'You shall love your neighbor as yourself.' you are doing well." In other words, keep it as best you can—but don't bet your eternal life on it! James goes on to say that whoever keeps the whole law, and stumbles in one point, has become guilty of all of it. So we are to speak and act as those who are judged by the law of liberty, rather than the old covenant, because we're now under grace, not law.[208]

Lewis Sperry Chafer reaches the same conclusion with regard to the second great command. When referring to the same three passages he says, "In no sense is the law applied to the believer by these three Scriptures; they merely imply that the law is fulfilled by the exercise of that love which is most vitally the duty of every child of God."[209]

Please feel free to contact the author at tweaver@tscnet.com

---

[206] Romans 13:9-10

[207] Romans 8:3-4

[208] James 2:8-13

[209] L. S. Chafer, Grace, The Bible Institute Colportage, 1939, p. 104.

Ordering Information

Additional copies of *The Gospel Solution* can be ordered for $18.00 per copy, which includes shipping and handling. ($19.30 for Washington State residence with WSST.)

Please order from:
      True Light Press
      3912 Steelhead Dr. NW
      Bremerton, WA 98312
      1(360) 830-2734

Credit Card Sales - 1 (800) 479-3208

FAX (360) 830-2436

Five (5) copies or more;
$14.75 per copy which includes shipping and handling. ($15.85 for Washington State residents with WSST.)

All funds must be in U.S. dollars
Prices subject to change without notice.

Visit our website at www.gospelsolution.com

Ordering Information

Additional copies of *The Gospel Solution* can be ordered for
$18.00 per copy, which includes shipping and handling.
($19.30 for Washington State residence with WSST.)

Please order from:
      True Light Press
      3912 Steelhead Dr. NW
      Bremerton, WA 98312
      1(360) 830-2734

Credit Card Sales - 1 (800) 479-3208

FAX (360) 830-2436

Five (5) copies or more;
$14.75 per copy which includes shipping and handling.
($15.85 for Washington State residents with WSST.)

All funds must be in U.S. dollars
Prices subject to change without notice.

Visit our website at www.gospelsolution.com